I0830562

A BRUTAL ATTACK ON DEMOCRACY

(The All-Time Enemies on the March)

By

J. Pelegrin

OM PUBLISHING n.y.c.

Three political forces are trying to destroy the USA, as we now it!

----------------o0o----------------

1-Democrat Party. (Postmodern Liberalism.)
2-Communist China. (State Capitalism)
3-Radical Islam. (Terrorism)

----------------o0o----------------

Know their strategy.
See their common goals.
Research the backgrounds.
Recognize the coincidences.
Acknowledge their inconsistencies.

Greed is the driving force.
Authoritarianism is the weapon.
Totalitarianism is the system.
Fear is the tool.
Money is the key.
Power is the ultimate goal.

After the Pandemic, the riots, looting and street violence, the plot will continue…

A book like no other.

A BRUTAL ATTACK ON DEMOCRACY

(The All-Time Enemies on the March)

A BRUTAL ATTACK ON DEMOCRACY by J. Pelegrin

J. Pelegrin

A BRUTAL ATTACK ON DEMOCRACY

(The All-Time Enemies on the March)

A BRUTAL ATTACK ON DEMOCRACY by J. Pelegrin

A BRUTAL ATTACK ON DEMOCRACY by J. Pelegrin

Synopsis

Three political forces are trying to destroy the USA as it is now! Two are foreign, and one is domestic, although under foreign influence. The three are together against a common enemy: The United States of America and Conservatism. Our country is in grave danger, and the American People and the World's community need to get smart and not let ignorance prevail. Education about history is now a must. We need to be sharp and recognize the perils at sight. This book attempts to make the public aware of the present evil plot. The author's comments and books are banned on Social Media, Google, AOL, and other outlets under Postmodern Liberals (Democrat Party) control.

Greed is the driving force; Authoritarianism, the weapon, Totalitarianism is the system, Fear, the tool, Money, the key, and Totalitarian absolute Power, is the ultimate goal; Communist China's style. Billionaires, High-Tech CEOs, Postmodern Liberal Politicians, in command of the Democrat Party, and Radical Islamists are together in an odd coalition. They will share the Booty in a bloody battle among the winners. They are trying to destroy Donald J. Trump as a first step. After eliminating the first obstacle, they will focus on the USA destruction to change our country into a Totalitarian Society, with a Big Government, which it's Political Elite, will dictate norms that regular people would follow without questioning or opposition. No need to think. Collective behavior is desired. The elite will do it for them, as they have learned the style from Communist China. They enjoy the profits of doing business with the Asian Giant without the guilt of exploiting workers themselves. Chinese do it to their subjects, used to survive in dire conditions for centuries, and as a first installment sent us the Coronavirus, Made in Wuhan, China, for export. We will never know if it was intentional or a dreadful mistake. The Democrat Party didn't waste time and mounted a fraudulent election, with millions of votes by mail, without any signature or Identity verification, dead people, illegal immigrants, and even scanning the same ballots up to ten times into the voting machines, also suspected of data manipulation in Joe Biden's favor.

J. Pelegrin has identified the strategy. The present work is uncovering the plot, recalling history, consulting the ancient Vedas, and exposing the daily maneuvers by the actors involved in what we call, without a doubt, the most significant treasonous attempt to damage the United States of America. The Media helps by lying and outpouring massive fake news while hiding Donald J. Trump's achievements. Active Obama holdovers keep hitting from the darkest "Shadow Government." sabotaging the President's actions daily.

"A BRUTAL ATTACK ON DEMOCRACY" (The All-Time Enemies on the March), a book like no other!

FOREWORD:

Supreme Court Justice Robert Jackson, appointed by **President Franklin D. Roosevelt**, wrote in the foreword of the book "Law in the Middle East" (1955): "Islamic Law offers the American lawyer a study in dramatic contrasts. Even casual acquaintance and superficial knowledge reveal that its striking features relative to our law are not likenesses but inconsistencies, not similarities but contrarieties. In its source, its scope, and its sanctions, the law of the Middle East is the direct opposite of Western law."

---------------------------------------oOo--

The **'Free Exercise Clause'** of our Constitution states that Congress cannot "prohibit the free exercise" of religious practices. The Supreme Court of the United States has consistently held, however, that the right to free exercise of religion is not absolute.
For example, in the 19th century, some of the members of The Church of Jesus Christ of Latter-day Saints traditionally practiced polygamy, yet in Reynolds v. United States (1879), the Supreme Court upheld the criminal conviction of one of these members under a federal law banning polygamy. The Court reasoned that to do otherwise would set a precedent for a full range of religious beliefs including those as extreme as human sacrifice.

The court stated that "laws are made for the government of actions, and while they cannot interfere with mere religious belief and opinions, they may do it with practices." for example, if one were part of a religion that believed in vampirism, the first amendment would protect one's belief in vampirism, but not the practice.

---------------------------------------oOo--

A BRUTAL ATTACK ON DEMOCRACY by J. Pelegrin

13

In my mind hangs the idea of why, in 1801, the Muslim, who are Islamists, engaged in a war with the United States and it was contested by two Presidents, why now, our Judges are defending a consuetudinary foe that continues to decimate our people and attempting to defy our Constitution and Lifestyle?
I am no Constitutional Lawyer, but it makes common sense that we have to revise our Constitutional Laws and to be more Patriots, rather than continue to defend others in detriment of our people.

J. Pelegrin

A BRUTAL ATTACK ON DEMOCRACY by J. Pelegrin

TABLE OF CONTENTS

21-Introduction

21 -An Unexpected Visitor: The Coronavirus shock.

24 -A Plot To Destroy The USA. As We Know It.

29 –The Democrat Party Started A Witch Hunt.

29 -Some Background Information. Why The Vedas, now?

38 -The Danger Ahead.

41 -Prologue.

41 –No One Saw It Coming.

42 –The Bernie Sanders Dream.

44 –A Difference Between Blue And Red States.

46 –A Brief Review.

49 -CHAPTER 1

(Establishing Political Correctness)

49 -The Election That Changed The World.

49 -Liberals Messing With Education.

49 -The Alliance.

57 -Hollywood/Nazi Connection During The Depression.

58 -Education's control Is Part Of The Liberal's Plan.

60 -Today's Education Fiction.

60 -The California Chaos.

61 -Political Correctness.

65 -Defining Postmodernism.

66 -Black Lives Matter and Antifa enter the game.

68 -The New Liberal Education Mentality.

68 -Defending The Student's Feelings?

70 -Free Speech, No Longer Available.

69 -The Teacher's Complaints.

71 -Today's Leftist Campuses.

72 -The Campuses Safe Spaces.

72 -Dangerous Alliance With Islam.

73 -The "Resist" Movement.

74 -A Genderless Society?
76 -Everybody Get A Medal?

79 -CHAPTER 2
(The Plot)
79 -The Strategy.
79 - Postmodern Liberal Movement In Action:
79 -Their Plans To Destroy Western Civilization.
86 -American Families Are Against Genderless Society.
91 -The well-planned Theft of the Century.
94 -If it ain't broke, don't fix it!
94 -Democrats Founded the KKK in 1865.
96 -Mainstream Media's Obsession To Defeat Trump.
99 -Co-Existence But With An Order.
102 -White Male Supremacy Syndrome.
102-Sanctuary Cities And Illegal Immigration.
107 -The Trump Era.

109 -CHAPTER 3
(Communist China - A Philosophical Battle)
109 -A Virus Made In China.
112 –Merging Of Ideologies.
113 -The Mutation Of The Left.
114 -Vedic Knowledge. Karma.
115 -Technology Advances Changed Communism.
121 -The U.S.S.R. Influence In Latin America.
123 -Consistent Failure Of Socialism And Communism.
124 -The Lenin Decalogue.
127 –China Awakes As Communism/State Capitalism.
130 -Does The Biological War Begun? Yet?
132 -How Communism Became A US Government Option.
136 -Communist Ideology Making In-Roads In The USA.
140 -Socialism Nefarious Consequences.
141 -The American People Need Education!
144 -One Reason Socialism And Communism Still Exist.

147 -CHAPTER 4

(The race to the White House)

147 -November 3rd, 2020, and beyond.

151 -Urban Disturbance Planned In Detail.

153 -Pelosi's Planned Election Reform.

156 -Following China's State Capitalism Model.

157–The Identity Politics Game.

159 -Totalitarianism: The Object In The Democrat Party.

161 -Obama Administration's Legacy Crumbling Down?

163 -COVID-19 Is Bringing Out To Light Liable Errors.

167 -CHAPTER 5

(Philosophical Controversy-The Vedas vs. Islam)

168 -The Difficult US Relationship With Islam.

168 -Obama: Islam Has Never Been At War With The US.

170 -The Eternal Conflict with Islam. A War Declaration.

172 -Islam's Goal: Establishment Of a Worldwide Caliphate.

172 -Abd Al Rahman's Warning.

174 -The Jefferson's Resistance.

175 -President Madison Finally Ended Muslim Extortion.

176 -History Education Is A Must.

178 -Is The United States Ready to Combat Islam?

180 -USA Must Revise Islam's Status In The Constitution.

182 -Insanity Continues.

184 -Postmodern Liberal Movement's birth.

184 -The Democrat Party Metamorphosis.

186 -Conservatism Ideal Keeps The Balance.

187 -The Personal Hatred Against Donald J. Trump.

188 -The Snowflake's Complaints.

190 -The Vedic Philosophy Teachings.

190 -The Genders.

194 -The Mainstream Media Fake News.

195 -Democrats and the KKK. The year 1865.

195 -What Democrat Party and Postmodern Liberals Want.

199 -CHAPTER 6

(The Vedic Knowledge)

195 -Why The Vedas, Now?

205 -The Need To Consult Conservative Standards.

206 -The Vedas, A Source Of Ancient Wisdom.

208 -The Most Trusted Source Of Knowledge.

211 -The Vedic Philosophy Teachings.

211 -The Genders.

214 -Jesus Christ Learning the Vedas?

215 -The Great Western Civilization.

218 -Democrats Need to Find an Identity.

221 -A Fierce Battle: Traditions vs. Postmodernism.

223 -CHAPTER 7

(Our Future - China's danger.)

223 -The most significant hoax -Russian collusion.

226 –The Most Urgent Measures.

231 -Our Dependence From China.

228 -A Different Communism - Worse Than The USSR.

237 -The US Greatest Challenge.

240 -Democrats Obsession With Absolute Power.

241 -Market Capitalism Clashes With State Capitalism.

239 -America's Future Is At Stake.

244 -The Conspiracy Is In Full Speed.

247 -Evolution, Not Revolution.

249 –The Author's view of the World.

251 -Important Words From The Author.

253 -EPILOGUE
(Islam: An ever-present danger)
253 –Three Contenders In The Battlefield.
255 -Postmodern Liberals/Islam, US Constitution's Enemies.
258 -Islamic Laws Are Clashing With Our Constitution
258 -The Postmodern Liberal Ideology is against Islam.
259 -Dangerous Islamic Infiltration To Destroy The USA.
263 –Old Barbary Pirates Are The New Islamic Terrorists.
265 -Some Additional Highly Controversial Facts.
268 -Koran Is Incompatible With Our Constitution.
269 - Postmodern Liberalism/Islam: An Unholy Tie.
270 -Identity Politics, A Failed Strategy.
272 -The Inevitable Talk Involving Islam.

277 –ABOUT THE AUTHOR

281 –OTHER BOOKS

A BRUTAL ATTACK ON DEMOCRACY by J. Pelegrin

J. Pelegrin

A BRUTAL ATTACK ON DEMOCRACY

(The All-Time Enemies on the March)

Introduction

Several dozens of books are published about our Current Affairs; Most of them focusing on detailing activities by individual actors in the political arena.

I took a different approach until now, ignored by all writers, based on my History and Ancient Vedic Scriptures knowledge. I studied them for over fifty years, under my Spiritual Master's guidance, Bhaktivedanta Swami Prabhupada, also known as the Guru, that introduced the famous group "The Beatles" into the Vedic knowledge.

So, be prepared to read a philosophical approach, with fact-checked historical information and a personal opinion.

21 -An Unexpected Visitor: The Coronavirus shock.

Because of the COVID-19 Pandemic, that has affected the whole World and surely will radically change our lives, this book I am writing now, in self-imposed quarantine, is continuously evolving in concept, tenor, politics, social life, and people's lives around the World. We are living in a critical season, full of surprises.

Writing from Midtown, Manhattan, sadly, where 1/4 (25% of the United States victims infected with the virus reside), I see our streets desolate, which inspires a sense of destruction, forced loneliness caused by the latest import from China: The 'Coronavirus.'

Without trying to suggest conspiracy theory, mostly blaming China's people, which I like and respect because of their many qualities through thousands of years of their unique culture, it is necessary to recognize the facts, or at least what we know.

At the same time, seeing the reality of some of the Chinese people's habits, especially eating everything that walks, crawls, swims, or flies, is bringing chills to my skin.

Watching some live videos of the "wet markets," where all kinds of animals are sold life, in cages with the sole purpose of killing them and become a meal, or already dead and chopped, it is frankly disgusting, at least to me, a vegetarian.

It is something we cannot call civilized in any way, and it is easy to understand how something like the COVID-19 was bred or created right there.

The other part of the story: How the virus was spread out to the World, causing the Pandemic we are suffering at present.

We can call it a mistake, a series of errors, an irresponsible act, or all of them. However, the intentionality is a question we will never know, and if it were some of it, people involved in it would deserve millions of years of going to hell. Of course, as said before, we will never know the truth.

Educated people recognize that a Communist system is capable of causing genocide or mass murdering. History tells that at least one hundred and thirty million people were killed by Communist regimes in the last one hundred and fifty years—no doubts about it.

So, could this be an attempt to weaken the rest of the free World by a biological attack? It is hard to believe, but also a possibility based on previous acts. I prefer to think otherwise.

However, doubt hangs in my mind like a horrific nightmare; The recall of a dream, like I, never had in my long life on this Earth.

I believe we will recover from these dreadful moments; our economy would indeed quickly rebound from the ashes. Especially the World will recognize our civilization is good for humanity, how we treat animals, even the ones people eat. (I am a Dairy-Vegetarian for 50 years), and refuse to criticize meat-eaters, simply because I am not qualified to judge anyone.

Nevertheless, there are limits. Our culture is being updated and upgraded by the day, and we prioritize our human nature to achieve better standards daily.

Western culture is not perfect, but we can't overlook our effort to improve it through the centuries.

Investors all over the Planet know that, and the comparison with the actual situation will, without a doubt, improve the USA ratings.

Our country's economy will bounce back. The World will compare the political systems, and the USA will be victorious once again. Now with more force, after people, Worldwide, realize that they can trust our political system, backed by an imperfect but ever-evolving and improving Market Capitalism. Unfortunately, some wrongly called "Democrats" are trying to change it, just for a reckless, insensitive "power grab obsession."

You just read the book's central point, revealing a hideous political plot never before devised in US politics. It is something that would make our Founding Fathers' hairs under the wigs stand up like sharp stilettos.

We should hope this act of God, sending us the present Pandemic, through Karma, personal, or group liability will be a teaching lesson for us at all levels of culture, education, and economy. We must learn the lesson and assign the guilt to the real perpetrators in a variety of responsibilities accordingly with the facts.

These are not times to play politics. I hope everybody understands it.

However, from the Speaker of the House Nancy Pelosi to the minority Senate leader Chuck Schumer, including the rest of the Democrat Party members, is part of the nefarious plot to destroy President Trump and the United States of America as we know it. We have never seen anything like it in the History of our country.

Schumer had the nerve to say on National TV, regarding the "Run-Off" in the State of Georgia: "First we take Georgia, then we change America!" Who wants to change the most beautiful country on Earth?

The hatred Democrat Party members display against President Trump is out of this World, and it is like extracted from a horror science fiction movie.

Democrat lawmakers insist on charging against the President, lying, and creating obstacles to his job, trying to save the American people's lives. It is like it for the last four years.

24 -A Plot To Destroy The USA. As We Know It.

Although there is an in-depth research on every fact explained here, this book is about the author's evaluation and opinion, honest and maybe partisan; I am a "Liberal-Conservative."

However, not a lie is said in these pages. The reader could find some disagreements, but good faith has been my motto.

I know it sounds brutal, maybe unreal, but the facts confirm the existence of a plot to destroy the USA as we know it. It is real. We will discuss the actors, their ideology, intentions, and background (History is the most crucial part of the scheme.)

The partners are three groups: Postmodern Liberalism (the new identity assumed by the Democrat Party,) Socialism/Communism, and Radical Islam. Let's be clear that Postmodern Liberalism has hijacked the old Democrat Party, and it is in full command of it.

First of all:

The Liberal Movement, in my opinion, has mutated into what I call now: Postmodern Liberalism, with some exceptions of traditional Liberals who became pariahs inside the Party.

Throughout many years of evolution, the change occurred due to the last 2016 election, where the old traditional Democrat Party fell out of decisive leadership and collapsed.

The Liberals stepped on the gas and, taking advantage of the situation, pushed their agenda, entirely leaning to the left, dragging with it, most of the old traditional Democrat Party.

Bernie Sanders, once labeled as a dark, unattractive Socialist, acting in fact as Communist, took the idea to the American youngsters, mostly uneducated "students," desperately seeking "free stuff" and the giveaways abundantly offered by the old Communist fanatic. Sanders has no practical way to finance them without bankrupting our country.

Bernie curiously spent his honeymoon in the USSR, enamored by the "Revolution," that has stuck in his mind, and still is pushing with great conviction, despite that Socialism/Communism has failed every time a country applied it. Bernie got stuck in the 1960s.

However, the old career politician said in a recent Town Hall: The USSR has never been Socialist? He needs to unveil the USSR acronym: United Soviet Socialist Republics.

Recently, the Senator from Vermont sung praises to Fidel Castro and his Communist Cuban Revolution.

Postmodern Liberals also introduced the idea of seeking a convenient alliance with Islam, fighting a common enemy: The Conservatives in the GOP.

We will see the connotations of this coalition later in the chapters. Also, analyzing the discussion of irreconcilable Islamist differences with our Constitution and Lifestyle, and History tells the truth!

I carefully tried to avoid a personal negative opinion about Islam, preferring to expose facts, so that the readers could form their own opinion without my influence.

I am not an anti-Islamic person, although I disagree with the practices. I will explain the different forms of Islam later.

The new Postmodern Liberalism is a radical approach of the Liberalism we all knew and probably argued with but estimated viable in some cases. I consider myself a Liberal-Conservative, meaning that I study Liberal proposals, and accept some, rejecting others, nowadays it has mutated into a very different animal.

In many instances, something interesting came out of those discussions, enriching some aspects that moderately helped change our Society's traditions.

The newly proposed style implies a violent attempt to go to uncharted territories, where our Society's typical lifestyle is being breached, making many people feel uncomfortable and displeased with those modifications.

Democrats have entered a coalition integrated by The Democrat Party, Liberals, Academia, Mainstream Media, The Left, Washington Establishment, Hollywood Elite, Deep State, and the LGBTQ, which together became, in my opinion, the Postmodern Liberalism.

Unfortunately, they are pushing the most extreme anti-Conservative sexual oriented craze based on ignorance of History, science, and philosophy. As a result, Postmodern Liberalism hijacked the Democrat Party.

In an unfortunate attempt to challenge President Trump, the alliance is now defending issues like the MS-13 (praising them as similar to our grandparents arriving in the US, an absurd comparison made by Speaker Pelosi.

Democrats are promoting illegal immigration as a way to enroll new Democratic voters. They are instituting the Sanctuary States in Democratic Governed cities and states (protecting criminal illegal aliens.) They also want a borderless country, allowing immigrants from any land, including Radical Islamic terrorist places, to enter the US freely to acquire rights equal to the natural citizens immediately.

Not even the actual COVID-19 Pandemic slowed them down. Democrats want to increase taxes and undo the recent Trump Administration tax reform that had pumped the economy by the creation of new 7 million jobs, as well as other issues that, in the past, were condemned by the Democrat Party when it used to practice a mostly centrist ideology.

The existing Pandemic has not changed the Democratic politician's minds. They still don't care if the illegal aliens coming into our land are healthy or not.

Right after the 2016 election, they implemented a witch-hunt after Donald J. Trump, at the same time that the mainstream Media vowed, "The impeachment has begun," only 19 minutes after the Media released the 2016 election results.

Now, we just learned, through Inspector General Michael Horowitz, that during the Campaign, the FBI, under the Obama Administration led by James Comey, one hundred days before the election, placed a spy inside Trump's Campaign and maybe two or more.   Stephan Halper, a US citizen, Cambridge University professor with residence in the UK, was one of them. The other "informant" remains unknown at this time; The placing of the Mole was inspired by "Code Name Crossfire Hurricane": "The Secret Origins of the Trump Investigation," as the New York Times recently published.

DOJ Sources affirmed Obama's Administration paid Professor Halper one million dollars through the US Department of Defense to collect information about Trump's Campaign and others.

Deep incursions in the Trump campaign affiliates led to several interviews at the Trump Tower with active members. President Trump denounced illegal surveillance early in March 2017.

At that time, FBI officials downplayed any claim of spying inside the Trump Tower.

Recently, in May 2018, former NSA James Clapper said on TV: "it is a good thing the FBI spied on the Trump campaign."

Officially, the FBI said the "informant" got in touch with the Campaign to protect the then-candidate from Russian spying inside the organization.

However, if the FBI were concerned with Mr. Trump's safety, the correct would have been to make him aware of such a situation and warning him of its perils.

By keeping the "surveillance" secret, the actions became "Spying" into a campaign opposed to the Governing Party.

Inspector General Michael E. Horowitz confirmed it in his recent report.

Although the information seems to have occurred years ago, it is worth remembering the events to keep the coherence of the actual "Coup D'etat" attempt.

Significantly, Clinton's Campaign was not "protected," in a similar way, while it was public that the Russians breached into the DNC's computers. It is also notable that the DNC decided to make their computers unavailable to the FBI's requests.

So many lies like we've never seen before in the FBI and the DOJ is a severe discredit to the Obama's Justice Department, which has held an apparently impeccable prestige until that date. Now, we know it is false.

President Trump won the 2016 election under the slogan "Make America Great Again," and many Campaign promises that he has been fulfilling so far despite the fierce Democratic politicians' opposition through the "Resist" movement.

Unfortunately, many of those conquers are ignored by the people's majority because the Mainstream Media hides the result from them. They only publish negative aspects of the Trump Administration.

The President is the target, and all the Democrat Party's power, means, and efforts are focused on reaching only one goal: Destroying Donald J. Trump and his Administration. Not only that but destroying the USA as we know it. They want to convert the USA into a European country model and eventually going Communist.

The failed Impeachment attempt by the House, dismissed by the Senate, is proof of the "hoax" attempted by Democrats.

They have abandoned on the path, a political platform that could have had eventually helped them to regain the House, Senate, and White House, their biggest dream and obsession since 2016.

At present, the GOP is gaining terrain after the Impeachment's failure.

Polls show the progress despite a frantic battle with the Mainstream Media and the Left, helped by the Radical Islamists now, present in the House of Representatives, known as "The Squad."

"A BRUTAL ATTACK ON DEMOCRACY" is a narrative reflecting the US's current social/political situation. Its chapters detail the devilish plot by the mentioned coalition, which defines the perils of the alliance; I call Postmodern Liberalism, menacing to destroy not only Donald J. Trump, but also the whole country and the Western Civilization.

That is precisely what Marx and Engels suggested in the Communist Manifesto of 1848, and Lenin reaffirmed in his Decalogue in 1913.

It is also what the Islamists have fixed in their minds since the seventh Century: The Earth's domination through a Worldwide Caliphate. So, they are ganging up against the President's plans to Make America Great Again! The World is watching in anxiety!

So, let's start with the details.

29 -The Democrat Party Started A Witch Hunt.

A witch-hunt initiated on November 9th, 2016, has slowed down a Congress that, lacking a GOP majority (in 2018, Democrats obtained control of the House), has prevented implementing the President's plan altogether. I took the liberty to rename the Movement that hijacked the Democrat Party as Postmodern Liberalism. Accordingly, the present development is an entirely new version of the old World's understanding of traditional Liberalism. I will get into details of why in the following chapters. The alliance between several different groups, some of them vehemently opposed to Conservatism, is not surprising. The names have evolved through the times, in various fashions aligned with the World's actual regions.

The old phrase: "My enemy's enemy is my friend," is still valid.

The Left gathered together the entire Conservatives' traditional enemies inside the coalition we call Postmodern Liberalism.

They are all of a very different breed and hate President Trump and his supporters for various reasons. That is the common denominator, so they decide to unite to help each other.

29 -Some Background Information. Why The Vedas, now?

Since the beginning of the nineteenth century, the founders of the Quantum Mechanics: Nobel Prize winner, Laureate Niels Bohr (1885-1962) and Erwin Schrödinger (1887-1961), and later Werner Heisenberg (1901-1976), stated that "Quantum theory will not look ridiculous to people who have read 'Vedanta.'" (the conclusion of Vedic thought.)

Schroedinger went a little further, writing in his biographical work: "Vedanta teaches that consciousness is singular, all happenings are played out in one universal consciousness, and there is no multiplicity of selves."

The brightest mind of our times: Albert Einstein, acknowledged his regular reading of the Vedas, recognizing the absoluteness of Krishna, the Supreme Being.

Robert Oppenheimer (1904 – 1967) stated: "The Vedas are the greatest privilege of this century."

Strangely, the Vedic philosophy has remained apart from the main discussion; I ignore the reason.

However, because I have acquired a vast knowledge of the Vedic philosophy over fifty years of studies under an erudite teacher, I insist we must evaluate the present analysis. It is too valuable to dismiss it and the World's dire situation; I believe it requires going back to consultation basics.

I must admit that Vedic knowledge is not simple to extract by reading the Scriptures. However, once it is done, it is easy to understand, concrete, and straightforward.

The Vedic complexity, flowery language, the citations, personalities, demi-Gods, fantastic places, and a significant portion of metaphoric language make Vedic understanding quite intricate. However, once one recognizes and familiarizes with the writing style, it becomes passionately addicting and immensely educating.

I was lucky enough to be introduced to Bhaktivedanta Swami Prabhupada, and most importantly, his philosophical work, wisdom, and kindness. Prabhupada is a Worldwide recognized authority in Vedic knowledge.

After engaging in servicing the Supreme Personality of God, Lord Krishna, he accepted me as his disciple, which changed my life entirely and forever.

So, the introduction to consciousness was the key that allowed me to enter another dimension: The Spiritual World.

However, nowadays, a particular phenomenon is dominating our Society: the most significant sociopolitical division ever is driving our lives insane, and causing a human disrupting feeling, as never occurred before.

The antagonism between the mutating Liberal ideologies, which I call now the Postmodern Liberalism, and the Conservative Movement, is dangerously increasing the hostility at present times, reaching the hatred zone.

Conservative thinkers are no longer allowed to speak at most Universities, mostly in control of the Postmodern Liberals. They violently attack them consistently.

So, my thoughts cannot get away from the current times, which significantly dominates the scene and keeps me focused on what is happening at present. I hope I do not become repetitive in excess, although I believe the repetition of the issues helps me understand, as Prabhupada used to say.

The drug culture is the favorite weapon the Western culture's enemies are using, trying to destroy it, and the extreme sexual liberation completes the scene to real chaos. China flooding our streets with opioids, Fentanyl, and other heavy drugs is an example.

They know the spiritual weakness that prosperity brings to people, and Western Society has fallen into the trap.

The providers are well-identified in the political Left, Islam, and the totalitarian left-wing. The mafia runs the drug distribution ring, a highly controversial bunch. Most of the heavy drugs keep coming from China and Mexico; Sometimes, in triangulation with other countries.

The materially successful fools and the losers are their clients; The LGBTQ helps. It is a wide variety of political styles incompatible between them with a common denominator; the hatred for Trump and his supporters.

I would like to establish right here that my opinion about the LGBTQ is not homophobic at all. As a Jazz Dance student for many years, and a successful professional musician, I shared space and relationships with Gay people, having a deep camaraderie and many friendships. I believe people should be free to choose the way they want to live and be respected. However, as they have the right to choose, I also reserve my right to a dissenting opinion, something that, at this time, due to 'political correctness' is difficult to express.

I consider the LGBTQ a political arm of the people they affirm to defend. Nevertheless, they have become highly demanding and pushing their lifestyle, which transgresses many' moral principles.

Morals have been, and I hope it continues to be, the pillar of a healthy society that has maintained the World's population growth and evolution. The contrary is not optimum and is in strong opposition to the excessive liberties the Postmodern Liberals want to push down our throats.

Western Civilization women, caught up by their economic success, restrict the newborn, avoiding dividing the cake into smaller pieces. In the Islamic faith, baby's production is at full speed ahead. Their motto:

"In the end, Islam will prevail because our women bear more children than any other group."

I remind you that the Koran's primary purpose is conquering the World to be an Islamic Caliphate.

The City of London is an example. For the first time in History, the original White population is in the minority. The Islamist community on the rise as crime is also on the increase overlooked by Muslim Mayor Sadiq Khan.

Western Civilization's people, by restricting the newborn, are undermining the defenses against the all-time enemies.

Recently, Alexandra Ocasio Cortez, the Squad Leader, has vowed and counseled women to avoid having any newborn; A controversial, anti-human statement.

Postmodern Liberals insist on making the modern World a genderless society. An ignorant option! Something scientifically impossible where they only seem to care about the "feelings." They disregard reality and science.

While this is happening, their allies are frantically working to take advantage of the system's weakening.

But, who are the opponents of Western Civilization?

A coalition has been formed by Postmodern Liberals (including the LGBTQ), Democratic Party, Mainstream Media, Communists, Socialists, Anarchists, Fascists, Nazis, and the odd addition of Islamist, unequivocally opposed to the rest.

As said before, I call the group Postmodern Liberalism, but inevitably bound to the new edition of CCP's China, including their State Capitalism. The High-Tech executives lead them, many of them subscribed to the LGBTQ, as always looking for social recognition. It is no longer enough the social tolerance to their questionable public behavior.

Their aggressiveness is evident, helping up with millions of dollars Pete Buttigieg's failed Campaign, which was strongly backed by the Mainstream Media and Silicon Valley's executives. Pete's Campaign failed, but surely will be rewarded with a substantial bone on the eventual new Administration if Biden is elected. He could be named US Ambassador in Beijing; A terrible mistake.

Now, people, especially conservatives, are required to change their minds and applaud their increasingly disruptive public lifestyle and the shift into an impulsive liberality that is degrading Society based on morals as we know it.

It seems the goal might be a kind of modern "Sodom and Gomorrah." They actively and violently ignore the rights of Conservatives to differ.

Remembering my youth in South America, I could recall many clashes with the prior generations. Fortunately, my dear parents were the kind of individuals who always took the cultural changes naturally, understanding or trying to understand the young people's need for those changes.

With practically a lack of factual information, South-American youngsters tried to copy the changes generated by another entirely different culture, coming from the USA and Europe.

Unfortunately, the Vedic knowledge was absent from our region at that time.

South-American countries never suffered the horrors of wars like the US or Europe.

The only information received at the time of the World Wars, Korean War and others, was only acquired by watching the newsreels showing previews before the theaters' feature film.

The information was reduced to a couple of minutes and always sided with the US Government.

Hollywood was pro-Government at that time, although in the 1930s, the Hollywood elite had a weird closeness to the Nazis. (The Hollywood connection.) I will get into some details in a later chapter.

The radio shows gave more detailed information about the World's developments. Books delivered the results of those experiences and changes in a more comprehensive and sophisticated way, but of course, with some time delay because of the news distribution's physical nature.

Since my youth, I have always had a sincere eagerness to know more about life, the Universes, and the human presence on Earth.

My craving to know about spiritual being came later in my

life, mainly because, at the time, thinking outside the box presented some fear to enter an uncertain mind status.

Religion had a part of this concern. I always thought that Christianity (Catholicism at that time) had considerable control over the creation issues while reading the Bible was not encouraged.

As a teen, I remember asking some priests why we would not read the Bible more often. The answers indicated that the leadership (La Curia) was concerned that the filigrees would misunderstand the Bible writings, or it could open a can of worms by generating unwanted questions, challenging to be evacuated.

Besides, there was almost no information about the Vedas or the Eastern culture and much less about Islam. Later in my life, I had the opportunity to study in detail, mainly related to the Vedas.

However, some students were interested in History, especially the Barbary Wars around the end of the 17th Century and beginning of the 18th Century, when Muslims had a common practice of kidnapping US ships, holding passengers and crews for ransom, and selling them as slaves.

These barbaric practices and the US ships' taxes drained the US economy on 10% of the Gross National Product for some time.

Those years were undoubtedly a dark period. In South America was no different.

For some reason, the teachers, philosophers, and other educators felt that people were coming from the dark ages and unable to understand reality at sight.

Except for certain elites in Europe and the US, the knowledge was slowly starting to be available to the average folks.

Of course, a few avid readers seeking information of all kinds were able to form a nucleus or an elite of intellectuals that were secretively gathering on exclusive joints, as Coffee shops, Jazz clubs, or reading clubs, quite tricky to access without an insider's introduction.

Somehow, through my musician's skills, a brief activity in the Independent theater, and in general, by hanging out with older people, I kept an increasing expansion of my knowledge.

Music has always been a mind opener. The maths in it, which I discovered later in life, notably when the digital era unveiled the equations in the musical phrases and even in the sound vibrations, opened an incredible parallel World that earlier in my youth I could not precisely detect. I could've only felt it.

The vast ocean of sounds, although defined as Harmony, Melody, and Rhythm, contains an endless wave of alternatives that make it a Science, including Physics, Mathematics, Geometry, and other aspects of Science and Philosophy.

Discovering the algorithms in the music, already established by Pythagoras and revealed to some privileged musicians at the time, was little by little uncovered and made available to others through different means. The latest one, developing digital music, is based on what the Genius of Pythagoras masterfully designed centuries ago.

That knowledge was made available within the timed development of science, which today our scientists manage to make public after years of intense work.

When one thinks of those incredible minds, it only recognizes that they were advanced souls responsible for the future's education. If anybody doubts God's existence, they must surrender to the Creator's idea before these facts.

However, I do not mean "religion," but science, the science of God's creation, something very different from religion, as it is commonly known.

We could go back and pay attention to the thinkers, poets, sadhus, and philosophers who helped write the Vedic Scriptures on the East and the Greek documents like the New Testament, the Septuagint, the Greek Old Testament, and the Torah translation.

It is hard to imagine those days, where human life had a small value, regarded as disposable. When ignorance dominated the scene, and knowledge was a privilege enjoyed by a few, born in wealthy families or protected by patrons or sponsors of the arts and sciences.

Gaius Cilnius Maecenas, a wealthy poet and patron of the Roman Empire artists, started a trend followed by many other wealthy people, art lovers, sponsoring and protecting many developing new artistic talent.

But the particular knowledge that some prophets, thinkers, philosophers, and poets made available through the ancient scriptures is a significant treasure that today continues to be enjoyed, enlightening our lives.

Modern scientists are beginning to acknowledge those individuals that, illuminated by the Creator, poured their vast knowledge into those documents.

However, we must lament the loss of a significant part of that legacy, destroyed by barbarians and war incidents or the loss of almost the entire life of Nicola Tesla, a genius, vilified and ignored because he wanted people to be the recipient of his inventions for free.

Tesla did not want the military to use his knowledge to jeopardize the Planet, and others, who enjoyed the credit without deserving it, later pilfered many of his designs.

Also unfortunate is the absence of data about Pythagoras, whose life was a source of fantastic knowledge in music, sciences, and philosophy.

It was difficult for me, starting writing this book for a few reasons.

I thought writing about my experiences could trigger a dangerous collision between ego and humbleness. After consulting with many of my friends, practically all of them counseled me to go ahead and not only to do it but also to write it in the Spanish Language. As some said, you have acquired a vast experience in life and must tell it, just because numerous people would like to read about it. It humbled me.

I believe people are inclined to read about real issues.

I usually do not explain myself and, overall, do not apologize for my statements.

So, please take these paragraphs as lightly as you can, because,

in the end, I am a little shy, although I must overcome that feeling to tell you about some interesting issues.

I intend to inform you and entertain you, at least, and keep you updated about the facts, as I know them.

So, be prepared to read some opinionated ideas, especially in politics.

These times are heavily politically charged, and remaining impartial is almost impossible, especially when a declared Liberal-Conservative.

Nevertheless, I will try to keep separate the material life from my spiritual self.

Although I have a conservative base, I am pro-changes, making me a hybrid kind of Liberal-Conservative, a unique breed.

Looking at the word Liberal in the Oxford Dictionary: "Willing to respect or accept behavior or opinions different from one's own; open to new ideas." I could resume it on "Being open-minded to changes."

Furthermore, the Postmodern Liberal Movement in America today is like a bulldozer that advances, attempting to destroy every trace of traditional behavior. They try to replace it with controversial thoughts and practices, ignoring many natural laws and scientific facts, favoring feelings over realities. They are blurring the lines.

Due to Society's status nowadays, it is quite tricky to avoid current issues while having an opinion about them.

So, I hope the reader will find my writing style exciting and will be able to see the point through the clouds.

That is why I advise you to be prepared for a controversial mix between past, present, and future, with a personal opinion, that you might love or hate, but I hope you will never find dull.

38 -The Danger Ahead.

The Postmodern Liberal Movement is already causing damages, and a Civil War is plausible. The controversial result of the 2020 election, evidently tainted by stories of fraud, grossly mismanagement, irregularities, including unconstitutional changes by State Courts, usurping Legislative rulings.

The current times are among the most important since the creation of our Nation. The external political forces, Democrats are attempting to operate a radical change, which I am sure most Americans do not desire. Many ignore the dreadful consequences.

Communism, a project coming from the sick mind of Karl Marx and Fredrich Engel, initially tried in the old USSR, materialized its in-roads to the USA through the Cuban Revolution. However, the Soviets opened up a collateral project in my birth country Uruguay. So, I was a witness to such development in my hometown. I will bring details in further chapters.

The United States has been mostly a conservative bastion through religious thought. However, a different "religion" is pounding at our doors, menacing our standards, and attempting to dominate us by force. They've been doing it in the East for 1400 years. Now the invasion is in motion, right at our doors. Islam keeps on the move, thru the Radical Wing led by Iran with increasing force, now invited by the Postmodern Liberals, to be part of the coalition to destroy our President and our Nation, as we know it.

Some challenging times lie ahead, and we need to choose the right path while fighting against the evil forces to keep a necessary balance.

So, I decided to keep comparing the present with the past and a vision of the future. I hope to have made the right choice.

You will judge it.

However, Coronavirus's unannounced intrusion has taken our people and the World's population by surprise. The Pandemic is forcing us more dramatically than any previous war, to come to a temporary stop that is changing already our lifestyle like we never imagined, and who knows the extent of the changes in the future.

To begin with it, no longer our usual salutation kissing, embracing, fist slapping, high-five, fist-bumping, and similar will be routine in the future, or at least for some time. Instead, the usual Eastern-Asian bow-down, hands together, or head bowing will probably be the new norm. Be ready for a drastic change.

Democrats desperately want a permanent lockdown to blame President Trump for the health calamity, as well as the economic disaster.

They have the most flawed Presidential candidate possible, a man who does not remember what he ate for breakfast and stuttering, most of the time incoherent, confusing names and situations. A recent one, after named a cabinet member, Xavier Becerra, two hours later, Joe mispronounced Becerra's name, horribly, undescribable. That is why his campaign directors limited his air time from his basement to seven minutes, developed a virtual campaign to make-up for the candidate's handicap. Of course, they counted on the valuable Mainstream Media's partnership, that sweeps under the rug any embarrassing or compromising issue.

Meanwhile, the Blue States Governors are doing their part, keeping their States closed or limiting the citizens' liberties.

One of their biggest mistakes is to keep schools closed until next year.

They are not thinking wisely!

A BRUTAL ATTACK ON DEMOCRACY by J. Pelegrin

J. Pelegrin

A BRUTAL ATTACK ON DEMOCRACY

(The All-Time Enemies on the March)

Prologue

(The Army's in the philosophical battlefield)

41 -No One Saw It Coming.
The American People never considered the possibility of a threat like the present one.
Moreover, the existence of an internal political force like the Democrat Party, to turn against our Constitution, was never a serious chance it could happen, until now.
Democrats have always been leaning to the left, middle of the political road option, at least until they lost the 2016 election.
Starting a little before that, when Bernie Sanders, an old Communist militant, a fan of the former USSR, who spent his "honeymoon," of all places, in USSR's Moscow, made a bid to get the Presidential nomination.
We all know the end of that contest, so I will avoid repeating the events. The Democrat's puppeteers knew Sanders wouldn't make it thru the end, manipulated results, and chose the manageable Joe Biden.
After Donald J. Trump won the Presidency in 2016, Democrats went berserk, and derangement syndrome developed rapidly and out of control.

Unlike previous elections, the 2020 campaign started the day after learning that the new President was not a Democrat.

However, Sanders' ideology was kept in the shadow, with the promise that if Biden were successful, the new Administration would reward Bernie's extreme dreams.

42 –The Bernie Sanders Dream.

Bernie's giveaways to the potential voters, which in 2016 were incredibly generous, consistent with a Socialist/Communist program, was cheered by the youth during the primaries. Still, not enough voters accompanied Sanders through the end.

Besides, as we know, there were some dirty tricks from the DNC, like the "super-delegates," that forced Hillary to be the nominee.

Bernie didn't stop working on his platform, and he thought that by adding the new voters in 2020, with some adjustments, he could have another chance to be the nominee and face President Trump in November.

He didn't stop working on his platform; with the help of the newly elected Alexandria Ocasio Cortez, who developed what is called the "Green New Deal," put together an insane Communist platform. He rebranded him and his movement as "Democratic Socialism." In my opinion, a controversy since Socialism is not democratic, per se.

His new label: "Democratic Socialism," caught momentum, and immediately most youngsters, mainly students, began a love affair with the old Socialist, acting like a Communist.

Sander's giveaways were precisely what the uneducated youth wanted. Forgiving student loans, free tuition, free Healthcare even for illegals, food stamps, and free housing, free this, free that; the old career politician offered perks that Marx and Engels never mentioned in their Communist Manifesto.

It was an excess of giveaways, like not the most prominent demagogue in history ever offered in an electoral campaign.

Communism is not a giving philosophy. On the contrary, people suppose to work for the Government and dedicate their lives to the one Party system, only rewarded with meager pay to keep them alive merely. No social or health benefits, like in the USA.

Bernie, counting on the economic bonanza created by Donald J. Trump, with record employment, over 3% GDP, and the lowest corporate taxes ever, saw an opportunity to spend big money. The Trump tax-cuts triggered the repatriation of capital and the opening of new factories in the USA. So, Bernie was ready to dilapidate that wealth to achieve his Communist dreams; he treasured for decades.

Because his numbers were better than the other twenty-some pre-candidates, the DNC saw an opportunity to beat Trump in 2020.

They will deal with Bernie's Communist dreams at a later date.

What they needed at the moment was momentum, and they thought Sanders could provide it.

The Ultra-Liberals began supporting the lefty independent, running under the Democrat's umbrella.

Meanwhile, with the powerful help of the Mainstream Media, they threw the kitchen sink at the President and starting with the "Russian Collusion," which they extended for almost three years, in an appalling Mueller's investigation.

In the end, Bob Mueller's probe proved to be only a hoax.

Democrat politicians alternated with various false sexual accusations against Trump, featuring all kinds of lies, slander, and fake news, while we reached the Democratic primaries time.

Additionally, we recall that 19 hours after the 2016 election, The Washington Post published a headline saying: "The impeachment has begun." A significant promise that kept the Media and Democrats looking to find a motive for such impeachment.

Meanwhile, Adam Schiff, and Jerry Nadler, in the background, were furiously preparing the impeachment. The scenario was ready, and they only needed the main ingredient: A motive.

Finally, they grabbed the famous phone conversation between Donald Trump and the Ukrainian President, and bingo! They began to put together the articles of impeachment.

In January of 2020, while in the Democrat's mind, the only thing was the impeachment, a tiny virus entered the scene, mostly unnoticed and, of course, far less important to Democrats than to impeach the President, their most treasured dream.

In jeopardy by the Democrat's plans, Trump learned the bad news coming from China and immediately, on January 31, declared a National Emergency and banned travel to and from China, right in the middle of his worse nightmare: An Impeachment.

Finally, after a three-ring Circus, the Senate acquitted Trump on February 5.

On February 24, Speaker Pelosi appeared on TV on a street event in Chinatown, San Francisco, inviting people to go out on the streets to celebrate the Lunar Chinese New Year and show Chinese people that everything was calm and healthy.

Nancy said nothing to fear on TV, embracing people at the parade without a Mask or other precautions.

On March 12, additionally, Trump banned travel between the US and 26 European countries.

It is hard to understand why Democrats claim that Trump started to act too late against the COVID-19.

Meanwhile, the Coronavirus coming from Wuhan, China, showed the first victims, increasing by the hundreds daily, and we all know the rest because it became a Pandemic and the worse nightmare to our country and the World.

44 –A Difference Between Blue And Red States.

While in January 2020, Democrats and the MSM were busily Occupying 98 % of their time trying to nail Trump with the Impeachment, Dr. Fauci declared that he thought the Coronavirus was not that important. Despite that declaration, Trump had a brilliant idea to enact National Emergency, stop traveling with China, and then extend Europe's measure. That decision saved thousands of lives.

Despite that intelligent move, Democrats and the MSM are continuously lying, saying that 'Trump delayed the action against the virus for too long.

We must understand the COVID-19 is a new strain, and not even the expert virologists of the World know much about it. The World knew no cure, no vaccine, or treatment at that time, and while around the World, there was a frantic activity trying to find a remedy, there were only minor developments to help us. Finally, thru Operation Warp Speed, Trump fathered the "Trump Vaccine."

Also, the Blue States were unprepared for a Pandemic. While they wasted taxpayer's money giving away billions to the Union's Pension Funds, and wasting millions on stupid investments as Gov. Cuomo's did in New York State.

Since taking office in 2011, Gov. Cuomo has consumed more than $10 billion in public funding and tax breaks in the name of economic development; All of the investments significant failures. However, none of the States under the Democrat's Government did foresee Health problems and left supplies and equipment to empty, so there was nothing when the Trump Administration needed them badly. No Ventilators, an expensive machine, no emergency supplies, nothing. So they falsely blamed Trump for the Governor's lack of foresight.

Fortunately, with the help of the 1973 War Powers Resolution, the Trump Administration got the assistance of many industries and Labs. They quickly acted to manufacture equipment and supplies to face the health crisis.

In the beginning, Gov. Cuomo demanded from the Trump Administration 40.000 ventilators; a quantity later found inaccurate and excessive.

The Federal Government never failed to supply a ventilator to any patient in need of it in the whole country.

Ventilators' existence is now in excess, and the Trump Administration is helping various countries in need of expensive and sophisticated equipment.

Democrats overlooked Cuomo's administration failures, and his co-partner, the worse Mayor of all times: Bill De Blasio, both mishandling the Pandemic, which in New York State is the largest in the country.

Cuomo made a big mistake ordering Nursing homes to accept elderly infected with the Coronavirus, putting in danger thousands of older adults in healthy condition living in those facilities, instead of utilizing the Ship Hospital that Trump made available to him. Over 7.000 seniors died as a consequence of Cuomo's mistake.

Also, the 2.900-bed hospital the Military Engineers built in the Javit's Center, and other facilities the President fulfilled after Cuomo called on President Donald Trump to approve the construction of 4,000 additional hospital beds across the city, have not been used suitably.

A terrible move, politically detrimental, will haunt the Governor all his life.

Finally, Trump recalled the Hospital Ship USNS Comfort, which was not used by the Governor's team.

46 –A Brief Review.

In Chapter 1, I will be detailing some of the issues that brought me to many conclusions and defined the course of the events trying to change our country to something that our Founding Fathers did not want.

Although the Founders did not know Communism, Totalitarianism, Authoritarianism, Despotism, Cruelty, and other terms alike were known; They were born with humanity.

Communism, a political philosophy developed in the 18th Century, adopted most of them and exercised them politically, producing a hideous form of Government that deprives people of the main reasons we are born in this World. Freedom, free speech, liberty, and human rights, especially the pursuit of happiness.

Karl Marx and Fredrich Engels were Atheists, totally materialists, and ignorant of high philosophical principles, especially of Consciousness, the element which links the human body and the soul.

In my opinion, that disavows anybody to govern a country, what to say about ruling the World, as they pretend.

Of course, Authoritarianism and Theology, featured in Islam, are embedded in their beliefs since the seven Century and practiced with cruelty until nowadays by Radical Islam.

A savage understanding of human life punishes violators of Islamic religious rules sometimes with death is despicable behavior, even when the violation is against God's rulings, as they affirm.

Also, the way they treat women as second or third class citizens considered men's property, and sexual or servitude objects is a despicable practice.

Despite that, Communism and Islam are incompatible since the first is Atheist. At the same time, the latter is based on God's belief. Our Democrat Party found a similar goal in both philosophies: They both hate Democracy. In this particular case, they also hate Donald J. Trump because he is a Liberal-Conservative and against Totalitarianism and Authoritarianism.

But the strangest case is that the US Democrat Party renegades even of its name. They are going against centuries of history and many personalities that constructed a genuine Democratic organization of prestige in the USA. They are now siding with Communism and Socialism after having a commercial experience with Communist China that enriched several of its members.

They are now aligning with the Chinese Government to exploit the Asian laborers and farm-workers to provide cheap craft to the Billionaires owners of factories and High-Tech corporations doing business with the Communist, now ruling the Asian giant.

Based on the belief that "My enemy's enemy is my friend," the three of them, Socialism/Communism, Islam, and the US Democrat Party, are engaged in a kind of partnership, which focuses on destroying President Trump and the United States of America, as we know it.

Their plans are obvious, and although all the three groups want exclusive domination of our country, two of them will not stop at that because they want the World's absolute power, and they will not stop at anything less than that.

That is the sad situation with our country today, in the middle of the Coronavirus Pandemic. Blue governments are experimenting with suppressing many rights and putting in practice some of the bans in the insane "Green New Deal."

Also, a self-imposed, and many times State Governments quarantine makes our Cities and Towns look empty, desolate, and helpless.

Democrats poisoned the most critical election of our lifetime with manipulations; They well-planned chaos, confusion, and fraudulent voting. They certainly succeeded.

Democracy, mainly Constitutional Democracy, we must protect by defending the written Constitution and preventing modern lawyers from changing its articles. They are invoking the false pretext that our Charter is a "Living Constitution" and therefore must change according to with extreme Liberals' changing wishes; I call them now "Postmodern Liberals."
The fight is on, the armies are already engaged in a brutal battle, and the mixture of philosophies practiced by the three rogue groups trying to destroy our country, the most successful Constitutional Democracy in the World's history.

J. Pelegrin

A BRUTAL ATTACK ON DEMOCRACY

(The All-Time Enemies on the March)

CHAPTER 1

(Political Correctness)

49-The Election That Changed The World.
49-Liberals Messing With Education.
49-The Alliance.
The 2016 US election was not an ordinary electoral act. The consequences have been unpredictable, shocking, and devastating for some people while promising for others.
Starting with Hillary Clinton, Bill Clinton, Barak Obama, and the rest of the Democrat Party, but much worse for the Liberal community.
It created: "The Trump Derangement Syndrome."
In a general panorama, the entire political scenario changed. Hillary Clinton turned to the left more than any other Democratic candidate before her. Still, the new leadership went so far to the Left that it encountered Fascism, Communism, and authoritarianism at its best.
We all know and experienced during the campaign; a much more critical political factor developed and helped make the changes even greater.

The Liberal Movement in the Democrat Party re-defined part of the leftist philosophy, adding a totalitarian fascist denomination. I now call them Postmodern Liberalism,
They refuse to admit it, although their behavior confirms it.
Democrats made a grave mistake not condemning the totalitarian practices of Black lives matter and Antifa. They display a violent activity. On the contrary, Democrats officialized their assistance and made it an intrinsic part of their violent arm.
After the catastrophic defeat of November 8, 2016, Postmodern Liberals practically seized power in the DNC. They forced its members, Congress-people, and their ideology, pushing them to a new frontier, adopting modern Liberalism with different content, mostly totalitarian.
BLM's now iconic phrase: Protesters in a Black Lives Matter march held outside the Minnesota State Fair over the weekend were captured on video yelling "pigs in a blanket, fry 'em like bacon," a statement that people viewed as targeting police officers.
Democrats didn't waste the opportunity to use the protesters as a valuable asset. They kept them unofficial, but as the central part of an illegal operation that rapidly acquired popular support in a population's sector. Postmodern Liberals knew that a part of the Black population would support a bid to provide them with a loud and violent help, especially to some of the unemployed, low income, and illegals.
So, BLM became a kind of "folk-hero," false defenders of the needy, in reality, a growing domestic terrorist organization servicing the Postmodern Liberalism that hijacked the Old Democrat Party. They received hundreds of millions of dollars in donations, from the poor to the Billionaires owning High-Tech corporations.
Almost immediately after knowing the BLM popular success, another, even a more violent group, appeared on the scene, this time hiding its roots. Marxist trained also, its members showed sophisticated techniques, especially torching police cars, Federal

buildings, and small businesses. Curiously, they did not touch any Mosques or Islamic Centers, or business.

Both groups began to show on the streets, perfectly coordinated. BLM initiated the "protests," and immediately, Antifa followed up, bringing weapons, fireworks, and other disturbance elements, that distribute them among the protesters.

They installed chaos under the Democrat Party leader's approval and encouragement. The Media labeled them: Peaceful protesters—a mockery of reality.

Each one of the Democratic Party members ignores the traditional DNC platform. They devoted their full time to resist the Trump Administration, the Republican Party, and the Conservative Movement.

Rapidly, Democrats planned their actions so well that the GOP should envy and learn from their techniques.

I do not need to address the harmful influence of Socialism and Communism throughout the world.

Latin Americans reading this book, especially, know the scope of these totalitarian ideologies, much better than the ordinary American citizen.

In America's Southern Hemisphere, they study the World's history in greater depth than in the USA. The experienced it on the flesh, with many Socialist and Communist regimes practically destroying countries' economies recently, has been devastating for Hispanic citizens. Concluding the case: They say that 'whoever burns with milk when he/she sees a cow, cries.'

After November 8, 2016, people began to separate some friends and families to argue and distancing from each other.

People changed their preferences and stopped talking to old neighbors. A whole series of regrettable issues came between the families, the acquaintances, and friendships in the country, and everything changed due to political discrepancies. The trend, rather than being an occasional fad, continues to grow with unfortunate proportions. The USA population is divided like never before. Democrats are trying to blame President Trump, but it is evident, Democrat leaders are to blame. They wanted the American people to feel uncomfortable, miserable, and desperately in need of a change. They lied, and lied, inventing stories against President Trump, and during four years, they sang the same tune blaming him for everything.

Never before in history, a President was so disrespected and viciously attacked every single day.

After the 2016 election, we entered a virtual civil war right after an election in which the country changes the Government through the people's vote. The decision of the Electoral College, according to the words of our Constitution, elects a President.

The media has a large part of the responsibility for social dislocation.

Mainstream "journalists," converted into Democratic Partisans, immediately shoveled fuel into the fire seeking power, creating the greatest disaster of all times, even worse than the racial hatred of a few years ago.

At first, Democrats were desperately looking for errors in the counting, irregularities in handling paperwork, and even some accusations of fraud by the Republican Party, for months occupied the news and the 'talk of the town.'

Everything became irrelevant, except for the discussion and arguments about the recent 2016 election.

Social life, conversations at work, near the water cooler, and even at the street level; people stopped talking about the electoral act's speculations.

As the weeks passed by and the Electoral College pronounced the final results electing Donald J. Trump as the 45th President of the United States, he assumed power on January 20, 2017.

Although many of us thought that the waters were calming down and the country would be taking its regular course, it did not.

Postmodern Liberals, who at that time had already taken all aspects of the leadership in the Democrat Party, continued to exert even more pressure, leaning more and more to the Left and adding support from other groups to their already declared "Resist" movement.

Democrats knew they needed something new to recover the Government. The first step was to take the House of Representatives back.

They exploited the fact that Trump was new and inexperienced in government affairs and organization.

They also took advantage that he brought many new people to his Administration. Those newcomers made many mistakes, especially trying to change the President's programs, which ended in many replacements and criticism from the Media, self-declared Democrat's partisans. Some GOP Senators like Mitt Romney, John McCain, and others started a movement called "Never-Trumpers," one of the causes that helped Democrats taking the House of Representatives in 2018.

The Hollywood elite also entered the rebellion. Liberals, naturally led by former President Barack Obama, Hillary Clinton, Bill Clinton, and senators such as Mark Warner, Nancy Pelosi, Chuck Schumer, and celebrities such as Oprah Winfrey, Robert DeNiro, David Axelrod, Harry Reid, Judge Sonia Sotomayor, ex-Vice President Joseph Biden, showed their massive support.

The Media and other personalities of our political and social life, especially in California and New York, also fully entered the "Resist" movement.

Almost instantly, a whole opposite front to the newly elected President made its physical presence on the scene, led by the Black Lives Matter and fascist group "Antifa."

Democrats' plans materialized. The entire country became a battlefield, relegating essential issues such as economics, employment, medical care, international relations, and other vital aspects of our lives to a second place. All efforts of Postmodern Liberals focused on consolidating the new movement, opposed and determined to derail the Presidency of Donald J. Trump.

Not even North Korean Kim Jong Un's daring attempts to initiate a nuclear war distracted Democrats from continuing the revolt against President Trump.

The Democrat Party made the "resistance movement" its only motive to exist and Impeachment the principal tool to unseat Trump and preventing him from being re-elected.

Democrat leadership decided Impeachment, only 19 minutes after knowing the 2016 election results. Then, they began to look for a motive.

They tried a few; The Russian Collusion, Derangement, unfit to be President, sexual false accusations, and many others, including the recent Impeachment failure, an obvious hoax.

The alliances did not stop there. The Postmodern Liberal Movement continued its support search and soon formed a strange bond with Islam. The well-known prominent supporters of terrorist organizations such as Al-Qaida, ISIS, Hezbollah, Al-Nusrah, Hamas, and dozens more, led by the Iranian clerics in power, have assumed the entire Radical Islam leadership. They have many activists in our country, even in the House of Representatives.

Despite the vast difference in their values and support issues, both sides are US conservatives' enemies. They decided to fight together. Although, if they might succeed in the end, Islam will inevitably overwhelm the Liberals by numbers and, of course, by the experience of 1400 years fighting for its radical and totalitarian cause. They will wait; no rush. They've been waiting and acting as they were allowed for centuries.

Remember that in our World, there is no force more potent than religion, and the fanaticism of Islam exceeds the average.

Armed with the rant of "Climate Change," an exaggerated view of the catastrophes that the World has witnessed for centuries, the fight began. The climate issue, although significant, is not the most important for the survival of our country.

As a matter of fact, in a recent poll by the Pew Institute, the issue "Climate Change" came in 18th place. Not a preferred subject among voters.

The search for clean energy and caring for the environment are tasks that we must closely watch. We must protect it carefully but without exaggeration. Still, we must make sure that other countries do not take advantage of us using regulations that could negatively affect our lives.

President Trump withdrew from the Paris Accord because other countries were abusing the United States that had, at the time, stricter regulations for us, but allow other countries to have better deals. The Agreement was detrimental to our economic development and favored other countries that follow the US from afar in the environment's care. China, India, and other countries are known as more significant environmental polluters; however, considered by the Paris accord as "developing countries?".

Let's face it. If the whole world does not take care of the environment simultaneously, it's irrelevant to sacrifice our people with regulations that others won't follow.

In any case, the USA holds the World's lead concerning conservation, preservation, clean air, and care of the environment.

After serious irregularities, President Trump fired FBI Director James Comey, which prompted a special prosecutor, Robert Mueller, with ample power to investigate the alleged Russian collusion. A definite hoax based on an apocryphal document named Crossfire Hurricane.

The three and a half years investigation did not found any "Collusion with the Russians." Still, on the contrary, Mueller continued looking for "a crime," any crime that ever existed on the part of the Republican Party or the Trump campaign. He did not find any.

Simultaneously, the liberals added the infamous "Collusion with Russia," a hoax that, after two years, was exhaustively scrutinized by the Special Counsel Robert Mueller and 19 Liberal Lawyers helping him, never showed any proof of being real. No collusion, no obstruction was in the report written by Mueller.

However, DOJ investigators indicate that the real collusion may have been between the Russians, the DNC, and Hillary Clinton. So, things have become murky in the Democratic Party now commanded by the Postmodern Liberal Movement.

Besides, Attorney General Bill Barr has appointed a special investigator, US Attorney John Durham, to look into the start of the FISA Court dealings, a criminal investigation. Unfortunately, despite the judicial and political attributions, the Durham process has been a timid attempt to uncover the dirt and still hanging in limbo. After everybody assuming that Durham would release the report before the 2020 election, he did not.

Senator Lindsey Graham is looking to initiate an inquiry of the Democrats with the Russians and the FISA affair.

Recently, A.G. Bill Barr made Durham a Special Counsel, which will be practically impossible to fire by the new Biden appointee as Attorney General, eventually.

The Media intervention has been and continues to be a significant force in the 2016 post-election struggle, has no signs of changing after the 2020 election. The hatred poured out by liberal journalists; we have never seen before.

Except for Fox News, the Media devotes practically 97% of their time to deprecating the Trump Government's actions or ideas and significantly tarnish the President's image. The opposition became a source of personal hatred against Mr. Trump, his family, and his team. Democrats kept attacking and insulting the President supporters in an actual witch-hunt that persecuted the MAGA followers, even attacking them inside restaurants, gas stations, grocery stores, and the streets. The personal hostility shown by some of the journalists siding with the Postmodern Liberal Movement turned unhealthy, unreal, making no sense. It is an unfair campaign by the mainstream media and Democrats that the President has named "Fake News."

Washington's Establishment hates the changes that President Trump had in mind. Even some Republican Party senators in the "Never-Trumpers," and some Congress-people keep battling POTUS. The group has reduced its members lately, and Trump slowly gained support after fulfilling most campaign promises, especially the economy, until the COVID-19 arrived.

Surprisingly, the US economy, although the Wall Street market has shown some days of deep plunging, followed by also strong rebounds, is considered by experts, including the Federal Reserve Chief, as healthy and robust, reaching the 30.000 marks lately, in November 2020, never shown before.

Some experts predict an unusual increase in investors' confidence in the USA and the Market Capitalist system. However, the possible Biden Administration has other plans that will damage our economy and increase the Chinese domination of the World's economy. If Biden enters the Oval Office, China will have its pet in the White House.

57 -Hollywood/Nazi Connection During The Depression.

As mentioned earlier, the Hollywood elite is in full support of the DNC, now hijacked by the Postmodern Liberal Movement.

It is significant that during the times of the US Depression in the 1930s, the big Hollywood producers worked closely with the Nazis to survive the economic crisis.

Hitler's addiction to Hollywood movies is widely known. Some historians say the Führer never fell asleep without first watching a Hollywood movie. At that time, Germany was the most important market for the American film industry. Any film projected in Germany's theaters ensured the real income to its producer desperately needed for survival.

Hitler even had an exclusive Ambassador in Hollywood, named Georg Gyssling, who frequently visited the studios and supervised the productions and their contents. Gyssling regularly inspected the new production's scripts carefully and even prohibited some of them from continuing filming or forcing changes that would negatively affect the reputation of his boss, Adolph Hitler.

Producers, unable to obtain money loans from American banks due to the economic crisis, found an essential cash source in the vibrant German industries, which considered the film industry very profitable and anxious to invest.

Despite the apparent ownership of the film studios by Jewish investors, the magnates opted for the convenient separation of business and religion. This close relationship with the Nazis probably left a legacy in the Hollywood elite, particularly about the Third Reich fanatic practices.

The closeness between Left and Right was, at that time, confusing, and its traditions sometimes superimposed at some point. Money was the main issue.

Both were totalitarians. Thus, the Postmodern Liberalism Movement is itself totalitarian.

Over the years, the Hollywood community has shown a controversial identity, where autocratic ideas appear at every step of the way, while money is always King.

At this time, it is not different. It helps a totalitarian movement such as Postmodern Liberalism, which supports an attempt to go against conservatives whose primary motive is to maintain Market Capitalism's fundamental principles and morals: reputation, respect, and economic prosperity.

However, it is not clear if the reason is to ruin our conservative bases or personal hatred towards President Trump. I am inclined to believe that they hate Donald Trump because he is trying to keep the country conservative against the Postmodern Liberalism's intentions to turn it into a modern version of Sodom and Gomorrah.

However, I doubt the Hollywood community understands or even tries to know the President's philosophy. In my opinion, we could synthesize as Liberal-Conservative, which means a traditional Conservative base but open to some Liberal ideas. Not like Postmodern Liberalism but like its old etymological meaning: Liberalism= "Open to changes and exploring new ideas."

However, I insist that observing the Ancient Scriptures' experience is wise advice to preserve our country's success and identity.

58 -Education's control Is Part Of The Liberal's Plan.

Postmodern Liberals' intentions have become even more radicalized and are pushing the movement further to the left, making the issues they are pressing stranger and shameful.

Simultaneously, they reduce the space between the Left and the Right in a threatening way. Turning to the Left all the way, it will find the hard totalitarian Right that dominates the Left utilizing money, power, and corruption. The winners are always the same: The wealthiest people.

The 1 % form the elite that prefers and loves totalitarianism, regardless of the political trench. Those are the Oligarchs that corrupt the Communists and Socialists rulers and monopolize the lion's share in any government. For them, people are only numbers without a soul.

Nowadays, it seems the Democratic Party is pushing towards an exact totalitarian leadership style where a big Government commanded by an elite of presumably privileged individuals would indoctrinate the masses to obey their orders without dissenting or even asking questions.

A similar government like China under Xi Jinping; he enjoys a lifetime President or Chairman title.

A clear example is an appearance in Congress of the very ambitious young woman, Alexandria Ocasio-Cortez. She, by chance, was elected Representative of The Democrat Party at 29 years of age.

In her first two months in Congress, she has already proclaimed herself the leader of the Democrat Party without having been serious opposition to her assumption.

The actual leader of the House, Nancy Pelosi, has remained mute. Immediately, AOC launched an idea, completely unreal, unrealizable by the exorbitant cost and its thoroughly deranged nature.

The plan, called "Green New Deal," demands the ban of all air commercial transportation and proposes changing the US energy matrix in ten years to renewable energy exclusively. Simultaneously, it shows an irrational philosophy that includes the total renovation of absolutely all USA's buildings and houses that depend on fossil or nuclear fuels. There is no known energy source for such a replacement, something utterly unrealizable since no technology allows the exclusion of fossil fuel or nuclear energy.

The AOC madness does not stop there. She has suggested that women should wonder if having babies is worth it because of climate change. Also, she asks for the elimination of all cows because their flatulent discharges are contaminating gases.

The proposal is too extensive and utterly undoable, so I will avoid detailing it at this time.

The huge problem is that Biden is wholly sold to such an idea, although he is trying to deflect his commitment to a lesser drastic sketch published on his website.

AOL keeps insisting that she and her movement (The Squad) will continue to lobby for adopting her idea.

60 -Today's Education Fiction.

Education is the first issue Fascist, Communist, or Nazi want to control. As history shows, one of the first measures of those totalitarian ideologies is the appropriation and manipulation of the educational system.

Totalitarian political doctrines need to command educators and manipulate them to indoctrinate young minds in their political philosophy. In the Postmodern Liberal agenda, indoctrination replaces education. We will show some examples.

60 -The California Chaos.

I was recently in Los Angeles, visiting friends. California, especially the cities of San Francisco and Los Angeles, is the greatest bastion of the Postmodern Liberal Movement.

Except for Hollywood and its surroundings, the Pacific coast, and other places where the rich and famous dwell, most of its population seems to be living off the Government's welfare.

Of course, it is not a crime to seek government help. The social assistance system supposes to temporarily help American citizens recover, redesign their lives, and contributing to the families to enter or return to a productive life.

However, Democrats, who were hijacked by Postmodern Liberals, are planning to create a parallel society, which has been restricted to "survival" instead of "living life" productively and dynamically, being pillars of our community. Of course, it is part of the Government's desired dependence, necessary to make people practically slaves of the new system designed by the High-Tech sector, conveniently supported by the Democrat Party.

The ill Democratic State of California Administration has been responsible for the enormous expansion of the homeless, drug addition, and Mental disease," in colossal proportions.

The longtime residents are reasonably alarmed and hiring private security companies to protect their properties.

Many migrate to other states with lower taxes and fewer regulations, totally disenchanted by the famous "California Paradise."

Postmodern Liberals are determined to impose a new division in the American people.

An excessive government with a vast bureaucratic block that 'works' for the State will make decisions about an impoverished society of dependent, uneducated people and increasingly heavy drugs.

The new welfare dependents will abuse the Government's social services.

One of the provisions on the AOC "Green New Deal" is that the Government will pay a basic salary to all citizens who can't find work or those who are unwilling to work (former Presidential candidate Andrew Young proposed $ 1.000.oo monthly) Alexandria Ocasio remarked. Unbelievable!

Capitalism may not be perfect, but it is undoubtedly the most effective system to grow and develop our World in freedom and justice. The United States is a good example, or was at least in the recent past.

Of course, undesirable human greed spoils the high characteristics of Market Capitalism. Still, unless we can change the person's nature and behavior, all we can do is continue to work to improve the system and society.

Democrats, in exchange, are proposing a mass of people embedded in a group thinking, obeying a bunch of bureaucrats, commanded by corrupt politicians concurring with the old Capitalists now converted in Oligarchs, enriching themselves by the Lefty Politicians' association.

Is that what the American People want? I don't think so.

61 -Political Correctness.

The now-famous expression: Political Correctness (PC), has lately been a way to keep society segregated, but under different standards, where the groups that once dominated are guilty and ensure that their members assume the consequent burden, of course, exaggerated by the new directives from the Left.

The Left is an integral part of the Postmodern Liberal ideology, as well as Fascism, which was initiated from the Left by Benito Mussolini, or Hitler's National Socialism, the Democrat Party of the People.

For example, in the field of education, conservative professors are segregated, only because they continue teaching science, as usual, observing hundreds of years of development and progress.

They continue to qualify the students in the old fashion way. While on the left, it is about indoctrination. With different rules, though, now enforced by the new leadership known as Postmodern Liberalism that has infiltrated and hijacked the Democratic Party, imposed leftist Socialist-Communist philosophy and then added Anarchist Fascist values to help to enforce them.

We must remember that Mussolini, the creator of Fascism, was a member of the Italian Socialist Party, and Hitler's Party was National Socialism, the people's party. Democrats have also made room to adopt the "Islamist ideology," which I refuse to call only "religion."

Islam has at least four facets:

1) Merchants (used as exploratory commercial penetration).
2) Military (following the settlement of the merchant, including the former Barbary Pirates, now called Islamic Radical Terrorists),
3) Political (after the military incursions, dictate the laws), and
4) Religious (the ultimate goal and destiny of all efforts): religious indoctrination.

They have been doing it for 1400 years without any changes. We will go into detail in other chapters.

As we can see, this new Postmodern Liberal Movement is an extensive agglutination of different ways of thinking and acting. Some opposed to the others, whose only common denominator is the opposition or antagonism to the conservatism and "liberal-conservatism," a lifestyle that Donald Trump proposes.

The most notable addition is then an absolute demagogic behavior: the application of "political correctness." Insults and especially the expressions: "racist, homophobic, intolerant, misogynist, radical, sexist, anti-immigrant, anti-LGBTQ," and many other willfully derogatory adjectives are exchanged across the aisle, deeply dividing our society today.

The hilarious stuff is that Democrats accuse Trump of being the divider.

This polarization often results in the wrong language, which prevents having smart communication.

The postmodern liberal coalition has flooded the atmosphere of lies with such a force that the word lost credibility in every way. They use lies to combating another lie and thus confuse and hide the truth.

It is, in fact, the glamour of totalitarianism. Although this pernicious fashion is in full force in big cities like Los Angeles, Chicago, New York, Baltimore, and others, it has not fully reached American society.

However, there is an open cultural war that conservative or traditional people face. They desperately try to defend our country's greatness built brick by brick for more than two hundred and forty-some years. It has been successful and productive for American citizens and the entire World.

The contribution of our Market Capitalist Society to the World is irrefutable proof of our success. The approximated thirty million illegals in the country, plus the millions waiting in line for a legal entrance to the USA, cannot be all wrong; they all dream of being Americans; Also, the hordes of people trying daily to enter our country illegally.

However, it seems to have been dramatically criticized and challenged by the inept Democrats in the last decade.

American Left-wing is trying to change the direction of our lifestyle. They ignore the accumulated experience for more than one hundred and fifty years since Karl Marx and Fredrich Engels devised the evil philosophy designed to replace God's creation standards, for a Godless system implanted by the Government, led by mortals as a guide and direction towards the future. I will expand on this later.

For now, the so-called PC (Political Correctness), represented by a distorted understanding of natural human behavior, is beginning to take over the centers of liberal education in the United States' major cities.

Parents rely on pedagogy in the United States, hoping that their children will learn the skills necessary to find good jobs.

However, some of those parents have a significant part of the blame on failing results.

Not all conservative parents are role models. Many of them are pushing for their children's performances to improve falsely, just for their satisfaction or to get better jobs for them.

Some would encourage cheating or lying to get better grades and try a whole series of tricks to satisfy their false pride. Others engage in buying favors, paying fortunes to enroll their kids in Universities. That is what we call the negative characteristics of some human beings. Parents send their children to high schools, colleges, and universities, pay more than sixty thousand dollars a year, and when young people return home, the only thing they can offer is contempt.

There are many reports and interviews of college and university students, with horrific results that show the absolute ignorance of the majority of the learners consulted.

The answers they have provided are a shame for our society. Most students have no idea about the basic knowledge that any elementary school child, 50 years ago, would have known in great detail. It is a real shame.

A sinister plot has been discovered, including Hollywood stars on the screen.

Here is what we know.

The FBI has found a criminal maneuver in which a registration manager at universities such as Yale, Georgetown, USC, Stanford, UCLA, Texas, and San Diego, named Rick Singer, has been accused of fraud. Singer submitted pictures of students with their faces in someone else's photo, showing evident superiority on sports, together with false statements and affidavits, to force his clients' acceptance into colleges.

By paying sums of up to one half million dollars in bribes to Mr. Singer, celebrities as actresses: Felicity Huffman and Lory

Laughlin, also accused by the FBI of fraud and other crimes, tried to force their daughters to register in a University.

It seems the mentioned entities weren't officially aware of the plot. One can understand that millionaire parents want to help their children to have a better future, but violating the laws and worse, passing over talented students who do not have millionaire parents is despicable behavior.

65 -Defining Postmodernism.

Postmodernity is ruining the life of the student. In general, a small number of young people go to high school, colleges, or universities to get an education.

At the end of the road, politics would probably help some of them improve their lives and the connections they could make, especially on prestigious educational complexes.

Most students know that some of their classmates would probably get an influential executive or government job that will allow them to hire other employees after graduation.

Of course, selecting these potential workers will be among the students who shared the same classes in universities or colleges.

It's natural. Executives seem to prefer to work with colleagues who graduated from a familiar source. Therefore, public relations are always a sure way to see future employment. That is why, as a student, it is essential to be "someone," intelligent, attractive, or maybe just a show-off; A superficial display of intelligence.

That is the conventional approach today.

The new progressive order has the intention to interrupt or prevent conservatives from making their point of view.

In states like Illinois and California, postmodern liberals are blocking any attempt by conservatives to expose their ideas, even by force and violent behavior, as we all have seen lately in TV news at UC Berkeley and others.

Destruction of private and public property is frequent, trying to stop any conservative speech. The police have not been able or willing to prevent the disruptors from doing so, and what is worst, punish them for preventing such disturbing behavior from continuing.

66 -Black Lives Matter and Antifa enter the game.

Democrats knew that they needed a drastic new plan, and it had to be bold, ruthless, and violent.

With the active help of BLM and Antifa, they engaged in the determined and meticulous destruction of President Trump and the United States of America, as we know it.

Right after the 2020 election, Senator Schumer yelled on National TV: "Now we take Georgia (referring to the run-off for two Senators to define the Senate's control) and then, we change America." There are no doubts Democrats want to end our success as a country for over 245 years and attempt to convert our Nation to a "one Party system" in which, in the future, a Republican President would be impossible. Democrats aim for a One Party Country. Just like China.

Postmodern liberals are trying to create a mass of people unable to face any difficulty in life, so; it will allow bureaucrats who work for the Government to act on their behalf and make all decisions for them, of course, under the High-Tech Billionaires' leadership.

Thinking is not necessary for postmodern life. That is scary!

An excess of liberal professors is the biggest problem.

Often, the professionals, who could not achieve success in the business world, accept jobs as educators and bring all the frustration caused by their lack of acceptance by a better-paid business community, probably too selective. So, they carry their disappointment to the educational center that hosted their liberal status.

Of course, this is not the case in general, although an undesired practice, increasingly frequent.

Liberalism used to be a progressive form of ideology (in the proper etymology of the word) promoting new ideas, changing old and fatigued norms.

Also, there are many Liberal-Conservatives, and I consider myself one of them, who believe in ancient teachings and rules, but who also accepts new ways of thinking, reviewing, and updating the basic concepts of contemporary life.

Like all things in life, if exaggerated, they become useless or even against the original intent.

That is what has happened with the Liberal Movement. It became so damn liberal, so influenced by the Atheist Left that it went in the opposite direction, creating a clash of cultures, with the aggravation of a violent fanaticism added.

An adverse electoral result that upset the relations between people is something totally unwanted. Among other negative aspects, it has separated people instead of uniting them, which we all should want. But the Democrat Party's plan is now different. An absolute power-grab to install a totalitarian form of Government designed and manipulated by the new Oligarchs of Silicone Valley, in tandem with the Washington swamp.

Part of the change is the excessive politicization of the LGBTQ, not satisfied with Conservative society recognizing their lifestyles, now in a bold campaign to promote the expansion of their sexual ideas, borderline with sodomizing and corrupting naive, innocent youngsters, willing to try different feelings and now messing with infants and very tender children.

Because let's face it. It's everything about feelings, ignoring reality, and past experiences with negative results.

Just take a look at what happened in Berkeley, CA., in 2017. The city is famous for being a place in northern California, on the east side of San Francisco Bay, and home to the University of California, Berkeley, the birthplace of the Freedom of Expression Movement of the 1960s. However, in recent events, freedom of expression was denied to several speakers, who invited by the Conservative Students, tried to spread their traditional thoughts.

The people's violent behavior on the Left caused damages worth millions of dollars, destroying public and private property, trying to stop the presentation of different speakers talking about their traditionalist beliefs.

The Postmodern Liberal Movement is trying to change the course of our incredible success as a Nation and replace it with an authoritarian system that promotes hatred and forbids opposition to its Left/Postmodern Liberal/Atheistic beliefs. It is not a positive result, we could say. They are ignoring the experience of the many countries that suffered the governments of Socialist and Communist systems.

The above is the core of the idea Democrats pushed in the middle of the 2020 summer, and with the help of BLM and Antifa, created Civil unrest, sometimes chaos, similar to a Civil War; we'll expand on the next Chapter.

68 -The New Liberal Education Mentality.

One of the selected practices of 'Political Correctness' is not saying the students' qualifications out loud in the universities' world. All grades must be confidential to protect the student's self-esteem, they say.

It is clear that knowing the grades of other students inspires debate and generates the impetus to improve performance, even though it also provides a filter that would separate the talented from the mediocre.

Competition is what has made Western Civilization and Market Capitalism preferred systems in the World. Indeed, the most successful and productive.

When we were students, I can remember that the performance of some advantaged classmates was an incentive to improve our effort. Seeing the advanced students who came to the front to tell their progress and the new developments in the subjects was a motivating and positive experience for many other young students and me. Having talented classmates was an honor and inspiration to improve our work and learning process. However, these days, things seem to be completely different under the new Postmodern Liberal ideology.

68 -Defending The Student's Feelings?

A story circulates in the student media. A girl comes home crying to her mother because another child was deliberately belching in her face, poking her with pencils in her hands and head whenever he approached her.

The mother complains to the school counselor. He tells her to be patient because she would not want to hurt the other child's feelings and asked her to think that he might have had inadequate education and that he "was not educated correctly."

That is the focus of today's educator leadership. They defend the aggressor, justifying their actions instead of punishing them and telling them they are wrong, that they must change their behavior and not be aggressive with their fellows. They call it "defending the student's feelings."

69 -The Teacher's Complaints.

Some good teachers have complained that they receive a "system average" rating on their performances, which only teaches ELA (English Language Arts and Literature). Therefore, if you are an incredible teacher of physics or mathematics, you are given the system's average performance, even if this means reducing the average of your evaluation. Teachers are forced, under liberal postmodern thinking, to share the qualifications with low-level teachers.

Everyone must share a summative assessment score, only in two categories of educators: Science and ELA. That is the concept of the new Liberal Educational Leadership.

That is how Marx and Engels thought, creating a disaster in all the countries where "Socialism or Communism" was practiced.

These evil characters are the basic construction of Socialism and Communism as a substitute for the personal capacity given to the individual by creation. Or even the progress that a person could achieve through their discipline and consistency by an average, dividing the collective efforts by a denominator whose result would give the same figure.

Of course, such a practice becomes completely artificial and demeaning to the more intelligent and gratifies those who have mediocre performance.

That is the philosophy Postmodern Liberals are trying to impose. They insist on the failed concept of Karl Marx and Fredrich Engels, of flattening individuality, to create a group where the personality is null, to exacerbate the sense of community. That would meet the Communist Government's goal of nullifying the person and forcing them to participate in an impersonal group with no desire to improve them.

Postmodern Liberalism and The Democratic Party are trying to eliminate individuality to impose collective thinking.

70 -Free Speech, No Longer Available.

Even at the lowest level, the rule's changes indicate the extent of the Left's push to accuse what they call the "white supremacy" of segregation and other crimes.

They define especially the white man educated as racist, intolerant, anti-immigrant, so their campaign aimed at silencing Conservatives who want to talk about Socialists' experience and their failures in countries where they have experimented with that ideology.

My birth country, Uruguay, is one of those. Happily, in November of 2019, the Uruguayan people realized the error and voted Socialism out, after fifteen years of disasters.

The infiltration of thousands of lefty teachers and professors in colleges and universities is determined to use their physical and mental power over their students to join and violently transmit the Postmodern Liberal message.

Recent events in California and Illinois show how they use their local publications on campuses to energize what they call "psychologically gentle minds of the students."

They claim to be generally offended by the slightest opposition to the Left's ideas. They regularly send a strong message to Conservatives, telling them that the freedom of expression contained in the First Amendment is no longer available.

President Trump has just signed an executive order that protects free speech in educational centers, under penalty of taking away economic support. It is worth mentioning that this Right's protection already appears in the Constitution's First Amendment. Recent events say in a booming and violent voice that public lecterns are only for the Left to express their radical ideas.

This behavior renders useless the decades that Liberals fought against evil ideologies such as Communism and Nazism, defending the Right of free expression, in those same universities.

71 -Today's Leftist Campuses.

Many university campuses have prohibited, under the threat of violent disturbances, destruction of public and State property, the presence of speakers such as; Charles A. Murray, Ben Shapiro, Nicholas Dirk, Anita Alvarez, Emily Wong, Jason Riley, Milos Yannopoulous, Ann Coulter, David Horowitz, and other conservative thinkers. They also banned my books, and I am considered an undesirable person.

Traditionalist teachers think that what is happening now is frightening. It seems that the desired fashion for education is for educators to remain in the freezer, while students will educate themselves, giving themselves their qualifications.

Under the postmodern liberal leadership, parents and students will lead the schools, and finally, the teachers will not be necessary. Silly, isn't it?

However, that is the attitude of the Postmodern Liberal culture. Totalitarianism has invaded the Liberals and the Democratic Party. However, there is still a big question mark. What is Islam doing here? We will examine this later on.

We can see an attempt to reduce the level of education, so there would be no competition at the top level.

Postmodern Liberalism's goal is that only a mass of mediocre students aspires to positions within the Great Government ranks.

It is a dark future for young people, a totalitarian result to imitate Communism, Socialism, Nazism, and Fascism.

Meanwhile, the offenses are so subtle that it would be necessary to modify the entire language to avoid conflict when speaking publicly.

Let's clarify that not all universities are like that, but at the pace they go, what the educators show, and the particular elections exercised by the Left's leadership, it would be a miracle that they do not contaminate the entire educational system.

The postmodern liberal tentacles are spreading at an alarming rate. Ignorance is widespread, and a false idea of equality is adding fuel to the fire.

A comment says that the dangerous thing is happening in some universities is a "real movement," based on a leftist philosophy, that struggles to globalize the World and eliminate all prejudices.

Unfortunately, they have taken a reasonable human spiritual transformation and turned it into fascist coercion, a necessary condition for a Godless state, which is its ultimate goal.

Once again, we must draw a line between God's creation and religion, two very different things. The science of God's creation is one thing; It is science and separates from religion, an option made by man to assemble and worship God.

Also, how would they explain a Godless society to their Islamic partners? We will review it later.

72 -The Campuses Safe Spaces.

University campuses' created "safe spaces" to provide students with an environment where they could discuss practical issues, although criticized because they control freedom of expression.

Said action is one of the objectives of the Postmodern Liberal movement, of course.

The Islamic culture is more noticeable every day in the universities and increasingly dominant; Now, they are demanding their own private space in the form of "safe rooms."

72 -Dangerous Alliance With Islam.

The above is the most dramatic. In the Democrat Party's circles, every day with more force and frequency, they talk about the formal inclusion of Islam as a fundamental part of the Democratic Party's political platform.

If accurate, that information would be a stab in the back to our Patriots that bravely fought against totalitarianism and Islamic theology since the 17th century.

It is worth noting that the President who preceded Thomas Jefferson, John Adams sold much of the US warships in the commercial market to avoid fighting Islam. History reports that Adams opposed a US war against Muslims. But under President Jefferson, our navy at the beginning of the Marines' Corp fought relentlessly to reduce the Muslim's power (The Barbary Pirates), who was the Mediterranean Sea shores inhabitants nightmare for several centuries.

Jefferson, under the slogan: "Hit hard without taking prisoners," "Smack-down, no prisoners taken," fought against the Muslims Pirates from 1801 to 1804. Finally, he managed to get the Pasha of Tripoli, the highest Islamic authority, to abolish the US gross product's 10% tax as payment and trade with the Mediterranean countries. They did not bother us again for about 200 years, until recently, 9/11/2001, when they attacked the Twin Towers and Pentagon.

73 -The "Resist" Movement.

Sadly, Democrats weren't able to recover fully after the catastrophic results of the 2016 elections, and the word "resist," as Hillary Clinton said, became the Democrats' obsession; A mantra that has been repeated daily with increasing emphasis and incitement to violence.

We just have witnessed the above when a volunteer from the Bernie Sanders Campaign shot Republican representative Steve Scalise at a charity baseball game's practice.

The mainstream media pointed to the issue as a deranged man, avoiding any connection with Senator Sanders' speech. Such an episode was a typical fanatical leftist against a Conservative, now, unfortunately, a familiar scene.

The apparent fact is that the fierce opposition to conservatism is growing, after the 2016 elections, increasing after President Trump's governing success.

Therefore, the battlefield must begin in the spheres of education, as totalitarian regimes usually impose (Nazis, Communists, Socialists, and Islamic). They manipulate young people through fear, lies, false news, slandering public figures, including sexual liberation, promiscuity, and any other means to suffocate the conservative movement.

Notably, ignorance leads to the protest of a crowd that, when asked why they are complaining, does not know the answers and just parrot clichés supplied by the Lefty leadership.

Traditional media helps with the megaphone, a massive team of "apprentice journalists," and the horde of monsters without God who preach a perverse message to help them.

Democrats' first objective was to add seats in Congress, which failed. Democrats lost about 20 seats in the House, while Republicans gained some 22, mostly conservative women. On the Senate, Republicans keep the majority; the primary aim was to obtain the White House in 2020. It is still in doubt.

Radical feminism is a big part of the Democrat's program. Although paradoxical, the leading liberal objective is a classless, genderless, and faceless society, embedded in collective thinking, devoid of individuality.

The scene has become so sensitive that communication creates a false, hypocritical, and uncomfortable situation. One has to observe the language deeply to avoid offenses, which borders on the ridiculous. It is a time of hypocrisy!

Political correctness is the tool. It suppresses words, potentially destroys sensitivity, and weaponizes the language. Postmodern liberals are creating an enslaving reality where they use expressions as weapons of mass destruction.

They banned many words from the English language, which makes it difficult to express in public freely. Fortunately, in the Spanish Language, the Real Academy is showing good leadership.

Sadly, in the English Language, one has to choose the expression of thoughts with a Postmodern Liberal manual on hand to avoid crashing and offending them.

However, among the black community, the word "nigger" is repeated every two words by blacks without anyone being upset. Curious?

74 -A Genderless Society?

Oh, wait! hinted a student. Do liberals not even recognize the existence of only two genders? How retrograde is the way you indoctrinate kids now?

Also, they point that intersexuality exists, right? There are multiple variations of sex chromosomes, gonads, sex hormones, and genitalia that do not agree with the binary understanding of sex. That is not even in dispute.

However, procreation is only possible if a male and a female have sex or sperm is attached to the female's ovule inside the uterus. The same happens with any other animal specimen.

Therefore, it is not clear what the problem is with the recognition of the two unique genres.

On the other hand, it could be a psychological malfunction that is clouding the understanding of so many people on the Left.

We can turn it over, backward, from side to side, from the inside out, but the genetic information stamped on each chromosome will not change. Until a new order, we will have to deal with only two sexes: male and female, female, and male.

The rest is a mere modification of the human being's psychological behavior, which in some cases can be seriously unbalanced with unpredictable consequences.

Of course, handling these situations should be approached with care and always trying not to disturb or offend the person through inappropriate comments or harsh attitudes, but still bearing in mind that "the right of one ends where the rights of others begin," simple and without complications.

However, the postmodern liberal culture prefers to make a big scandal, extending the prevention of clashes between both parties, suppressing the words, instead of requesting manners, and eventually accepting the rejections that people may feel natural if delivered kindly.

Human beings are not perfect, and although we must strive for perfection, we are not close to it.

In this case, manners are useful to improve relationships between people. Nevertheless, cutting out personal thoughts, avoiding expressions that can hurt other people's feelings that express themselves is not in any way a solution. The individual's speech is as crucial as the Right of the recipient to reject it. Freedom of expression is as sacred as the Right to refuse it by others.

76 -Everybody Get A Medal?

The truth shows that no one, ever, could have established a society not even close to what the Postmodern Liberals propose.

This highly arrogant community tries to implement the idea of "everyone deserves a medal." Therefore, there are no people left behind, not even at the cost of mediocrity, which seems to be the desired product.

Teachers should not criticize students who make mistakes because "somehow they are less capable," and God forbid the teacher to yell at a student!

In most cases at "Liberal Universities," educators are told to apologize to a spoiled idiot because he/she got upset after being punished for being rude to a partner.

That is our school system today. Well, not all, thank God, but if the error is not corrected, it will be a general fashion.

God bless the souls of my school teachers. They shouted at me to correct the mistakes I had made. But I learned.

Do not ever think of anyone mentioning that there are only two genders! Of course, there are only two genders! The whole liberal World will fall on your head, and the force of the community desiring to be genderless will crush you ruthlessly! You are destroying their fantasy.

Postmodern Liberals instruct parents not to reveal the sex of their children at birth and tell them to decide which way they wish to go when they grow up, which is criminal behavior.

It does not matter if you believe in Creation or Evolution's theories, although it could be a combination of both; gender is a thing of the past for Postmodern Liberals.

I remember reading the Lenin Decalogue of 1913, with instructions on seizing a country to Communism.

Article number one says 1) "Corrupt young people and give them absolute sexual freedom." Does it sound familiar?

I will publish the entire set of Lenin's Decalogue later.

The Left promotes that rules are not so simple but somewhat complicated by the proposed gender changes. For them, physical and psychological are the same, which at the moment it is an illusion; pure fantasy.

J. Pelegrin

A BRUTAL ATTACK ON DEMOCRACY

(The All-Time Enemies on the March)

CHAPTER 2

(The Plot)

79 -The Strategy.
79 - Postmodern Liberal Movement In Action:
79 -Their Plans To Destroy Western Civilization.

As described in Chapter 1, the new Postmodern Liberal's have made an Alliance: They have weaved a net against the Conservatives. The latter defend Western Civilization, the most beneficial influence on humanity in our World. Of course, it is not perfect.

However, the balance left by Western Civilization is highly favorable.

Among the benefits to our culture are the highest advancements in human rights, the progress of sciences, education evolution, and the positive improvements in human relations as the end of slave-owning in America. Unfortunately, there is still Slavery around the World.

Postmodern Liberals, on their part, are irresponsibly turning Left, pushing Socialism (one step away from Communism). Also, they are inviting Islam as an ally to help in the fight against the Conservative Movement.

They would do anything to satiate their obsession with taking Trump down and destroying the USA as it is now. Just read the Koran and Hadith to learn the truth of the Muslim's goals and philosophy. Besides, understand the real meaning of Socialism and Communism, now with the drastic changes implemented by China, and the core of the Postmodern Liberalism goals. Those two groups are the worse USA enemies, now adding the new Democrat Party, on its present totalitarian style.

Meanwhile, watch the remains of the old Democratic Party members submissively following the trend, leaving behind years of moderated center-left politics.

Democrats, after the 2020 election, are quickly regrouping and taking convenient positions to grab at least a small piece of the handle, that surely will help them enrich themselves. It is all about money, to eventually buy power, the ultimate goal.

The recent election of two Congress Representatives, Ilhan Omar and Rashida Tlahib, prove their ill intentions.

As soon as they took office, Omar aggressively attacked Israel in an unequivocal racist and poor ethical attitude, which the other Democrat congress-people did not dare to condemn.

Besides, the well-known Communist lover Alexandra Ocasio Cortez (AOC), and Ayanna Presley, two ultra radicals, also, conveniently Islam lovers, helped to form what we call: The Squad; A quartet of disgraceful USA haters. Let's remember that Communism and Islam hate each other.

Is it time for Jewish people to leave the DNC? Maybe. Think about it.

Many 'Old Democrats' are also siding now with Socialism, Communism, Anarchism, and the LGBTQ movement, in a genuine attempt to defeat Conservatives.

Also, they welcomed a Fascist group, paradoxically called "Antifa."

Not used to such a bullying crowd, conservatives are slowly reacting to the onslaughts from the Left, overcoming their peaceful nature, now are pushing back.

The 2016 Democrat's losses have been significant, and they continued to lose local elections in 2017. However, in 2020, the pompous announced "Blue Wave" failed miserably.

In 2020, the Democrat's House lost 20 members.

The Democrat Party, hijacked by the Postmodern Liberal Movement, displays a total lack of leadership, an obsessive dedication to derail President Trump, showing a complete absence of ideas to regain the people's favor thru significant issues, unattractive leadership.

Please notice that from our point of view, Trump won the election by a landslide. Still, the imminent fraud, yet not proved by hard evidence, it's starting to show little by little, although compromised by the election time-frame to decide the winner by the Electoral College legally. The US Constitution is frankly so complicated, moreover with the 50 States having local autonomy, their own Constitutions, and the power to manipulate laws that sometimes override the US Constitution. It is weird, but that's the way it is.

Also, some of the State courts, by Septiembre, 2020, modified the local electoral laws, mainly eliminating the voters' signature verification, as well as other rulings, to create the chaos and confusion reigning nowadays.

The present anarchy in the balloting places has allowed the ballot's stuffing, false votes to appear even one month after the election day, and an array of irregularities that benefit Biden and hurting Trump in its totality. No doubts, Democrats are perfecting the art of stealing an election; Not only that but erasing the evidence leaving no trace of their shabby behavior. However, some idiots, pulling suitcases full of ballots pre-filled in Biden's favor, hidden under a table, after Democrats' officials at 10:30 pm dismissed GOP "Poll-Watchers," spent all night stuffing ballots in the voting machines several times. The idiots forgot to turn the security cameras off, and that became evidence. Republicans say that the same procedure was used in other balloting places.

Trying to tempt the American People with Socialist/Communist ideas is not well received. Bernie Sanders and the other politicians of the same lefty ideology were left out of the scene during the electoral campaign, trying to hide Biden's partnership. Nevertheless, the claims to pay back the favors from the campaign's beginning are starting to show right after the election. Everyone is claiming a piece of the pie.

Democrats are only concerned with destroying President Trump to grab the Government's power. They have been unable to show a coherent political platform or any definite Government plans! Only "Resist," an entirely negative term, is in their minds. Additionally, they keep furiously looking for issues and inventing others to condemn President Trump of wrongdoings, until now without success.

The actual Pandemic our country is bravely fighting has not altered the despicable actions of Democrats. They keep pounding the President, doing everything they can to block every move Trump makes to save American lives and keep our economy from collapsing.

The release of the "Trump Vaccine," as I call it, is devastating news for Democrats. By all means, they are trying to degrade it, deny its value, and demonize it, even at the risk of people's death. They don't care about people. They only care about power.

They don't believe in America. They believe in Globalism. They don't believe in our Founding Fathers or our 1778 Constitution. They are traitors!

The Democrat Party's internal shows many reckless politicians, with various controversial electoral propositions that have departed the Party's traditional ideals for decades.

The new proposals, mainly led by Bernie Sanders, with the help of AOC, are Socialist/Communist and failing to say how they will finance them, maybe because there is no way to support crazy plans.

They chose a sugarcoated set of populist promises to fool the ignorant youngsters, so-called "Bernie Bros." lacking any experience in life, to seize their votes.

Joe Biden is repeatedly proving to be unable to show coherence in his speech, with his increasing daily gaffes, a total mess. Sometimes, the man seems to have lost track of where he is standing.

The Left has never shown any country that had a Socialist/Communist government flourishing experience. Venezuela is its last disaster.

Uruguay, finally, after 15 years of Socialist Government destruction, voted them out and returned to Democracy and Market Capitalism.

Bernie Sanders insists that the Nordic countries are Socialist in his lying speech, something those Nations deny repeatedly. Still, the corrupt Media keeps hiding the facts to hurt Trump.

Besides, note that the Nordic country's taxes are up to 70%. They are, in reality, Free Market economies.

However, the real issue is that all the giveaways, free stuff, pardoning students' debts, welcome illegal immigration, open borders, Medicare for all, free this, free that, really;? Nothing is for free.

Someone will have to pay for it!. In this case: The American taxpayer.

The Mainstream Media continue to cooperate with Postmodern Liberals, many of the Colleges' Directors, the University's faculty, and Administrators who are disrupting the Campuses practices in favor of the anti-Conservative mob.

The country is in a terrible spot, socially and politically divided like never before. With the COVID-19 Pandemic severely minimizing all fields, especially the economy, 30 million Americans plus are without a job. Compare the numbers with Trump's economy, a 3.5 % jobless rate until the Coronavirus rained in the parade.

Believe it or not, that is the dream of most Democrat politicians. We can remember the TV personality Bill Maher: "I am 'Hoping' For 'A Crashing Economy' So We Can Get Rid Of Trump, 'Bring On The Recession.'" Such a despicable statement is, unfortunately, the mood in most DNC politicians.

However, the actual economic crisis is not due to American finances' mishandling, but because of a Health Crisis that originated in Wuhan, China. Still, our economy remains healthy, temporarily affected by the COVID-19.

Unfortunately, Democrats use The Pandemic as a massive War weapon against Trump and the Republican Party, and why not to the United States of America as we know it and love it for 245 years.

An Anti-American campaign is in motion, with one of the eldest newspapers, The New York Times, in a leadership position. They insist on calling the USA a systemic racist country, now supporting a hoax they call the "1619 Project," an attempt to reframe American history, a false argument the New York Times' is trying to promote that the American's fought a Revolution to protect Slavery. In any case, the Party in favor of Slavery was the Democrats, while Republicans wanted to abolish Slavery. Abraham Lincoln, a Republican President, finally did it and paid with his life.

They also deny the United States of America's real foundation in 1774, together with our Constitution of 1778.

If those idiots were in China or even in Russia, there would be many rolling heads.

Postmodern Liberals, integrated by Democrats, some Independents, Socialists, Anarchists, Communists, Mainstream Media, LGBTQ, Hollywood elite, helped by the Islamist wearing a ship's skin, under a wolf's identity, in one side; On the opposite side, conservatives and moderates keep pushing to reject totalitarianism.

Curiously, the High-Tech Industry's Elite is also pushing against the President because he disagrees with their employment policies that favor immigrants to replace American workers with cheaper immigrants.

Democrats keep arguing in favor of open borders to invite Illegal Immigration into our country but do not allow them to live near them. There are no poor people's shelters in Beverly Hills, West Hollywood, or Malibu, of course.

On the other side, the Conservatives, working people, Middle Class, Christians, Hindus, Asians, educated Hispanic, European, a portion of Black's, Slavic heritage-related and, of course, the unavoidable 1%, except a part of the new High-tech-billionaires in Silicon Valley supporting Postmodern Liberalism, are enjoying President Trump's America First. Let's remember that President Trump, speaking before the UN assembly, clearly stated that "any President of any country is elected to put his country first." So, putting America First is not an attempt to diminish the other countries, but keep focusing on its people first. A President's obligation.

The Silicon Valley Elite desperately want to keep importing high tech engineers and workers from India (70%) and China (20%) to replace Americans for a fraction of the money they pay the locals.

They even force Americans to train foreign employees, and after they transfer the knowledge to them, they fire them without any consideration. Such is the hideous part of the American Capitalism I vehemently despise.

A significant portion of those companies profit goes to CEO's and their small elite close to the top. Most of the "imported talent" make between $ 70.000. and 100.000 dollars a year. They pay American workers a higher figure, so they want to get rid of them. Greed is the drive.

They are two well-defined sides, very different philosophies of life, where ancestry plays an important role, especially in keeping the traditions and old culture. They are opposing radical changes that will demean not only Western Culture but also Spanish, Asians, Slavic, European, and Hindu traditions.

It is a battle between the old customs and the radical new attempts to dismiss the safety standards of life, try some crazy experiments, play with feelings, and new unexplored games that will end damaging Society to irreparable consequences.

The Chinese are at the helm. The new attachment to their authoritative modified addition of "Market Capitalism" Western-style created their version of "State Capitalism" that enslaves their workers. It deprives them of even asking questions and paying them only enough to keep them alive, work, and survive in inhuman conditions.

Our Creator established which kind of ideas in our Universes we must adopt to keep orderly growth. God has delivered a conscious Legacy, perfectly coordinated and defined in his philosophy.

Unfortunately, many Postmodern Liberals deny Creation. They ignore that evolution is a consequence of Creation.

We must keep developing our culture safely, maintaining a common sense based on past experiences, and future guidance following tradition. Balance is the key.

Postmodern Liberals are ignoring the examples of recent degradation caused by some severe mistakes, like the AIDS spreading thru unsafe sex practices and sharing needles, and insisting on continuing to ignore the red lights.

They keep promoting a libertine lifestyle, which has failed in all past experiences, causing considerable damage to our Society.

Maybe they aim for a modern take of Sodom and Gomorrah.

86 -American Families Are Against Genderless Society.

The American family has been the primary component of Society. Keeping a traditional lifestyle is not only socially desired but also suited to religious practices — all religions counsel to preserve decency and restraint regarding sex life and personal relationships.

Postmodern Liberals accuse religions of being an obstacle to free thinkers, people opposing traditionalism, and welcoming new ways of relating to others, mainly through open sexual practice.

They ignore that so far, nobody has encountered happiness or total satisfaction through sexual intercourse only.

Additionally, widespread reckless sexual practices bring illnesses, cultural and social problems.

Those practices mostly bring difficulties to relationships because of jealousy and other mixed and confusing human feelings that always appear sooner or later.

The truth is, regardless of superficial opinions, that sex is a tool for procreation, the essential part of the animal and human life's survival; no one can deny it.

That is why the Creator made sex so appealing and unavoidable with the intended meaning to have intercourse between the two genders as the only means to create a newborn and an almost impossible way to avoid it. Unfortunately, people confuse the objectives as well as the results.

Instead, Postmodern Liberals have instituted a new idea: a genderless society — a total fantasy based on the pretended choice of gender by individual selection after birth.

It is a fictional way to express their dark and ignorant wish of adopting an alternative identity, which would only satisfy, in part, their imagination and feelings, but not reality.

Such a choice is only temporary make-believe that could meet their desires for some time until they realize that it is only an illusion. It is described in the Vedas by the word 'Maya.' Maybe the fantasy may remain for their whole material lives, but still fiction, like a dream.

So, being in 'Maya' means living an illusion.

A temporary feeling that would not make anything unreal, becoming real. It is, instead, a mental disruption.

The embattled "Planned Parenthood," the ultra-liberal organization accused of selling fetuses and baby parts for a profit, which also dedicates 80% of their activities to provide abortion services, has established new guidelines to define the gender of a newborn.

Furthermore, the controversial group advice instructs parents to tell children to avoid considering the sexual organs to define their gender.

In an open homosexual-friendly effort, the organization is stepping on the gas pushing for a genderless society in opposition to all religious groups and the scientific community, which has not changed the definition of sexual orientation or the gender assigned at birth.

The truth is, anyone that wants to change their gender is only possible as a fantasy and an unreal experience that would last only a moment, maybe a material lifetime, but it would not modify the facts.

People are born either female or male. There is no other option. Of course, they are allowed to "feel" the way they wish, but it will not affect reality.

However, individuals who want to live such a fantasy have the right to do it.

Nevertheless, the controversial part of the Postmodern Liberal philosophy is that they want others to accept fantasy as real while it is not; it remains only an illusion; All that effort, only to justify the wishful person's feeling.

Of course, the rest does not matter for their utter egotistic unreal thought.

Postmodern Liberals need to accept that a society based on feelings is only fiction that they can choose living, although still, it is not real.

The LGBTQ community is bustling, working to widen the acceptance of some new denominations that lately they have been trying to validate by including them in dictionaries, social media, and other fields.

The group is a dedicated community, initially created to fight for same-sex intercourse recognition in a Conservative Society, disgusted in part by some unexpected proposed changes, rated not acceptable by the community as public expressions of intimate affections. In my opinion, sexual relations should be kept private for heterosexual couples too. Let's stay sexual life confidential, please.

Although we must appreciate their effort to recognize de rights of the people they defend, they are confusing their boundaries. Moreover, here, I would like once again to remember an essential old thought:

"My rights end where the other people's rights begin."

The terminology used by these new Postmodern Liberals is broad and diversified; although they organize it to satisfy their community, it sometimes becomes controversial and confusing. Their will to bully Conservatives is not a nice fellow's attitude.

That is the case with the word "Gay," which in the

twelve century meant "happy." In the seventeenth century, Society commonly used the word gay to indicate "immoral," in the nineteenth century, it meant a "female prostitute" also (a gay man used to define a man who had sex with female prostitutes a lot).

So, terminology mutates and accommodates the purposes of the trend.

However, their central objective is to keep pushing for the acceptance of the ultra-liberal way of life and have the Conservatives increasingly acknowledging their escalating way for Postmodern Liberalism to be accepted and respected.

Those attempts do not seem to be changing the bottom line: Regardless of the different ways they are being described and named, our human race only has two genders, impossible to change after birth: female and male.

The pretended way of life may have dozens of sub-denominations, but the reality is the same, Male or Female.

Lately, they have been pushing trans-genders behavior, an even more outrageous fashion that a few confused people are living in their fantasy.

The bottom line is that Postmodern Liberals are determined to disrupt life traditions while Conservatives are defending the standards, based on past behavior, and keeping in mind the Sacred Scriptures wise advice.

These are all-time accurate guidance regarded by the majority and the Scientist's opinions, most of which agree with the Scriptures.

The United States of America has been the Free World leader by traditionally adhering to the conservative style, although accepting certain liberality within consciousness. I call it: Liberal-Conservatism.

That practice had its rewards, providing a long string of benefits that have made people as happy and prosperous as possible in this material world where we live.

The battle continues to keep equilibrium because the voters, electing Donald J. Trump, decided to restrain the path of liberal craziness and return to the more traditional lifestyle.

At least until January 20th, 2021, President Trump is determined to help stop the excesses, and it seems people are positively responding little by little to his ideas. But the heavy pounding of anti-Trump opinions by the Mainstream Media, and their acolytes, has been hideously heavy and convincing to the most ignorant people while hiding, burying the President's positive achievements.

The "resist" movement lead by the Democrat Congress-people relentlessly slowed the Trump Administration's actions by delaying and obstructing all its moves.

The House of Representatives, in the hands of an utterly crazy Nancy Pelosi, has been the principal cause of the Government's actions disruption.

Unfortunately, Democrats never realized that if the President loses, we all lose. Nobody wins.

Or maybe they desired the entire country to fail. Democrats had the idea to "Rebuild better," as they announced during the campaign. Let's see.

It is obvious Democrats hate our country as it is today. They prefer the Global World, and they want to destroy it to replace it with the Postmodern Liberalism style we are detailing here.

It breaks my heart to write it, but in the middle of the present turmoil, health-wise and economic uncertainty, some people on the Left are showing satisfaction with the possibility of our economy's collapse, which would bring our President down.

91 -The well-planned Theft of the Century.

Democrats used and abused COVID-19 as a weapon. As the majority-whip Congressman James E. Clyburn (D-SC) expression: "We shouldn't let COVID-19 go to waste."

They knew they would need a more efficient tool to "get rid of Trump,' as they say. Unquestionably, they used the Pandemic to the fullest extent, fruitfully.

So, a few months before the Nov. 3rd election, taking advantage of the states governed by Democrats and cities controlled by their majors, they made many changes to their electoral laws, some of them unconstitutional or illegal. In the State Legislature, those changes are only valid when performed by the local Congresses, not by the Governors, Mayors, or even the State Supreme Courts.

But because it takes time to do it right, they did it anyway, without the GOP's opposition. Of course, they had the Media supporting the move, arguing, of course, the COVID-19 excuse, disenfranchisement, racism, and the like.

The new changes included letting the ballots go without a signature or address verification, allowing dead people to vote, disregarding double voting, sending millions of ballots to people who no longer lived in the State.

Voting by mail is an old practice in the USA, but those, called absentee ballots, are mainly used by the service people staying overseas, on business, or many other causes. However, they send the ballots after the individuals request them. But Democrats, abusing of the Pandemic, mailed them to everybody they've got an address. The result was that many, or most of the ballots went to inexistent people, dead, absent, or unknown, and many other reasons, so the people who got those ballots, used illegally, on purpose, to help Biden. Republicans or Conservatives are known to refrain from illegal voting. Although it may be a small portion of disloyal citizens, the majority is against such a practice.

The confusion, distress, and fraudulent indiscriminate "voting by mail" gave them the false results of a rigged 2020 election. Democrats knew that the massive mailing voting would create confusion and chaos, and they warned people, thru the Media, to ignore the traditional results after the voting day. Their new ruling included changes that ballots arriving up to 16 days after November 3rd, and even postmarked on November 4th, will be valid; An utterly absurd order. Such an aberration is a mockery of US Democracy and the election laws.

In any other country, it would scream potential fraud!

Democrats did it masterfully! They created chaos, confusion, and the opportunity to extend the fraud into an army of bureaucrats favoring Biden, to enhance the scheme previously, and secretly spread thru the partisanship, which, by the way, are most of the election's average workers.

We know that government employees are Democrats in its great majority.

So the plan was executed flawlessly, in a way that it would provide an opportunity for the Trump-haters to innovate, and personally, imitating an ant community, cooperate with their grain of sand, to build a final mount of fraudulent votes.

But the Strawberry on the cake was the carefully crafted manipulation of the State Laws, inconceivably out of the reach of the Federal Government, especially being that affecting a Presidential election.

Unfortunately, Federalism is not a perfect form of Government. The founding fathers did not suspect that evolution would take us to this kind of shabby behavior.

Those were grossly the plans of Postmodern Liberals in the so-called Democrat Party of today.

Maybe, this was the alibi used, as we read from Marx's political philosophy, to bring Conservatism to rubles and, on top of it, to build a "Communist Paradise," a false statement. After 150 years plus, it has been an impossible dream, a flat failure, with dreadful consequences at every attempt.

However, personal desires, proper of Postmodern Liberal thinking, are commanding the actions against Conservatives.

If these measures are not corrected soon, the United States will be facing self-destruction, after being for two hundred and forty-three years, the model, almost everyone in our World, wants to follow. Except for the Democrat Party politicians, totally unaware of the reality the proposed changes will bring, and Communism lovers, all times passionate ignorants.

Of course, within the Communist philosophy, there are the oppressors (Government officials, politicians, oligarchs, military brass) and the regular people, the oppressed.

Right now, we are assisting a demented coalition rooting for the failure of President Trump's plans to unify the two Koreas and denuclearize the Peninsula.

They also criticize and diminish the peace agreement Donald J. Trump promotes in the Middle East between Israel and some Arab countries.

It is negative energy from the Democrat politicians who publicly mock the President's decisions. In the end, all they are samples of achievements by Trump's policies with the Koreans and the Middle Easterns. The USA remains at peace, with no new actual or future wars seen ahead, and the best World economy, despite the health crisis.

We must remind that changes take time, and to expect immediate progress in the negotiations is asking for too much.

In the past 70 years and many presidencies, there has been no world peace progress at all. The narrow path must end, and we need to encounter a center row that could satisfy the extremes without losing the goal. Trump is on his way.

Spirituality, once again, must prevail over the material way.

It only makes sense. We got to act smart!

We all must contribute to the re-alignment of the current path or face derailment, and who knows what other catastrophes?

We need a Liberal-Conservative approach to preserve the traditions, with an open mind to positive gradual changes to our lives, previous in-depth examination of the eventual consequences. Bad times are ahead.

Beware!

The tools are in the box. However, we must learn how to use them wisely and equitably.

First of all, we must revise our Constitution and adjust some of the amendments' interpretations, perhaps better defining its objects and subjects.

The United States of America has a purpose, clearly expressed in our Constitution. We must keep on the path designed by our Founding Fathers.

Millions, among millions, are desperately trying to live, study, work, and raise their families in the USA, under our present lifestyle, developing for over three hundred years. Are they all wrong? Or are we mistaken? I do not think so. So.

About 30 million illegals risked their lives to live in a "systemic racist USA," as Democrats affirm? Hmm.

94 -If it ain't broke, don't fix it!
94 -Democrats Founded the KKK in 1865.

We must remember, Democrats, in the past, have supported or even helped create movements like the KKK, the American Nazis and vigorously defended Slavery. Oh! They do not talk about it at all.

Over the years, the Democrat Party has been a staunch supporter of Slave-ownership. The Civil War was fought between the Republican Abraham Lincoln's supporters to Abolish Slavery and the Democrats to maintain the Slave Trading, among other issues.

History reminds us that Democrat General Nathan Bedford Forrest founded the KKK in 1865, and he was its first grand wizard.

The Republican Party was known in the past as the "Black People's Party," while the Democrat Party was the White People's Party.

Curiously, Democrats are trying to escape that past, which has managed through different tricks, to revert the trend.

Due to John F. Kennedy's alliance with the Black Community, in the figure of Dr. Martin L. King, the reversal was possible.

Do the American People have a short memory or blatant ignorance?

Coretta Scott King asked for help; President Kennedy sent his brother Robert to approach a DeKalb County Judge and successfully lobbied for Martin Luther King Jr.'s release. That started the dreadful Democrat Party's reversal and tilted the popularity scale to the DNC's side.

Dr. King has been the most visible and influential figure in the Black Community's history, and that was no small force.

Since the 1960s, the Democrat Party practically managed to erase its shameful racist past and conquered the majority of the Black votes at the time.

Barry Goldwater's extremism's negative influence helped the shift when the late Senator pronounced against the Civil Liberties Act.

In 1964, with the passage of the Civil Rights Act, President Johnson cemented the Black People's change that helped Carter, Clinton, and later Obama wins the elections.

However, in reality, the Democrat Party's core has not made Blacks advance in the North of the Country.

The former Urban League Director Vernon Jordan expressed his concerns during Carter's presidency: "We have no full employment policy. We have no welfare reform plan. We have no national health system. We have no urban revitalization project. "We have no aggressive affirmative action policy. We have no solutions to the grinding problems of poverty and discrimination."

Republicans, which, distracted by the appearance of Barry Goldwater, who practically destroyed the Party's relationship with the Blacks by denouncing the Civil Rights Act as illegal, confirmed the beginning of the Black voters' migration to the Democrat Party at that time.

Bill Clinton cemented the alliance, and the rise of Barak Obama definitively helped with racial approval, although he never did anything meaningful to help his race. He instead helped Islam advance, while his Town of Chicago sunk in a pool of drugs and crime, actually on the rise!

President Trump changed those dark days, and employment among Blacks before the Pandemic, which is not an economic problem, but a health crisis managed to show the best Black's engagement ever registered, of course, before the COVID-19 forced the country to close.

96 -Mainstream Media's Obsession To Defeat Trump.

The word 'fake' became common, and the news is bound to it. It seems that the word 'reality' is losing weight, and from the daily stated 'fake news,' we realize the Press and TV Networks want us to live in a fantasy world.

Although the Media defend itself from the President and his supporters' accusations, there is substantial doubt about their arguments.

Mainly, after over three years of charges, accusations, suspicions, and false indications of the "Russian Collusion" with the Trump Campaign, there is no proof of being real.

In a desperate attempt to feed those allegations daily, the DNC, helped by the Mainstream Media, continued a mad campaign trying to dismiss the President's Administration.

The MSM has decided to ignore the truth and keep repeating the word liar, attached to President Trump's anything.

It is like a deaf people's conversation.

So, liar, liar, liar, repeated a thousand times might become real, as Nazi Joseph Goebbels used to affirm.

The addition of some possible "Obstruction of Congress" used to fabricate a wishful Presidential impeachment has poured fuel to the fire that keeps the Media blabbing about nothing.

Simultaneously, the Democrat leadership insists on continuing the Impeachment effort even after the Senate acquitted the President.

In a grave mishandling of the actual news, CNN, MSNBC, CBS, ABC, Univision, and the major newspapers have almost ignored the recent Islamic Radical Terrorist attack in Manchester, UK, as well as other Islamist Terrorist attacks around the World.

They are also elevating the chief terrorist Qassim Suleimani, Master of Iran's Intrigue, to a martyr, denying Trump his victory over Radical Islamic terrorism. They are now trying to link President Trump to the "father of Iran's nuclear bomb," Mohsen Fakhrizadeh assassination.

Undoubtedly they praised Obama for killing Osama Bin Laden, although he slaughtered about 3.000 people while Suleimani murdered hundreds of thousands of Americans.

Meanwhile, they continue to pound with the illusory elaboration of allegations about the now-famous hoax, the "Russian Collusion" with the Trump Campaign.

In contrast, they do not investigate the real collusion between Democrats, Hillary Clinton, and the Russians correctly.

In a desperate attempt to feed those accusations daily, the DNC, aided by the MSM, continues a mad campaign trying to mud President Trump's Administration.

The DOJ shows that the Mueller's "investigation," now finished, after three years of interviews, has not shown any evidence of Americans' wrongdoing.

They maintain the same results as before: No proof, nothing substantial, and definitively no evidence to add to the subject.

Mueller, under the Law, quietly released the final report of the investigation to the Attorney General, William Barr. He, in turn, after ascertaining that State secrets were not divulged or endangering any person mentioned in it, could publish it or not, at his discretion, what he considered public and even Congress could learn. That is the Law.

The Media has gone Postmodern Liberal all the way, and it is even obstructing the people from learning the truth. The Liberal Journalists have embarked on open war against the President and the White House staff.

This fact is enormously aggravated by several leaks from the White House, by old holdover bureaucrats left by the Obama Administration. They have engaged in unfair inside espionage and disbursement of classified information to the Media.

Unfortunately, the publication of classified data is not a crime, although obtaining said data is a punishable offense.

So the Media can publish the unfairly obtained information, damage the Government's plans, and in many cases, jeopardizing lives in the Secret Service and other Security Agencies.

The New York Times has repeatedly breached the rules. It seems they are using the so-called "undisclosed sources" as an alibi to publish doubtfully obtained classified information, which becomes legal after washed by the "intermediate" intervention of the unfaithful Obama's holdover bureaucrats. It is sad and unpatriotic.

Keep in mind that it is practically impossible to fire a public official due to some government's old laws.

The New York Times, Washington Post, other large newspapers, the Press Agencies, and many Internet Blogs and

Google contribute to alternative news daily, many of them fake. Others come from "undisclosed sources" nowadays, a favorite way to hide or dismiss the origin and integrity of the information they publish.

These events contribute to an increasing loss of faith in the Press and TV news by the American people.

The known mantra that keeps the Postmodern Liberal movement going is "equality" or "diversity."

It is a questionable assertion, as performer Kathy Perry commented after the killing of 22 young children in the Manchester, UK venue by an Islamic Terrorist: 'No Barriers, No Borders, We All Just Need to Co-Exist.' Is this even real? Do the Radical Islamic faith followers think the same?; Of course not.

Consult history books, especially on the XVII and XVIII century, and learn what Islam's real goal is, especially the Radical branch, and the controversy with our Constitution. (See this book's Foreword)

Moreover, the fading performer Madonna, saying publicly: "Many times I thought to place a bomb in the White House."

In other countries, people go to jail or get executed for less than that.

99 -Co-Existence But With An Order.

There is no doubt, we all should co-exist on this Planet, but a Borderless World is not yet a viable reality. People are not all prepared and educated for that.

The USA is the potential big loser if that would happen.

Nevertheless, the Media insist on deviating from the subject. Instead of spreading the news as they come, they continue their agenda, mainly seeing President Trump as a "trial President."

The prestigious Journalist Bob Woodward, renowned for bringing the Nixon's Watergate case to the front pages, talked about the subject.

Mr. Woodward, a moderated Liberal, just labeled the Journalists as "smug," criticized the US Media for falsely labeling Mr. Trump Presidency "temporary." Mr. Woodward also described it as a state of "hyperventilation."

"I think there are so many people treating the Trump presidency as if it is a tryout or as if it is provisional," Woodward said. "Odds are, he is probably going to be president for a full term, four years, maybe even more."

During the Trump Administration tenure, the Media has occupied the airtime with 97% of an anti-Trump campaign. Their panels are a 9 to 1 rate of anti-Trump pundits, and the vitriol is abundant on their political shows, as we have not seen ever before. The absence of Conservative pundits or commentators on CNN, MSNBC, CBS, ABC, and major Newspapers, is disgusting, unfair, and unpatriotic.

It is an obsession, a fanatical fixation with a daily increase due to the frustration of not advancing on the allegations or adding any proof to the so-called "Russians Collusion" or the failed Impeachment hoax.

It could be hilarious if it were not pathetic.

Both the Mainstream Media and the Postmodern Liberal Movement are trying to impose the notion that a blanket of diversity and equality should cover the whole World, allowing flattening the human race and ignoring the natural values and virtues. Precisely, the flunked thought of Marx and Engels.

The idea seems to be, having a mass of people rejoicing in their mediocrity, happy with an absence of competition at any level.

The Mainstream Media, with its heavyweight influence, is adding fuel to the fire by dangerously twisting the information they provide to the American People. Fake News!

The COVID-19 Pandemic is undoubtedly ending the unsuccessful Globalization. It was a good try, ill applied, unfair, and premature.

The Planet is not prepared yet for such an idea. Maybe we could try in a century or more. We should not forget humans inhabit and rule our World. With Lenin's help, Marx and Engels dismissed human beings and their dreams of personal achievements, emotions, love, hate, but principally Karma. We cannot change those—God-given gifts.

However, here is a paradox: The corporations with Liberal leadership undoubtedly employ the crop's cream, not by equality but by excellence.

The practice is not questionable. However, the point is that not everything is about "equality," since competition is a choice, especially at the top — something Postmodern Liberals hate but frequently take advantage of it.

At home, Democrats and the Mainstream Media are trying to ignore the facts.

Instead, they continue to insist on the ill-famous "collusion with the Russians." After more than three years of investigations, they displayed no evidence of its existence and the Impeachment hoax.

Postmodern Liberals have assumed the political leadership in the Democrat Party, embraced by weak leaders. They, lacking attractive programs to move forward, rely on leftist grassroots activists to campaign against President Trump.

The Mainstream Media news concentrates their airtime on 97% dedicated to accusing the President's wrongdoing campaign, falsely.

In comparison, only 3% of their airtime they use to informing of the President's International or National successes and the message he is delivering to the people, so essential to the World's peace and the recovering of the US old lost prestige under previous Administrations.

The White House suspended Press Conferences for eight months, harshly criticized by the Media.

Now attending the Pandemic, the President and his technical team hold extensive daily conferences where the President answers journalist questions for hours.

But several 'journalists,' including MSNBC Rachel Maddow, suggest that Trump is using those events to enhance his political campaign; she says Networks should not air them. Indescribable dishonesty.

So, Trump stopped that modality and is trying something else.

Political Correctness is far more critical to the Media than the President's restoring the USA prestige and the political weight in the International scene.

They do not want the President to succeed.

They hate that idea.

Meanwhile, Barak Obama has resurfaced and keeping lying, throwing dirt at President Trump.

Obama also criticized Hispanic voters, accusing them:

"There's a lot of evangelical Hispanics who, the fact that Trump says racist things about Mexicans, or puts undocumented workers in cages, they think that's less important than the fact that he supports their views on gay marriage or abortion." He accuses Trump of putting illegals in cages while not mentioning that his Administration started the trend, and Trump is trying to stop it. Obama himself ordered to cage illegals.

102 -White Male Supremacy Syndrome.

102-Sanctuary Cities And Illegal Immigration.

Postmodern Liberals are trying, by all means, to make being white male a sin, 'horrible individuals that eat children alive, rape women and suck their blood, something out of this World, and unwelcome.'

They propagate hatred against Whites in Universities, Colleges, Schools, and on the streets of cities that support the arguably Sanctuary status, by the way, misinterpreted.

Sanctuary cities are supposed to offer shelter to illegal immigrants, who are afraid that Homeland Security and the INS could break up their families and unfairly deport some of its members, never to protect criminals.

It is surreal that said "Sanctuary Cities/States Law" would go against the country's Federal immigration legislation in such a controversial way.

The Mainstream Media, beginning with the Associated Press, changed its AP Stylebook to provide an exception, trying to modify the rules.

They wrote: "Except in direct quotes essential to the story, using the word illegal only to refer to an action, not a person: illegal immigration, but not an illegal immigrant." It is pure speculation.

We believe if someone enters the USA, violating the immigration laws, it becomes an illegal alien; A cause and effect.

If you do not like the Law, ask Congress to write a new one, but meanwhile, we must observe the current legislation.

Then, major U.S. newspapers such as the Chicago Tribune, the Los Angeles Times, and USA Today adopted similar guidance.

"The New York Times style guide similarly states that the term illegal immigrant may be considered "loaded or offensive."

Moreover, journalists frequently 'decorate' the rule to the particular circumstances of the person in question or to focus on actions: "who crossed the border illegally; who overstayed a visa; who is not authorized to work in this country." All the cases mentioned here became "illegal aliens," and those "journalists," I challenge them to try staying "undocumented" in Iran, North Korea, China, or any other World country, including Mexico, and see if they could write a story about their experience.

The Media is a significant contributor to the establishment of the Postmodern Liberal culture or New Liberal Politics, forcing changes accordingly with their personal views of the Laws.

At this point, we all know that written laws are, nowadays, manipulated like chewing gum.

Such practice is similar to "Legislating from the bench." (As it is the case with Judges who do not interpret the Laws as written).

Some journalists try to fabricate opinions and applying them to laws from their pens or pixels.

Meanwhile, nobody checks, and modern Judges, especially Liberals, are so political that their rulings are scary.

The result is a gross misapplication of legislation and a constant fight between the Federal and the Municipal Governments (including the City's dependent Police Departments).

Disobedience, citations of Constitutional Laws, Local Laws, and all kinds of resources are part of a fierce battle.

The absurd "Defund the Police" movement has proved a crazy idea. Many Mayors, supporters in the past of such craze, are now asking the Police for help. Meanwhile, Biden is trying to convince people that he never supported it.

Lies, lies, lies.

Meanwhile, some pro-illegal organizations assist people who enter the USA without the necessary documents to appear as legal, while they are not, and coaching them to claim asylum falsely.

At this point, I remember something I learned years ago. Possession is 9/10 of the Law. In this case, the practice also becomes nine-tenths of the Law. Moreover, that is what Postmodern Liberals are doing, especially in the Immigration case. Once people are inside our land, it is tough to deport them. Liberal lawyers have mastered the Constitution's manipulation on the issue.

The leniency that started around the nineteen-eighties has allowed a population of between twenty-five and thirty million people to stay in the USA without the proper documentation, whose majority is doing paid work. Also, millions of illegal aliens are taking advantage of the Social Security System, supported by taxpayers.

Some of them are paying a minimum amount of taxes, hoping that it could be of some help to obtain a green card and eventually citizenship one day.

From the human point of view, one can only feel sorry for the people affected. Nevertheless, from the Constitutional perspective, if we do not enforce the Constitution, then the US stops being a Republic since what it makes a Republic is the observance and application of the Constitution.

The problem has turned to a tacit invasion that has forced the President to declare a "National Emergency" after Congress denied him 5.7 billion dollars to build a southern wall.

We need to stop the flow of drug cartels and caravans from Central America; they bring crime, diseases, and some needy people.

Fortunately, due to President Trump and his team's extraordinary efforts, the Caravans stopped for now. The Senate and the Military helped, and Mexico's President sent 27.000 soldiers to the border to help us.

On the other hand, most undocumented people have jobs, and they contribute their skills to the successful development of business.

Depriving the business owners of those employees would be devastating for them and their families too. So, it is a big problem not easy to solve. The country needs some of those immigrants. However, an uncontrolled flow becomes an invasion, and that seems to be the case at present.

Back in 1974, for instance, when I arrived in the US, there was stricter control of immigration, and except for some rare cases, the enforcement of the laws was tight and kept order.

In part, because of the farmer's need for cheap labor to harvest their crops seasonally, they were allowed to bring temporary workers, called "braceros" or "pickers" from Mexico.

The State governments looked the other way and said practice generalized to the point of "convenience" and that American citizens did not want to perform such work, moreover, for low pay under the minimum wage.

Consumers also looked the other way because that practice made possible much lower produce prices in the supermarkets. Today, with harvesting machinery widely used, doing most of that work, those "pickers" are hardly needed.

However, the "coyotes" or illegal aliens' smugglers took advantage of the leniency and, together with the aspirant laborers entering the US, began smuggling drugs, making the southern border a corrupted place several thousand miles long.

They made the Southern frontier the most dangerous permeable border where the Drug Lords and also terrorists have a free pass to enter the USA.

Today, with the Coronavirus Pandemic, the danger increased exponentially, although the traffic between countries slowed down a lot.

What began with a convenient under the table deal then developed into a major headache.

The Obama Administration refused to face the truth, and the 44th President directed the Border Patrol to wash their hands.

They ordered them to "catch and release," which in reality means, 'do not even bother with the illegal aliens.'

No other country in the World has such an insane immigration practice that violates its immigration laws.

Very few people think that many undocumented workers are taking jobs from American Citizens or lowering wages.

It is also true that the country needs many of those people.

Because undocumented migrants offer their services for less money, they get no workers-comp or health benefits.

However, under the table payments and other secretive deals open a way to illegal accounting methods and cheating on taxes.

As we can see, the problems have engrossed, and there are winners and losers. Too much is too much.

We need to enforce the Federal laws, which was one of the issues featured in Trump's campaign; To be a country of Law and Order again.

The USA is a country of immigrants, undoubtedly, but how many is the limit?

When journalists ask undocumented people's advocates, nobody wants to answer, not even think of the question. How many immigrants are suitable for the country and its population, especially the illegal?

TV Anchor Tucker Carlson frequently asks his guests the question, but nobody has answered it to date.

Throwing a figure is tricky. Maybe the market itself will set the number accordingly with the offer and demand, a proven working equation.

However, the two sides must agree for that to happen, which seems to be almost impossible to achieve at this time.

Maybe one day, when we all mature.

So far, some estimates are indicating there are about 30 million illegal aliens in the USA.

Meanwhile, Democrats insist on open borders, believing that the new illegal immigrants will prefer to vote for them.

Would this be true? Not in my opinion.

107 -The Trump Era.

The Postmodern Liberal leader's utter ignorance, or the lack of concern for the results, other than beating the Conservatives, is hard to believe. It shows their leadership is so confused that they cannot identify what makes the Left, the Left, Fascism, and other political and social concepts, frequently wrongly mentioned or geared to mislead people.

The confusion is outrageous, and the adjectives utilized are mostly in disarray. The actors' complete ignorance is crucial.

The Democrat Party is without a visible head (Biden is only the puppet on the front stage). We believe the leadership is like a "blob," inconsistent, ever-changing in a constant fight for political power, where the money is the main issue. The High-Tech industry is financially successful enough to provide with ruthless leadership, where their addiction to low salaries, slave working conditions in China, and now attempting to make the

USA a similar setting. They keep pushing for hiring foreigns, preferentially Indians and Chinese, at much lower rates than they pay Americans.

Unfortunately, Senator Mike Lee, a Republican, is the author of a new Law that helps hire those individuals. Shame on him!

The President-elect has not specified his eventual Administration plans of Government. His peculiar electoral campaign from his home's basement was too protected, not allowing any hard-core questions from Conservative journalists. In sum, people voted Biden, attending calls from the Media demonizing President Trump for three and a half years. Just like a herd of sheep.

They still lack a plan and continue to throw dirt to the President, while Biden is choosing his staff entirely from individuals who worked in the Obama-Biden Government. It seems the aim is to have a third Obama Administration period. Biden is only worried about assembling the most Diverse, intersectional Cabinet ever.

Would that assure the "best Cabinet?" Not, in my opinion. The different philosophies and backgrounds will be a significant headache if ever enable.

Their hatred for President Donald J. Trump is much stronger than their love of our country.

Please note that some of the writing may look confusing, regarding the verb tenses, situations, and the real-time when people read this book.

It is not easy to navigate the turbulent waters of our Nation at this time. I am doing my best. I am sure smart readers will understand.

J. Pelegrin

A BRUTAL ATTACK ON DEMOCRACY

(The All-Time Enemies on the March)

CHAPTER 3

(Communist China - A Philosophical Battle)

109 -A Virus Made In China.

Among the thousands of items China makes and ships to the US, the Communist Government's irresponsible behavior sent us the COVID-19, with the dangerous consequences that are killing hundreds of thousands of Americans in fragile health conditions and some young, as well as people all over the World.

After the Chinese officials knew for months of the Virus decimating thousands of their own people in Wuhan, they allowed millions of travelers to go to the USA and Europe by airplanes and ships.

While the Government of China acknowledges 83.000 people infected initially, some witnesses from the Hubei Province estimate the amount over the one million victims of the Virus, and above 60.000 deaths. The figures released by officials are not trusted, so it is practically impossible to know the actual truth.

The Communist Government is, as usual, lying to us, hiding the status of the extremely contagious strain, and covered their casualties. They also destroy all data indicating the beginning of the crisis now where or how it started.

In January, the United States offered medical help to the Chinese Government, sending a team of scientists experts on infectious diseases as soon as they learned about the first cases. Still, they refused any help and prohibited any Americans from entering the Wuhan City region, the Virus's source; Furthermore, the Communist Government expulsed two journalists from the New York Times and The Washington Post.

They also punished some of their own journalists and scientists for revealing some information about the novel Virus. The Doctor who initially blew the whistle about the Coronavirus's existence disappeared, and at present, is considered missing. No one seems to know what happened to him.

Also, they hid all information about the novel Virus and deleted all data about the spreading of the COVID-19.

Recently, a University in China, owned by the Government, published a notice prohibiting the publication of any study or research about the Coronavirus unless Beijing authorizes it.

Communist regimes are well known for their secrecy and misguidance of all aspects of their Government.

This case is not different, and still today, it is impossible to trust the data they release and how many people are infected with the Virus.

They lie consistently to hide any information that could lead to possible criticism of their totalitarian ruling style.

Fortunately, their action was minimized by President Trump's quick action, in the middle of January 2020, banning traveling in and out of China to our country, later extended to Europe, after European nations had troubles controlling the infectious disease.

President Trump saved thousands of American people's lives by such an action, said Dr. Antony Fauci, the worldwide leading expert advising the Trump Administration on the Subject.

Nevertheless, today, the Media still criticizes Trump for not having issued an order of "social distancing" in February, when the President banned traveling with China. At the time, the whole Media labeled the President as "Racist," including Joe Biden.

Meanwhile, Democrats were fully engaged in the infamous "Impeachment." As a reminder, in mid-February, most Democrat Governors were against a Social distance or separation.

The Media's hatred for Trump is hard to understand. Well, they are rooting for the Democratic Party.

They hate Donald J. Trump.

Meanwhile, China's Communist Government mounted a worldwide propaganda campaign to blame the USA Military for 'having carried the Virus to Wuhan City.' A blatant lie our President said it is despicable, adding: "that will not happen in my Presidency," referring to the intentional smearing of our Military.

The Chinese Government claims that everybody should thank the Asians for "saving the World" from a worse situation.

However, people from around Wuhan City and the Hubei Province are saying that the numbers the Communist Government is publishing "do not add up."

independent information delivered the following data:

"The 84 cremating furnaces in Wuhan City, with 11 million people, are working 24/7. The manufacturers are delivering 2.500 urns every day to funeral houses."

"Seven funeral homes in Wuhan have handled 3.500 urns with ashes every day in one week, claim some posts on Chinese social media.

Besides, they had told families who lost members under the Coronavirus that, at the festival of "Quin Min," that started on March 23rd, ending on April 5th, were trying to "complete cremations" before the traditional 'grave-tending' festival ended."

A local estimate shows that they were delivering about 45.000 urns during that time.

Another resident of the Hubei Province, where Wuhan is the Capital, said that more than 40.000 died during the lockdown time. That is tens of thousands more than what the Government acknowledges at that time.

Today, the estimate is much higher.

Other zone residents say that the Government is paying 3.000 Yuans in cash, equal to 433.00 dollars, to keep the families quiet and avoid mourning their deaths publicly.

Everything leads to thinking the Communist Government headed by Xi Jinping continues to lie big time, hiding the reality of lives lost because of the COVID-19 Pandemic.

Communists have always been experts to mount propaganda machines to exonerate them from wrongdoings, lying, and misguiding the World.

However, nobody doubts that COVID-19 is "The Wuhan virus, Made in China."

Chinese Virologist Dr. Li-Meng Yan Claims Coronavirus Lab 'Cover-Up' Made Her Flee China and seek for USA's political asylum. She denounced the Chinese Communist regime for purposely spreading the Coronavirus for political and economic gain. Although not providing hard evidence, her assertion comes from a reputed scientist linked to the Wuhan science community and directly involved with the Virus itself.

In the past, similar cases have taken the names of the regions where they originated, Ej: Ebola, Spanish Flu, MERS (Middle East Respiratory Syndrome), Asian Flu, etc. Therefore, naming the Virus after the region where it started is not racial or unfair.

It is merely a fact.

Time and investigations on the issue will reveal some details, although we will never know the actual truth; This case is no different from other Chinese mishaps. However, by information collected around the World, actions of the Chinese Government, and recent declarations from Chinese officials, the Chinese Government enjoys the gains from the COVID-19.

The Chinese regime is totalitarian, without a free press, and granting no citizen's freedom or civil liberties.

Is this a Communist paradise? You will judge it.

112 –Merging Of Ideologies.

Postmodern Liberalism has a history tightly linked to the Left.

However, traditional Liberalism was rarely a "political party," although they were always a "sidekick" attached to different traditional governing groups or opposition, like an adjective to the Subject.

We can track Liberalism to four centuries ago. Still, in the late 19th Century, after the French Revolution, Classical Liberalism argued for a minimal size Government and individual freedom for action, almost a US Republican Party paradigm.

They aimed to allow individuals to develop themselves freely, although slowly.

Then, it gradually mutated into a center-left-wing movement, which with the times went so far to the Left that encountered the far-Right and melted with it in a Fascist mode. Its development is quite confusing.

Lefty Liberals only began to make in-rows into the US through the Socialist/Communist frenzy that invaded South America in the late 1940s.

Simultaneously, in Hollywood, 'the infamous ten motion-picture producers, directors, and screenwriters' who appeared before the House "Un-American Activities Committee" in October 1947 refused to answer questions regarding their possible communist affiliations, and some went to jail for Contempt of Congress.

A long time has passed, and a considerable change in demographics and political philosophy occurred. After the 2016 election, it mutated into Postmodern Liberalism, a hybrid mixture of many different and controversial ideologies, sharing a common enemy: Conservatism.

The shift is a political maneuver trying to recover the power lost by Democrats in the 2016 election. That is what we call a hijack.

The most outrageous is probably the utilization of violent Fascist techniques at rallies, showed by the organized groups, "Antifa" and "Black Lives Matter." They focus on depriving the Conservatism of the free expression granted in the First Amendment, in contrast with the fierce defense of the same First Amendment by Classic Liberals, led by students and professors at the University of California, Berkely in the 1960s. What a change of direction!

113 -The Mutation Of The Left.

We can locate the birth of the Left at the French Revolution 1789-1799, as the anti-monarchists' Montagnard and Jacobin, deputies from the Third Estate, sat to the left of the presiding member's chair in the parliament.

The leftist movement took birth to oppose the French Monarchy and all European Blue Blood ruling.

This habit, which began in the Estates-General of 1789, solidified after the 1848 Revolution. Few people supported it at the time.

However, the influential Communist Manifesto authored by Karl Marx and Friedrich Engels, published in 1848, pointing to the class struggle, predicted that a proletarian revolution would eventually overthrow bourgeois capitalism and create a classless, stateless, post-monetary Communist Society.

At that moment, Left and Right's political terms were also established in the USA, although they remained the property of specific small intellectual groups.

The Marx-Engels manifesto theorized about how to reach a classless and stateless society. Both authors asserted without considering the actual human condition, passions, greed, ambitions, talents, virtues, intellectual capacity, and so many attributes and negative qualities that are not easy to define, although they are real.

114 -Vedic Knowledge. Karma.

Marx and Engels's most neglected issue was Karma, not widely known or even acknowledged, especially in the West and Eastern European land at the time.

Of course, in time, Karma has been accepted as the essential spiritual issue in a person's life by revealing the Vedic knowledge spread across the philosophical and academic circles in the United States and Western World.

However, neither the authors of the Communist Manifesto deemed humankind's future development, which holds an awful controversy within the Postmodern Liberal Movement, hard to decipher.

The Communist philosophy lines got severely blurred and confused by the advance of science and technology, which turned many trades and occupations obsolete, leaving the new groups without a particular side — Left, center, or right.

Marx, Engels, and then Lenin, who was the strategist for the Communist ideology application, lacked basic Philosophical knowledge, especially about the spiritual life.

Their studies and developments were utterly materialistic and completely ignoring the spirit soul, its existence, and, therefore, its consequences and extent.

Their only superficial philosophical knowledge strived on the speculations of the highly materialistic German and French philosophers.

The great Albert Einstein was the exception, confirmed by his vast understanding of Vedic Literature and philosophy.

Einstein's famous expression:
"God does not play dice with the universe." It is self-explanatory of Albert's thoughts about God.

(We will expand on the Vedic knowledge in a future chapter.)

Therefore, as time passed and the regular changes happened, Marx and Engel's speculation about life in society became obsolete for many.

The technological discoveries, advances, and inventions took their uncertain theories about the classist society and the optimal solution by surprise and turned them absurd.

Moreover, what to say about the inexorable coming of a "Robotics Era," turning millions of human jobs unnecessary.

115 -Technology Advances Changed Communism.

The factories, a primary worker's symbol and bloody battlefield to defend their rights, are nowadays automatized, in alarming development replacing humans with robots, mostly doing a more thorough and efficient job.

If we were to follow the Marx and Engels Communist predictions, we probably had missed most of the great inventions that have enhanced our lives in the last one hundred and fifty years. The new generations could not survive without them.

It is impossible to stop scientific and technological knowledge.
They are part of humankind's development.
It is not deniable that the Marxist ideas became fashionable and even fanatical, at the time, bringing a division among people in many countries around the World.
Communism became violent with the Bolshevik Revolution, then exported it throughout the World. Their bloody battles we all have heard or knew throughout history have left a disastrous, deadly mark. History is telling it as it happened.

Communism has left a horrific balance:
"History shows one hundred and thirty million deaths, plus in the hands of Communism, until the end of the XX century."

We must acknowledge that Russia, later the USSR was a special place with unique problems of wealth distribution, misery, famine, and a corrupt aristocracy, decrepit, and worn out.
However, Marx and Engels' Communist ideology rather than a permanent theory, today, we see it was a temporary and incidental shift that provoked a primary worker's awareness and changed the private owner/worker relationship in Russia for the worse. Nevertheless, Totalitarianism, a government system that is centralized, dictatorial, and requires complete subservience to the State, remained the foremost choice of authoritarianism enthusiasts.
At the beginning of the nineteenth Century, the business owners oppressed workers; working conditions were poor and, in many cases bordering on slavery.
So, Communism raised awareness and, in a way, helped, later on, to correct some of the problems or at least to recognize them, although the human lives price paid was excessively inhuman.
However, Communism did not improve the people's life quality and only transferred the abuse of workers from the private sector to the State.

The USSR Communism treated peasants and laborers like slaves. China's Communist present ruling reinforces the fact. Worker's oppression, a lack of free press, and suppression of liberties are the evidence.

However, consider that Chinese born under the Communist ruling don't know what Democracy is.

So, they are contented with the system because they don't know different. Subjects believe the State and its Government are taking good care of the people.

History says:
Socialism and Communism Have Never Made a Worker Happier.

The Communist State and the Oligarchy are much worse bosses than Monarchy was.

Communism killed more than 130 million people in the Twenties Century.

Also, the corruption among the leaders exponentially increased and spread out, creating favoritism for the Oligarchs. They immediately side with the Government officials that grant all contracts to the "businesses supporting the Communist System," making Oligarchs an essential part of Communism.

They handle the money and grease the palms of corrupt officials.

(That also occurred in Nazi Germany, where the Industrial Titans helped construct the Third Reich (1933-1944) and grossly profited from it.)

A Royalty, anti-democratic system replaces the totalitarian rule named Communism, a much worse option.

The Latin American Continent, but especially the South American part of it, since the 1940s, had a love affair with Socialism and Communism thru the intellectual community.

At the end of Nazism in Germany, the favorite places where the Nazi elite chose to hide and plant new roots were in South America: Argentina, Brazil, Paraguay, Uruguay, and Chile.

Also, Nazism and Fascism have been a powerful aid to propagating that political ideology in the USA. We must recall those are totalitarian styles of Government.

Hitler, Stalin, and Mussolini were partners at some time.

A cloudy myth was forcing its way into the World's society.

The nature of the economy, and land distribution, inherited from Colonial times, has always been an issue of discordance.

Criticism about land partition and assignment inequality has always been unclear, causing Military clashes between countries and unrest among the populations.

At the beginning of the Twenties Century, several Latin American groups of discontent citizens began to gather, forming leftist cells that grew and propagated, connecting through political and underground organizations, many times clandestine, but all of them under the guidance of the Communist ideology, always financed by the USSR.

The "International Socialist" order in Europe and later the "Foro de Sao Paulo," in Brazil, an organization to offer guidance and support to the leftist groups in Latin America, was founded by Fidel Castro, the Cuban Dictator for over fifty years, and Lula Da Silva, former leftist Brazilian President among others. (Lula was lately indicted for corruption and jailed. Now freed from confinement)

Thru these types of channels, some of these leftist groups became formal Party's and convinced the embattled workers that they needed a change, and the Leftist was there to help them.

The Communist propaganda spread the false idea that the workers should be the government heads and the economy's rulers.

However, the generally poorly educated laborers proved to lack the necessary knowledge to handle such monumental tasks. They had to seek the help of the better educated and powerful Oligarchs.

Corruption rapidly took over, and the "Capitalists," now converted into "Oligarchs" (the new Capitalists in the Communist communities) with the support of the corrupt Lefty leadership, in conjunction with the authoritarian Military brass, assumed control of the economy.

USSR Communist leadership quickly confiscated the aristocratic Russian royalty's old properties, dachas, farms, factories, and other means of production, usurping the wealth creation sources, and imposed widespread corruption that they shared with the Military in control of the Communist Party. They established one Party-State. No opposition allowed.

The leftist leaders promised a Communist Paradise, a classless society with equality that was supposed to answer all the people's problems.

Communist propaganda invaded Latin America.

Almost all countries in the sub-continent began a love affair with the Left that ended with many having Socialist or Communist Governments; All of them disastrous in the end.

They were Influenced by Fidel Castro's Cuban Revolution, which through a false romanticism, gained fame and prestige among the intellectuals of the World, sick of the Cuban Dictator Fulgencio Batista's excesses, supported by a considerable part of US politicians and people in the business community.

The Communists took advantage of a historical moment when the Conservative movement exceeded its power by creating too many wealthy individuals who oppressed the factories and farmworkers.

Capitalists, Oligarchs, and other influential groups, which do not have shame nor political sides, and only go where the business is flourishing, quickly got behind the Socialist and Communist movements to "aid" their affairs, only changing hats in the Market of "managing the wealth."

The USSR acronym means Union of Soviet Socialist Republics. The use of the word Socialist as a replacement of Communist when convenient for the leftist cause is evident.

The Left did not waste any time. Through the intellectual community's support, avid for changes but mainly charging against the all-time hated conservatives, found fertile ground in Latin America's embattled lower class in a pre-technological society.

Once again, the rich got richer and shared the profits with the Socialist/Communist politicians and military brass.

The slow region's development (Latin America) was the perfect laboratory to try building a new society, which Marx and Engels envisioned in 1848 when they wrote the Communist Manifesto.

Some European countries, absorbed by the USSR, had already put in practice Communism under the rule of the Soviets, although the results were somewhat disastrous.

Marx and Engels never figured out how to successfully manage Communism after they took power. They did not have the necessary vision to perceive the future or avoid corruption, maybe because they never considered the spirit soul as the center of the individual, feelings, talents, miseries, or Karma. They were gross materialists. Or maybe they counted on corruption as a totalitarian tool to control the masses? Hmm.

So, Latin America was next. The reckless, sometimes oppressive political system existent in the southern part of the American Continent offered a fertile ground where the seeds of Communism could have germinated and a political product harvested successfully.

The lack of South-American people's high education and spiritual knowledge did the rest.

Meanwhile, in the USA, politicians finally acknowledged the real threat of Cuba's Communism under Fidel Castro, especially after the Russian missiles reached the Island, and pointed them toward the US mainland, followed by President Kennedy's reaction, which almost ended in a nuclear war with the USSR.

The South-American local worker's unions gained prestige among the country's populations. People were beginning to evaluate a radical change that could improve the new workers' living conditions: Communism.

The greed and reckless behavior of local Latin-American Right-Wing politicians opened a straightforward way for some needed changes, and the "Communist philosophy," until then feared and rejected, became an option to be considered.

The People's question in their minds was: "What about if we change government styles?" The actual State of their economies was pretty bad, and although the top-rated raw product coming out of the South-American land fed the entrepreneurs' 1%, they did not share with their workers in a fairway or any way.

The complaints were loud, and the upper-class individuals disregarded them, enjoying visible excesses on numerous European and North American personal shopping tours and a lavish life at home. The workers had a lousy existence, overworked and underpaid; many times hungry and sick.

"The core of the Communist philosophy calls for the annihilation of Capitalism, to the point where over the ruins, they would start building an entirely new Communist Paradise."

A vast array of small clandestine lefty movements appeared all across Latin America, mainly with members that, after some training trips to Cuba, returned to their countries, formally converted into Leftist's subversives fighters, or "urban terrorists."

121 -The USSR Influence In Latin America.
The USSR had a significant impact on the Uruguayan group of Urban Terrorists named Tupamaros, the first of its class worldwide.
USSR Montevideo's Embassy had a side door on the premises, dedicated to free traffic, allowing a constant flowing of some selected individuals, identified as Communist militants, definitively working full time; some were on the Embassy's clandestine payroll.
The Communist ideologists had chosen the tiny, although most prestigious South American country at the time to be the base for the Latin American spreading of Communism and an eventual penetration into the USA.
The Uruguayan Government, not used to this kind of opposition, in disarray by the continuous criminal acts increasing by the days, adopted some military measures that took some time to become active.
By 1972, the terrorist movement collapsed, although, in the previous year, the MLN-T (Tupamaros) managed to legally

establish a Political Party they named Frente Amplio (Broad Front).

However, after a few years of urban guerrilla activities, most of the Tupamaro's leadership went to jail. Others escaped to European Countries, taking with them a large booty they had amassed from the criminal acts performed in Montevideo, the Uruguayan Capital, and other Uruguayan cities.

They were robbing banks, businesses, kidnapping people for ransom, and other illicit acts.

A few years later, those funds helped the Left win an election and access the Uruguayan Government, which lasted 15 years. Finally, another election act, in 2018 ousted the disastrous Leftist ruling.

But, for some time, the smallest, although at the time, most educated South-American country, became an essential pillar of the Lefty political establishment in the continent. Unfortunately, Socialism's ruling practically destroyed the economy, social fabric, and Republican infrastructure in the past, many called "the Switzerland of America."

Meanwhile, US Politicians completely disregarded the facts, paying little attention to the remarkable growth of the Left in their backyard, as they used to call Latin America.

We must acknowledge that in the USA, the Postmodern Liberal Movement was only in its beginning, influenced by the rise of Communism in the South-American land and the southern part of Central America, began the massive immigration of Latin Americans to the USA, mostly through Visa's overstay.

A large part of the undocumented immigrants from South and Central America came to the US carrying with them the seeds of Communism, implanted in their minds, and most of them, with hatred against the US in their hearts caused by Communist propaganda, and some US Government excesses throughout the World.

Although the new immigrants knew that living and working in the US was going to improve their lives and families, many of them had in mind to help the Left gain power in the Capitalist Empire.

US politicians had a hard time understanding that despite the good economic reasons the American Lifestyle offered. People outside the USA often regretted the American way of doing business. Distrust of the Capitalist system, through some Multinational Corporations, which cooperated with South American corrupt politicians, was abusing the granted privileges, and exploiting the local labor force. The Left continually vilified those Corporations, placing negative propaganda on the streets.

So the usual cry in Latin-America: "Yankees go home," turned into "Do not bother, we will come to your land!"

Today, those who migrated to the US years ago have proved that while they significantly improved their lives, especially economically, seeing now that the families they left behind in their birth countries are currently going thru horrible times, hungry and suffering unbelievable penances. Venezuela is a clear example, but others like Uruguay, Argentina, Ecuador, Bolivia, Brazil, and Nicaragua, are also symbols of the destruction caused by Socialism and Communism.

123 -Consistent Failure Of Socialism And Communism.

The Socialist/Communist experience has been catastrophic, and all countries that have experimented with leftist rulings have collapsed or on the way to collapse.

However, the Capitalist's Elite does not understand that somehow, Communism is a reaction to the excesses of Individuals in the Capitalist community. The excessive payments typically received by CEOs and some other high executives have no comparison to the compensation of the rest of those companies' employees; Something to think about it and correct.

Also, the exploitation of workers in other parts of the World, which includes children, practiced by some large corporations, like Sport shoe manufacturers, is a despicable example of human beings' abuse. It is understandable that in some regions of the World, families need children to have a job to help them to survive, but abusing minors is vile. Coincidentally, most of the factories where they make the products are in Communist countries.

Examples like Venezuela, in complete chaos despite having some of the largest oil deposits in the World, is one of them.

Venezuelan citizens are hungry, homeless, unable to obtain the necessary articles to healthy living, are now on the streets fighting the Government with their bare hands, without weapons, after a brutal dictatorship ruined their vast resources economy and confiscated their guns.

Again, the Vladimir Lenin Decalogue became fashionable, and they confiscated the people's weapons!

Americans must defend the Second Amendment from Democrats who want to take it away. The Founding Fathers meant using guns to protect people against government excesses.

Cuba, the most notable Communist failure, is still under the more than sixty-year-old Castro family's dictatorship. The Island now has its first "Non-Castro family" President, although there was no change in politics.

Democracy is back in Chile after a brief Socialist period.

The ouster of a leftist President in Argentina; is now back by after an electoral mistake.

The impeachment and removal of Brazilian President Dilma Rousseff and her corruption scandal, also the indictment of former President "Lula Da Silva," recently released from jail, has returned some of the South American countries to a kind of Democracy, not fully implemented yet, but promising.

The new Brazilian President, Jair Bolsonaro, emulates the Trump doctrine at the moment, and it seems to be obtaining success.

Other South American countries continue fighting for the shake-up of evil governments that have survived only because of their vast natural resources, despite the corruption established by the Left.

124 -The Lenin Decalogue.

A document called "The 1913 Vladimir Lenin's Decalogue," which some people say is a hoax, but because it is so accurate, painting an incredibly realistic picture on how to take over a country, looks and sounds truthful to many others and me.

The document makes people's skin creep. Said record has been around for decades and is the guidance for all the leftist movements in Latin America.

We have witnessed the disasters caused by these leftist guides on how to override any government and convert them into Left-wing. They always start with the same mantra: the Revolution, the defense of workers, women, the elder, together with a consistent attack on the "Yankee's Capitalism" and the Establishment.

South-American people, particularly the less fortunate, weak, and uneducated, have always been brainwashed by the Left and became staunch supporters of the Socialist and Communist Parties. Also, many lefty students go to Universities not to study but to engage in politics. Something I never expected to see in the USA, but is, unfortunately, today's reality and the Postmodern Liberal Movement's model strategy.

History, once again repeats itself.

The new immigrant youth in the USA is being indoctrinated with the same tools created by Marx and Engels, put in practice by Lenin, intensified by Mussolini's Fascism, and with some influence of Hitler's National Socialism. They all have a common denominator: Totalitarianism.

The Left in the USA has developed this powerful tool to brainwash the illegal immigrants coming from Latin America, as mentioned before, with their brains embedded in the Socialist/Communist myth. They keep saying that the leftist system is for the workers' defense, poor people's justice, and fairness when in real life, the only beneficiaries are the political leaders, Union bosses, the Military Brass, the Oligarchs, and their loyal, foolish unconditional followers.

Here is the famous Lenin's Decalogue, Lenin wrote in 1913:

"Manual to Seize Control of a Society," used in the 1917 Russian Re-Revolution (The October Surprise) usurping power from the original Russian Revolution, which occurred earlier in the spring of that year.

1.   Corrupt the youth and give them absolute sexual freedom.

2.   Infiltrate and take control of the mass communication media.

3.   Divide the population into antagonist groups; encourage arguments between them over social issues.

4.   Destroy the people's confidence in their leaders.

5.   Talk all the time about Democracy and republic, but when the opportunity arises, seize power as a dictator.

6.   Cooperate with the drainage of public funds, discrediting the country's image, especially overseas, and create panic within the population by launching an inflationary process.

7.   Encourage strikes, even if they are illegal, in the country's key industries.

8.   Promote riots while conspire to prevent intervention by law enforcement.

9.   Cooperate actively in destroying the moral foundations of society, honesty, and trust in the Government's promises. Infiltrate other parties with your own people, forcing them to vote for what is useful to your own Party's interest.

10.   Register everyone who has firearms to confiscate them when the time comes, preventing them from opposing your Revolution.

Notice: (The author only suggests the above's authenticity, knowing that many sources have questioned it as false. However, the contents are siding with Vladimir Lenin's philosophy and the

Communist practices so, it could well be coming from his mind and pen.)

I am detailing these facts because, believe it or not; these continue to be the root of what nowadays is the propeller, part of the Postmodern Liberal Movement in the USA and Canada.

One must keep in mind the strong influence of Latin Americans or Hispanics in North America. Socialism entered the United States from Latin American revolutionary politics through illegal immigration and Cuba, although Cuban immigrants are mainly escapees from Castro's regime.

127 –China Awakes As Communism/State Capitalism.

It is all about power; Personal power, the ultimate human individual goal. Money is the vehicle, but power is the big and ultimate prize. Sometimes is personal; others collective, although a person is always at the top and in command.

Meanwhile, quietly but surely, in the last years of Mao Zedong, around 1978, China was developing what many Western commentators described as "State Capitalism."

They adopted a mixed system that keeps the center of Mainland China, where the farms and factories are strictly Communist, with the population surviving on the borderline, fighting famine.

More than 30 people usually sleep in the same small room, in miserable conditions. In contrast, in the coastal cities, some selected people enjoy 'Capitalist-like' enterprises in partnership with the Government, experiencing some exclusive "luxurious" privileges.

This kind of economic system allowed the Asian giant to rapidly developing a massive improvement in production, finances, and resources, where the naive US leaders fell into a trap.

Some previous leaders may have illegally benefitted from the Chinese's paybacks, as we later discovered. Joe Biden and his son Hunter are under grave suspicion to have profited unlawfully. The mainstream media continues to sweep the case under the rug. The abundant evidence presented by the "New York Post" was practically "killed" by Social Media and TV Networks. Twitter and Facebook banned all mentioning of the facts, and Google suppressed the newspaper's article immediately.

A few weeks after the article, a former Hunter Biden's partner Tony Bobulinski told his story, that also accused Joe Biden of participating and profiting from the venture on the Tucker Carlson Tonight's Show. Still, no other Media outlet even commented on the witness' declaration. Maybe Mr. Bobulinsky came out a little too late with the information. It was only a few days before the election.

Doing business with China presents a controversy.

On the one hand, the US consumers got the benefits of buying much more with their money in China, where the Communist regime exploits workers sinfully. At the same time, millions of Americans lost their jobs because thousands of local factories were closing or transferring their operations to the Chinese country. The Asian laborers earn a fraction of what the US pays its workers.

Most Americans fell in love with Chinese products because they offered low prices while delivering acceptable quality and American designs. Business people got greedy with the generous profits coming from the Asian Giant, and politicians began receiving contributions from the Asian Giant to their campaigns and some in their private accounts.

In addition to learning the Capitalism business, now owned by the Communist regime, the Chinese rapidly learned bribing and massively spread it around.

However, US business people still do not have full access to the tightly restricted Chinese Market.

Universities and their executives receive tremendous benefits from the Chinese Government while enrolling thousands of Chinese students in universities and colleges paying full tuition.

Some politicians are also profiting by participating in joint ventures or simply 'helping' the Chinese to expedite lucrative business in the US, utilizing their official positions in the Government.

That seems to be the case of Hunter Biden, who went around the World, including China, selling his father's influence as Vice President of the United States of America.

In 2017, President Trump denounced the dire situation and began imposing tariffs on some of China's imports to recover from the extremely disadvantageous trade balance, unfair to the USA.

As Mr. Trump often says: such a situation is not entirely

China's fault, but the foolishness and lack of business vision that some former US Presidents allowed to happen, especially Barak Obama-Joe Biden Administration. The presumptive incoming Government already seems to be "a third term Obama-Biden." The primary selection of Uncle Joe's cabinet indicates it.

Because of excessive regulations, high taxes, and other measures taken by the Obama Administration, the unbalance of trading with the Asian Giant grew disproportionately in detriment of our country, losing millions of jobs after thousands of factories moved to China.

Due to the actual health crisis, the declared Pandemic because of the COVID-19 or Coronavirus epidemic, we, Americans, sadly found a terrifying reality.

China commercially dominates the USA because our past leaders, mainly the Obama-Biden Administration, sold us out!

Maybe they did not know what they were doing, and forgot to look for us! Alternatively, perhaps they knew and did not care.

Politicians and Business people just saw the quick profit, got greedy, and bribed by the "Elite," and the Asian Communist Government betrayed us and gave-us-away to China.

"The USA Business Elite, especially Hig-Tech executives, has more in common with a totalitarian Communist government than with the US Constitution and the American People."

The Democrat Party Establishment at the beginning of the 2020 campaign encouraged candidates leaning to the political Left. Nevertheless, once Bernie Sanders won the first caucus and primaries, they realized that they were making a big mistake and rapidly decided to support Joe Biden massively, despite all the blunders and lack of coordination the former VP shows daily.

Let us remember that Bernie Sanders is not a "Democrat."

"Not one of us," as many Democrat contenders in the primaries, have said.

They made Biden the Democratic Party Nominee, endorsed by Barak Obama, in a quite timid way after a thunderous silence! Bernie also has in mind the old Communist philosophy, not the 'updated" format the Chinese are practicing with the addition of "State Capitalism." During the campaign, we heard Sanders still condemning Capitalism as an evil form of economic development. He got stuck in the 1960s Communism, at least in his discourse.

130 -Does The Biological War Begun, Yet?

Sources are now saying the Coronavirus came from a Lab in Wuhan, Province of Hubei, in China.

Curiously, the Lab, where they investigate and manipulate viral strains, is situated across a small pond from a large "Wet Market," where, as mentioned before, they sell all kinds of animals, wild and domestic, for food. In this Market, the vendors sell dead animals, or they kill the livestock crammed in small cages at the customers' request, in-situ.

The scene is gross and highly dangerous, displaying pieces of meat on top of each other, with insects flying and crawling as well as rodents and other predators around the place.

One can imagine that the Virus, also transmitted by air, could have reached the Wet-Market and rapidly infected many of the products sold there, and therefore workers and customers. The Coronavirus seems to travel in tiny water droplets thru the air.

We can also imagine that some Lab employees already contaminated with the strain may have been the Market's customers and spread the Virus around.

We know that the first victim, a male employee of the Lab, infected his girlfriend, and she also spread the Virus around to others.

Of course, due to the hermetic silence the Chinese Communist Government exerts on their policies, these are all speculations.

However, there is a solid belief that China purposely developed this particular strain to compete with the USA.

The result went the wrong way, in part because of the policies of China's Government, and the lying and secrecy, especially in the first six days after they discovered the first cases, which allowed millions of people to travel to Italy, and the USA, carrying the strain, contaminating thousands more.

The whistleblowers, at least two of them, have disappeared, unable to be found. Also, the Communist Government of China destroyed samples and data, especially the first strain specimens and even the data concerning the testing or investigative work.

Some people even believe that it could have been a test on virus control, demonstrating the Chinese supposedly superiority over America on the matter. If that was the case, it was a catastrophic failure.

Although the Asian giant has developed some remarkable results in technology, infrastructure, and science; Still, because of its totalitarian Government, the expansion is not methodic, coordinated and observing social freedom, human rights, liberties, and especially a "Bill of Rights," similar to America.

They rule the country in an absolute totalitarian way, authoritarian and without granting any rights to the population. It is either you are with them (the Government) or against them. Moreover, if it is the latter, people are in real trouble, even losing their lives, as it commonly happens.

For people accustomed to living in the USA, it is a horrific scene. However, if you were born there, and you have not experienced it differently, you get used to being continuously watched and monitored. Humans adjust to all kinds of lifestyles.

Capitalism is not a perfect system. However, it is the best-known way to achieve happiness, to make some dreams come true, and to live in peace, enjoying, as our Pledge of Allegiance reads: "I pledge allegiance to the Flag of the United States of America, and to the Republic for which it stands, one Nation under God, indivisible, with liberty and justice for all."

Unfortunately, the manipulation some Lawyers make of our Constitution is disgraceful, allowing some to disrespect our Flag, our National Anthem, and even the Constitution itself.

In my opinion, having experienced living under a Lefty ruling, I deeply reject the idea of having in the USA a Socialist Government. If we fall into such a trap, it will take many years of suffering under Socialist or Communist destruction to be able to go back to our roots. If we can reverse the course, the damage that Lefty governments would have done will be irreparable. I have seen many examples. It is devastating!

However, being under Socialism and Communism, which are the same, there is another type of ruling that is as bad or worse than it.

Islamic ruling is the other big menace to our freedom. Both are the worse enemies we are still facing, now associated with the Postmodern Liberalism that has hijacked the old Democratic Party.

I will expand on Islam in another chapter.

132 -How Communism Became A US Government Option.

We know Bernie Sanders, the Vermont Senator, and career politician who now calls himself "Democratic Socialist," since his youth is a fan and lover of Marx and Engels's political philosophy. He praised Fidel Castro's Communist regime. Note that Socialism is not democratic at all.

Thru the years, he continues repeating the classic Communist rant over and over, which he knows so well, that echoes the same phrasing like a tolling bell.

His arguments are not new. Marx, Engels, Lenin, Stalin, and down the line, the rest of the Communist ideology established a series of slogans and issues that kept the Lefty propaganda untouched throughout the years.

It always starts with the workers' defense, condemnation of Capitalism, the Unions as the worker's strength, the need for a revolution, equality, and many others we all know: the Communist rhetoric building blocks.

For Bernie, those words defining the Communist Ideology myth, he is continuously reminding us for decades; they are the supposed marvels of the anti-Capitalism movement.

The American people, mostly uneducated and poor, still believe that the proposed system will bring them positive changes.

However, history says clearly, that it is the most incredible hoax politics has developed in the World's history.

There is no country on the Planet that, after applying the Communist or Socialist political system, the workers and poor people had benefitted from it. Not even one!

Only corruption, poverty, unemployment, and enriching the wrong people: Politicians, Military Brass, Union leaders, and Oligarchs; Moreover, Socialism is just one step away from Communism.

Sanders won the Nevada caucuses, he brags, with the "Latino votes." However, those Nevada Latinos are not coming from South America, and therefore, they lack the current knowledge of the Socialist disasters that left their families in distress. Those Hispanic immigrants are mostly ignorant of politics. They are only looking for "Free stuff from the Government," which Sanders is recklessly offering out of control, and that, if applied, will bankrupt our economy.

Looking at the last example of a Communist Government, China offers a clear picture of totalitarian, authoritative behavior. They keep their people under constant scrutiny and monitoring all their moves, with millions of cameras, government workers in charge of the surveillance, maintaining citizens inside a large prison within the Asian giant.

Contemporary slavery is the proper word to define the "Communist Paradise," as Marx and Engels describe it initially, and Mao Tse Dong imposed it in the land by force in 1949. Over forty-five million people died under the famous "Leap Forward," either assassinated, tortured, or victims of the Great Famine (between 1959-1961.)

Let us remember that Socialism emerged after the 18th Century Industrial Revolution that transformed mostly rural, agricultural societies in Russia and Europe into industrialized, urban ones. Earlier in 1789, the idea of Socialism appeared with the French Revolution but later solidified in the Marx-Engels Communist Manifesto of 1848.

Until then, goods that had been painstakingly crafted by hand started to be produced in mass quantities by machines in factories, thanks to introducing new machinery and techniques in textiles, steelmaking, and the beginning of technology.

Under Socialism, some labor leaders took advantage of the changes and began organizing Unions to assembly workers, promising to defend them from the factory owners who were abusing laborers, paying them little, and demanding unreasonable efforts. However, Communism does not encourage "Unions.'

Of course, for some, it was, in theory, the most magnificent idea ever. Communism must create a massive entity called State, perfect and spotless, managed by human beings in real life. It is hardly ideal and full of human defects and corruption.

Then, in 1848, Karl Marx, the German political philosopher and economist, became one of the most influential Socialist/Communist thinkers of all time.

Along came Friedrich Engels, with similar ideas to aid Marx. Together, they published in 1848 "The Communist Manifesto," which criticized those earlier socialist models as utterly "utopian" dreams, unrealistic and weak.

Marx affirmed that earlier Socialism lacked the strength and power necessary to take down Capitalism, bring it to rubles, and on top of the debris, constructing a "Communist Paradise,' where the State will own all businesses.

The establishment of Socialism then promoted the idea that workers should be under Government sponsorship, the factories' owners.

Marx Manifesto did not propose that people had the right to free education, healthcare, housing, and many other privileges. Those are additions by the western followers, Communist wannabes.

He mentioned abolishing private ownership in favor of State-owned, and all of it, administrated by a humongous Nation created to do the job.

In real life, Socialism is equal to Communism. The only difference is that while Socialism allows some individuals to own properties and small and medium businesses in partnership with Government, Communism keeps ownership of the land and all enterprises.

Nevertheless, today's Chinese Communism is allowing particular Private-Sate partnership.

Under Socialism, some countries have elections to choose Presidents and Congress members, while Communism allows only one Governing Party and has no polls because there is only one Party.

Sometimes they allow some electoral events to choose local authorities, although very rare and subordinated to the "one-party state."

The Chinese Government system imposed an innovation, creating what many call "State Capitalism," with Socialism on the coast, and Communism in the rest of the country, but all under the big umbrella of a totalitarian Central Government in Beijing, which owns all businesses and infrastructure.

When we think about how that system could be imposed in the USA, probably thinking it could be attractive, after two hundred and forty-some years of complete democratic elections and institutional freedom, really? Think again, please!

Marx argued that there was a history of class struggles in the past and that the working class (or proletariat) will inevitably triumph over the capitalistic class (bourgeoisie), finally wining control over the means of production, forever erasing all classes' problems.

Marx did not consider people's human nature, with their ambitions, desires, family, friendship, miseries, anxiety, and overall: Karma and spiritual life as an essential part of the individual.

His ultra totalitarian views considered humans as robots, born to work for the Government and die miserable, frustrated, without fulfilling or at least trying to achieve personal goals in search of happiness.

Here is where "the pursuit of happiness," embedded in the US Constitution and Bill of Rights, makes a big difference.

Marx and Engels dismissed that human beings are all different from each other and with diverse individual desires and rights accordingly with Karma.

136 -Communist Ideology Making In-Roads In The USA.

Greed is playing a role in the modern attempt to establish Socialism in the US. -Politicians are the main actors.

Little by little, we learn that many on both sides of the aisle are engaged in treason acts, receiving money primarily from China's Communist Government and other foreign powers.

Mike Bloomberg, the former NYC Mayor, is a vivid example. He admitted: "I have business with China. They set the rules, and if we do not follow them, then we are out of it!" That is an acknowledgment of complete submission to the authoritarian nature of State Capitalism.

Money is the only goal that turns the rest of the issues irrelevant, even patriotic feelings, to the United States of America.

That is, precisely, what is destroying Market Capitalism and our Country: Uncontrollable greed and a disdain for the Constitution and our lifestyle.

Billionaires could not care less about American Workers, and the Democratic Party glamorizes foreign workers' employment, legal or illegal. Simultaneously, they encourage local workers' replacement with the H-1B Visa holders coming mainly from India and China.

Prestigious Universities enjoy substantial contributions of funds in exchange for allowing a significant amount of Chinese students, paying full tuition and fees. Besides being part of the learning process, they steal and deliver critical information to the Chinese Government, mainly military and technological developments.

The amount of Chinese students enrolled in US Universities is continuously growing at an alarming pace.

Although the daily scene's peaceful appearance seems to be innocent, the reality is scary and dangerous. Thousands of Chinese spies keep sending our secrets to the Communist

Government. The Democrat's rant helps them big time by glamorizing Bernie's political philosophy at the helm.

Prestigious universities are holding Billions of Dollars in Cash, received from Communist China and other governments as bribes to educate hundreds of thousands of Chinese students, which at the same time pay full tuition to them, personally.

There is no secret that the Chinese Government intends to dominate the World and displace the USA from its leadership on all fronts.

A questionable appropriation of some small islands in the South China Sea, where a massive military construction is underway, includes a large airstrip. Artificially, they are expanding the land.

Also, recently, the leasing of an entire island in the South Pacific Ocean, near Australia, concerns the US and its partners.

3.2 million people live in the South Pacific Island complex. These are Cook Islands, Fiji, French Polynesia, Kiribati, Marshall Islands, Micronesia, Nauru, New Caledonia, Niue, Palau, Samoa, Solomon Islands, Tokelau, Tonga, Tuvalu, and Vanuatu.

The Chinese Communist Government is building a massive military complex that has alarmed the USA and the neighbors in the region.

The in-roads to the US the Chinese are achieving are alarming and point to their domination intentions, which severely menace our strategic position and humanity's liberties.

Chinese investments and loans to the US are reaching scandalous proportions, as well as the purchase of American debt, threatening the country's economy to become too dependent on China's money.

By the way, its origins are an extensive business relationship with our country for decades, which enriched China and put the US in debt.

At the same time, the Chinese have kept stealing technology, inventions, mechanical design, intellectual property, military ideas, and high tech devices. Our politicians are only watching from afar, and some are getting bribes to look the other way.

Factories like Foxconn and Pegatron use sensitive technology designed mostly by Apple engineers and others. They leak tech secrets to others around the World, creating a black market competing with us.

Such a situation is a much worse threat to our National Security than Russia was in the USSR days.

Besides, the Russians never achieved the Chinese people's skills in manufacturing.

During the USSR time, Russian product was imperfect, rudimentary, and almost laughable in some cases.

The size of Russia's economy is tiny, comparing it with China.

Over the past five decades, because our population got used to enjoying the products made in China, relatively inexpensive, with acceptable quality, our governments kept encouraging American entrepreneurs to open new factories, even at the cost of growing unemployment in our homeland.

We must consider that the Chinese worker's wages, on average, are about 10% of what an American craftsman earns. That is the main reason the Chinese product is so inexpensive.

Furthermore, under the Communist ruling, workers cannot even complain or ask for a raise. They live under slavery conditions, without proper healthcare or any other social benefits.

In his second term, Obama, through a massive regulation craze, provoked the closing of thousands of American Factories, and the migration of millions of American jobs to China, Mexico, and other countries. The move allowed popular articles to be inexpensive, which made the American consumers happy, of course, disregarding the future consequences we are learning now.

Our country's health system is dependent on 96 % of Chinese production and other countries in a minor percentage.

Penicillin essential ingredients are 96 % manufactured in China, the same with most prescriptions, including Diabetes, Heart Disease, High Cholesterol, or any other critical drug to keep the American people healthy.

Also, medical supplies as gowns, gloves, masks, gauzes, mechanical survival equipment as ventilators, scans, radiological equipment, and thousands of devices essential to our good health.

Not only in medicine, but National Security items like parts for Military aviation, ground Military equipment, components for radars, even missiles, and nuclear devices are "Made in China."

If what was said is not stupid on our part, trusting our National Security to Communist Government, then I do not know what would be.

Our Lawmakers need to wake-up from their "siesta" and begin earning the high salaries we, the People, pay them.

If the Communist Government of China decides to close its big hand, the whole American population will be trapped inside the fist.

This case is the greatest failure of past Governments, and the American voters deserve part of the blame.

The House of Representatives today is a pit of Postmodern Liberal snakes playing politics while receiving thousands of dollars from the American People they do not deserve.

Recently, President Trump, through executive orders, removed many of the regulations imposed by Obama and, together with a severe reduction of corporate taxes, managed to allow many large companies with factories in China, to return to the USA and open thousands of new plants, generating thousands of new jobs.

Such moves significantly impacted our economy, lowering the unemployment rate to 3.5 %, the lowest ever, just before the Coronavirus dreadful infection spoiled the Party.

Consequentially, the worker's wages increased due to the business's difficulty in finding qualified laborers' help. High-Tech executives hate that. They prefer to import labor from India and China, paying them much less than paying American workers.

Unfortunately, the COVID-19 Pandemic temporarily ruined the trend.

The US needs more immigrants, no doubt about it, but as President Trump insists, the new immigrant's selection should be among the more qualified people. As Trump affirms, immigration must be based on merit, not recklessly as the Democrats want, to enroll new voters, but orderly and selected accordingly with the country's needs.

We all hope the present Pandemic could soon be under control, and our economy could rapidly recover even to a higher standard we had a few months ago.

140 -Socialism Nefarious Consequences.

The old traditional Democrat Party has radically moved to the far left. So far, it has encountered the most totalitarian Communist ideology, now in the Chinese style, the despotic Fascist doctrine on the right and the autocratic Islamist Theology, with its unique totalitarian practices.

However, how Islam reconciles with the Postmodern Liberals is a mystery since their philosophies are very far apart.

Democrats ignorantly turn their faces the other way. Islamists know they could not live with most of the Postmodern Liberals lifestyle. Gay life, women's liberation, Atheism, Democracy, elections, sexual freedom, genderless society, widespread drug culture, and many other aspects we all know the Democrats love, Radical Muslims hate.

Besides, Islam is not welcome in the Chinese Communist country. More than one million Uyghur Muslims are kept prisoners in a Chinese concentration camp; they call Re-education camps.

Scores of radical Liberals have taken center stage, acknowledging the 'new' Liberal's takeover and the indoctrination by the new Postmodern Liberalism ideology via Political Correctness.

They are changing education centers, unfolding destructive practices, featuring violent and wholly undemocratic behavior.

As I write, these vandals are suppressing the First Amendment Free Speech right, destroying public and private property, burning American flags and Police cars, beating their opponents, and spreading complete chaos in the education system, as exposed in Chapter 1.

These New Postmodern Liberals promote equality, a genderless society, promiscuity, and education disarray, as previously described.

They befriend terrorist organizations, want welfare for everyone, including undocumented migrants. They have plans to extend free State Healthcare to all illegal aliens, and an array of issues that a few years ago were considered unacceptable for our country, including a borderless Nation, now, with the Pandemic, confirmed like an insane idea.

Naturally, Postmodern Liberals forget we were at war with the Left; President Reagan labeled Communism as the "Evil Empire." The labeling still applies.

141 -The American People Need Education!

Now, Conservatism needs to implement a "Road Warriors" front activity.

In our opinion, it is necessary to start a campaign geared to educate the public about the situation of our society and the perils at sight if Democrats manage to implement their "totalitarian" plans.

Education, education, education, is needed now, more than ever before.

The World's history, especially in the 1400 years of Islamic invasions and destruction, must be exposed, publicized, as well as Socialism and Communism history, intentions, and goals. People need education. A smart saying!

"People who forget their past are condemned to suffer their mistakes all over again."

The Conservative Movement needs to become a real Movement to engage everyone that does not agree with the Lefty/Liberal/Islamist/Anarchist alliance. They all have a common denominator: Totalitarianism.

People must have a home; we need to fight for that ideal.

The times of "taking things for granted" ended. We live in a different world now, and if a few months before we were unsure, the Coronavirus import from Wuhan, China, is an undoubted confirmation that we are in a whole different World, active now.

We need to keep fighting for our conquests. Democracy, Republicanism, and Freedom are not gifts.

We have to earn them every day, or we are bound to lose them.

Conservative activism is necessary, now more than ever, because the twisted minds of the Postmodern Liberals are inching in, while Conservatives rest on the assumed freedom!

So, we must consider that our enemies would try to take away from us whatever we do not defend.

Philosophy is an old but new weapon Republicans must use against Postmodern Liberalism. Education about historical facts, especially the relationship with Socialism/Communism and Islam, needs to be published, adding Postmodern Liberalism.

The American People need to educate about the past.

Please, be assured when I write about repealing Islam regarding their actual politics, not the philosophy. The Clerics in command are trying to apply the rules thru the original intentions. Islamists must adapt to modern times like other religions have done it.

Moreover, even the lesson that we have learned from the COVID-19, although maybe not yet fully digested, that all the unnecessary, brutal, inhuman killing of animals that triggered the Coronavirus on the wet markets of China must stop, we better revise it right now.

Moreover, Scientists have discovered that a tiger in a US zoo carries the Virus, so other wild animals in their habitat also do. The found could mean those wild animals could be natural carriers of Coronavirus, undetected until now because their very occasional contact with civilization was rare. But in China, because the intense killing of wild animals for food is widespread, the Virus encountered a path to human lives.

Chinese people need to learn from other philosophical schools on how to respect life, including animals. Reading the Vedas could be a good source of such knowledge.

We are in this World to share it, not to destroy it. The Planet's destruction will occur in due course of time. We do not have to rush it.

The United States of America is the most prosperous Constitutional Republican Democracy on the Planet because of our past and present goals.

It is not the country that the Liberals want to make based on European and Communism China style, a failed experience on immigration, demographics, society, and economics.

The USA is so divided, especially on race and religion, with one group (Radical Islam) that opposes any compromising because their scriptures continue to be misinterpreted by the Clerics in command, mostly Iranian, backed by the Postmodern Liberal's ignorance of the facts.

Politically, the persistent pounding of totalitarian Communism, now seen in China's bullying escalation, should teach us a lesson.

Allow me to repeat:

Education, education, education, is needed now.

However, the said situation could only change from the inside.

The countries involved must eradicate the proposed extremism—something it will take various generations to accomplish.

Democrats need to think, re-think the issue; especially the Mainstream Media, with their highly influential megaphone, must stop the childish behavior. They must see that our country has reached the actual status because of our philosophy of life, not for what the Postmodern Liberal Movement is offering now.

The US population must look to our neighbors in South America and see the disastrous results that Socialism and Communism have left, and what to say of Communism's most significant failure in the USSR and Eastern Europe.

All of the lefty Government's history experiences have brought pain, corruption, death, financial crisis, and indebtedness but overall a sense of despair, depression, and distress.

Some South American people, the latest victims of the Left, do not even have the money to buy a ticket and get out of the misery they live.

Venezuela is a vivid example. A country among the biggest Oil Producers is in such a state of necessity; it is hard to understand. They are hopeless, without a future, and stuck in the Socialist/Communist Government's corruption, still trying to follow Cuba's steps.

Seeing those experiences, the US Middle Class must learn that the Postmodern Liberal Movement now controlling the Democratic Party is a poisonous trick. Some very wealthy people manipulate the scene to keep the power under control and completely disregard the ordinary citizen's welfare.

One of the most evident operators is George Soros, a billionaire speculator interested in creating distress and commotion.

Sometimes it reminds us of Nero, the Roman Emperor, who burned the City of Rome, to watch the fire from his palace in the Mountain and enjoy the chaotic sight while playing the Lyre.

Also, the Hollywood elite, with their hidden Nazi philosophy baggage from the 1930s, are exercising their power, spreading the illusory way of life, the fantasy through an excess of Liberalism and sexual freedom that has brought only corruption and a lower lifestyle to the World.

However, those Oligarchs in Hollywood and Silicon Valley keep amassing fortunes while not paying decent salaries to most workers.

They only keep some minorities of employees handsomely paid, that are super loyal to the bosses and their philosophy. Liberalism is not a bad word, although the new concept of the "Postmodern Liberalism" with its sinister alliances definitively is.

Maybe the COVID-19 Pandemic, forcing social distance, could modify the reckless sexual relations practices and focus people toward a more philosophical approach. Who knows?

144 -One Reason Socialism And Communism Still Exist.

At one point or the other, most people had thought of the possibility to change Government style to the Left in its two variants: Socialism or Communism. It is a natural thought in some people's minds. People like Bernie Sanders and other Lefty politicians have developed over the years, a script that sounds very attractive, especially to youngsters and uneducated folks, ignorant of history.

The consistent inequality that allowed Bernie Sanders to raise a (multi-racial, multi-cultural, multi-ethnical movement,) as he often mentions, has a compelling reason.

The Capitalists individuals' greed, the vast fortunes accumulated, frequently acquired in suspicious ways, thru illegal practices, taking advantage of inside trading, and other dubious means, are harmful. People see the enormous differences of bank accounts balances between the Company's executives and employees, at times scandalous, unfair, and stomach-turning.

So, that is a significant reason for the existence of Communism, Socialism, and now, in China's example, what many political pundits call: State Capitalism; A combination of Socialist Capitalism and Communism, highly totalitarian, authoritarian, and despotic.

The Elite owners of the new technology companies dominating the World, and sharing Trillions of dollars in profits, are enamored with contemporary State Capitalism China's style and are abandoning the old-time Market Capitalism in practice in the West, to jump in the wagon of China and his totalitarian Government style.

Of course, they love authoritarianism, with its totalitarian practices and the Subject's indoctrination to obey their orders without question. They seem not to have time to lose bargaining with the workers, elevating the sharing and curbing their appetites for luxuries, extravagant lifestyles, and overall: power. That ultimate elixir: being closest to God! Yeah, power is the ultimate goal of a human being. Moreover, those Billionaires are so attached to the idea of absolute power that not getting is unthinkable! The horror!

Those are the same entrepreneurs who transferred the manufacturing of 96% of the Medical Supplies and Drugs essential to our survival to the Communist Government of China; Of course, with the help of Obama, Biden, and in part by Bush and Clinton.

The result is hard to describe, and it was discovered accidentally by the Pandemic lashing at our country at present.

We are discovering that we are totally in the hands of Communist China, our greatest enemy; trying to dethrone our country from the present influential status is unacceptable. The USA is fomenting Market Capitalism, Liberty, Freedom, and Justice for all.

The Chinese want to expand their despicable human slavering system, while we all are seeing them abusing most of their citizens to benefit an Elite of authoritarian despots.

Their greed became so uncontrollable that even knowing that by their attitude, they jeopardize the very existence of the USA, we keep doing business with them. High-Tech executives' insatiability for personal power and economic gains are more potent than their roots, the American Constitution, our Laws and Order, and our philosophical background full of pride and honesty.

Welcome to the new reality. Morals are dead; human decency is no longer critical; freedom of speech is out of fashion, in their way to obtain power. A sense of misery has invaded those corporate seats and corner offices, overlooking what they utterly disdain:

The American People.
Our Founding Fathers.
Our Constitution.
Our way of life.
Our Flag.
National Anthem.
Our history for two hundred and forty-some years.

They are the ones fighting for a Constitution other than the one written in 1787, but one that they could change to their desire to acquire more power.

It is sad. Very sad!

J. Pelegrin

A BRUTAL ATTACK ON DEMOCRACY

(The All-Time Enemies on the March)

CHAPTER 4

(Elections have consequences)

147 -November 3rd, 2020, and beyond.
WHEN DEMOCRATS STARTED TO MAIL MILLIONS OF UNREQUESTED BALLOTS TO EVERYONE, THEY GOT AN ADDRESS; I knew what the election result was going to be; confusion, chaos, and tons of fraudulent votes.

In 2000, President Jimmy Carter and Secretary of State James Baker expressed their strong opinions against Mailing Voting, assuring that such a practice was a call for fraudulent voting.

They included illegal aliens, invented names, addresses, signatures, included dogs, cats, other pets, dead people, and folks who had moved to another city. They engaged in harvesting votes by paying third parties to collect them, knocking on every door they could—a real call for fraud, a disaster.

Modern Democrats, especially Nancy Pelosi, who fought hard to be the Speaker of the House, had in mind the main object of her duties, an electoral reform.

Mailing voting was the central point of her aim, and the unfortunate COVID-19, sent from Communist China to the World and us, was the grain of sand she needed to finish building her castle of dreams.

The Coronavirus was the "Joker card" Democrats needed to initiate the dreadful change they had in mind for some time. They wanted to change the whole United States lifestyle, and especially the Constitution.

So, the new Virus delivered by the Chinese arrived just in time to expand their ambitions to kill Democracy in the United States and replace it with a Totalitarian Government, Communist China style.

We have written about the core of their new political Philosophy in previous chapters.

President Trump and many other politicians warned vigorously about the pernicious consequences of massive mailing voting. In a bipartisan 2005 report of the Commission on Federal Election Reform on the subject, President Carter and Secretary of State James Baker were thus: "Absentee ballots remain the largest source of potential voter fraud."

Voting by mail has been allowed for years, but always at the voter's request, and following four steps:

1) **Register to vote. Of course, being a US citizen.**
2) **Request your mail-in ballot.**
3) **Fill out your ballot — correctly.**
4) **Return your ballot.**

The Democrat's intentions weren't to follow the existing rules but to make their own new rules, and preferentially create confusion and distraction.

A major mess, and premeditated chaos, to serve the Democrat's dark purpose: To steal the election from President Donald J. Trump, who history will judge as to the best US President of modern times.

Democrats announced a BLUE WAVE that did not happen, and the Tens of Thousands of people assisting Trump's rallies, for the first time in history, multitudes, tens of thousands of people acclaimed a US President chanting phrases like "WE LOVE YOU." Trump received 74 million votes, 10 million more than in 2016, doubled the Black's and Hispanics' votes.

In some states like Nevada, Pennsylvania, Wisconsin, Georgia, and others, Democrat Secretaries of States, without consulting State Legislatures, suddenly changed the rules, mainly eliminating safety issues and controls, to fit Pelosi's plans.

They proceeded then to eliminate the bi-partisan ballot's signature verification, refusing to allow Republicans to confront the signature on the ballot envelope with the one in the voter's registration.

Besides, they extended the arrival of ballots set to 5 pm on Tuesday, November 3rd, to Friday at 5 pm and changed the old rule of having the envelope postmarked before November 2nd, to be counted if arrived even 16 days after the election day. Also, even in the case that there was no postmark, to validate the votes anyway.

Examples are clear; Democrats wanted to assure confusion would reign, so they could also smuggle suitcases full of ballots previously marked for Biden, as recorded in a Georgia's video. They hid the bags underneath a table with a black hanging tablecloth, reaching the floor. By 10:30 at night, and after dismissing the GOP poll workers arguing there was a plumbing malfunction, they started to do the planned work. Four female Democrat poll workers proceeded to pull the suitcases from under the table and fed the voting machines with the ballots inside, scanning votes several times (sometimes 9 or 10 times the same sheets for hours thru the night.

All these actions are registered in a video by a security camera shown on National TV, seen by millions of viewers. Nevertheless, nor the FBI, DOJ, or any other investigating agency, is looking into the case.

Another unusual issue is the complete absence of voter ID or other means to identify the voter and address verification.

As we can see, all the changes were focusing on creating chaos and disorder, to illegally feeding the voting machines scanning the same ballots several times, that several witnesses under perjury testified.

Another way to stuff the machines with fake ballots Democrat poll workers used was the connection of USB sticks, previously written with fraudulent votes with Biden's name.

It all looks like a well planned and coordinated operation to hurt Donald J. Trump and make sure Joe Biden was the winner.

Unfortunately, we don't know the operation's head, neither the mastermind, but there were too many coincidences for a repeated series of the same issues.

In some states, like Georgia, Pennsylvania, and a few others, the Constitution specifies that any changes to the electoral Law, only the Legislative body can do it. Not the Secretary of State, Governor, nor anyone else.

However, the proposed changes were elevated to the States' Supreme Court by order of the local Secretaries of State instead.

Five of its eight members are Radical Democrats. Over the weekend, they issued an order to implement the changes, something unconstitutional and unlawful. Again, the Legislators are the only ones that could operate such changes, not the Courts.

In some states, an additional measure: a notice of the proposed changes in two local Newspapers, should be published twice, and if nobody opposes them, they would be sufficient.

As we can see, Democrats planned and executed a very messy operation to facilitate the intended scam.

It is sad and embarrassing how Democrats, with the help of the Media, High-Tech executives, Academia, high education executives, the Sports stars, and the Entertainment elite, have divided this country.

The reason: a power-grab they will waste doing the wrong things as they have already announced.

Our beloved country is severely wounded, and the perpetrators, we all know who they are, probably, will get to set Biden in the White House.

Indeed, we can see in the mid-term election of 2022, the House of Representatives will go back to Republicans. I don't doubt severe mistakes by the Biden Administration will trigger it. I only hope the balance of Power (a Republican Senate) will mitigate the damage.

GOD SAVE OUR NATION!

151 -Urban Disturbance Planned In Detail.

During the electoral campaign of 2020, most people, not only in the USA but worldwide, have seen the violent videos showing the destruction of private and public property, police cars' torching, and the attempt to burn down Federal buildings, Catholic Churches, Supermarkets, and small businesses in many US cities, for an extended period of 120 days.

The violence, bullies, crime, looting, police officers' targeting, and private citizens wounded or killed, were out of this World. They resembled similar situations in third world countries we, Americans, witnessed in the past but never thought we could be victims in our land.

Despite the Mainstream Media, now partners with the Democrat Party, in a bid to take President Trump down, have meticulously hidden the evidence filmed by private independent journalists.

The Media has not shown those videos and ignored the consequences. They didn't even mention the riots and labeled some of the incidents as "mostly peaceful demonstrations."

No wonder the American Public dropped the Media's credibility down to less than 20 %.

Despite the Democrats ignoring the protests, that started with the death of George Floyd, which triggered a series of riots that Democrats tagged and promoted as "peaceful protests."

At the same time, Black Lives Matter appeared on the scene to back the protests with rants against the Police Officers in a violent manner. They chanted: "Pigs in a blanket, fry 'em like bacon." Immediately, another more violent group, "Antifa," appeared on the scene, after BLM conducted an early rally. They brought trucks and vans loaded with arms, fireworks (used as weapons against Police officers), studs, banners, and other urban-war paraphernalia they distributed among the BLM members.

The Antifa terrorists, trained on the Marxist ideology (by their own recognition), using subversive techniques, destroyed anything in their way. The only purpose was: destruction and people's intimidation.

Sources estimate the damage caused by the disturbances for 90 days in over two billion dollars. Of course, the human losses, the personal life-time savings lost, massive stock of merchandise looted from stores are impossible to evaluate. They torched hundreds of vehicles, in addition to hundreds of police cars destroyed or burned down.

Despite the incredible damage caused, the Media remained silent, ignoring the consequences, and kept labeling the evident disaster as: "Peaceful Protests." An utterly lie and hypocrisy we've never experienced before.

We knew those disturbances had a sole object. To inflict fear, insecurity, and disgust that Democrats, thru their megaphone, the Media, blamed President Trump.

It is suitable to state that Trump's White House is limited by the Constitution to defend only the Federal buildings, like the Courts and others. Still, he could not intervene on the rest: Private buildings, businesses, and even Police Stations depending on the Mayor's local offices. To do so, a request from the Governors or Mayors is necessary. That never happened.

Of course, those politicians in these "Blue cities" actually promoted disturbances in cahoots with the Democrat Party and the Media.

Only under the declaration of "Sedition," an extreme measure Trump declined to use, could the Federal Government sent the National Guard to restore the Law and order.

So, the devastation continued for over four months. The damages extended to hit all kinds of victims, indiscriminately, but mainly hurting small business owners that in horror saw their life-time savings going up in smoke. But the terrorists didn't care, with only one exception: curiously, they did not touch a single Mosque or Islamic building.

The riots continue, although, as expected, stopped a few days before the election. Then, the other chaos commenced—the 2020 presidential election - a well planned rigged electoral act.

Democrat Governors, blaming the COVID-19, also closed the public and private schools, increasing the pressure on children, and the parents that had to keep watching and teaching some basics to their kids, and therefore couldn't go to work.

Children are almost invulnerable to the Coronavirus. Their immune system is robust and protects them against infection. However, they need to stay in touch with the schools, their friends, their teachers, and not stopping the learning process. But the teacher's union, a very influential group led by Democrats, refused to keep working while they kept receiving full payment.

153 -Pelosi's Planned Election Reform.

The United States Constitution determines that we are a country formed by fifty states, each with its governors, city's mayors, and even their own Constitution. Therefore, the President has limited Power to exercise his/her authority in those states.

That is why they used COVID-19, purposely to mislead the public. From the beginning of the Pandemic, Democrats established confusing information. They insisted on the President's failure to dictate more drastic measures to isolate people, fulfill equipment, and therapeutics to First responders, health fighters, nurses, and doctors. They were lying. Trump did those and more.

At the same time, they refused the President's help in every aspect, opting to enforce each mandate from the State governments. It was a disloyal game they kept as long as they could, principally, ignoring, or dismissing Trump's extraordinary effort: "Operation Warp Speed" a vaccine development. Even now, we learned that Pfizer Lab. purposely delayed publicly announcing the venture's success until a week after the election. Once again, we can see the confabulation, now including the vaccine makers, to help Biden's team over President Trump's.

The World had never seen before such a widespread hatred against a President that fulfilled all his campaign promises, and more, except the ones he could not, because Democrats, with their Congressional Power, stopped or denied.

Trump's 2020 campaign featured "Law and Order," a phrase familiar with the United States of America, its Constitution, and the American People.

However, for Democrats, "lawlessness" is acceptable, and they supported it with facts on various cities' streets, as described above.

President Trump continues his promise to get as far as he is allowed to uncover the illegalities of the 2020 election.

However, most courts are full of Radical Liberal judges, and bureaucrats Democrats dominate the electoral system.

Regardless of the outcome that nobody knows how long it will take, I am writing this book, with the information available, focusing on the values, history, philosophy, the social consequences, and whatever I can write to tell the truth as I know it. The World must know the truth.

Unfortunately, the Mainstream Media, and Social Media, banned me and even prohibited my books or articles denouncing the attack on our Democracy.

Of course, the run-off election of January 5th will be determinant of the Senate structure. The contested Presidential result will also be unknown until the battle is over; A problematic situation that I am trying to overcome without stopping my writing.

Anyway, there is National consideration that we can't stop examining whatever the next Government will be.

China, for instance, is determined, and now with extra force, trying to take advantage of the apparent weakness and our 2020 troubled election. They are stepping on the gas in every front.

The Director of National Intelligence, Rep. John Ratcliffe, expressed his concern with the recent Chinese Government actions according to his classified information that can be public.

There is no secret the Communist Government of China wants to dethrone the United States economically, militarily, scientific, technological, and any other significant worldwide influence possible.

Since President Xi took the Government, his most important goal has been to out Power the USA in any way conceivable.

The Chines have flooded our country not only with the merchandise they manufacture but with China nationals, as students, merchants, diplomats, scholars, and any other positions.

They are mainly focusing on spying, stealing the USA technology, trade secrets, medical investigation, military parts, technological medical equipment, drugs (legal and illegal), and whatever they can take from us.

They have been doing it for years, while our politicians are sleeping their naps, or in many cases taking bribes from them, to look the other way, or when possible helping them to achieve their goals. All for money, the Chinese learned to spread around like butter.

Recently, we are learning; Chinese officials are threatening some American politicians in the Senate and the House with the possibility of exposing their links to China's Government. China has been bribing them for years, helping them to advance over the USA in all fields. There are many nervous politicians at this time.

Senator Diane Feinstein employed a spy as a chauffeur for 30 years, former Congressional member Joe Lieberman, Ed Royce, and others come to our memory. And now we know Congressman Eric Swalwell has refused to say if he had sex with an alleged Chinese spy — claiming the information is "classified."

Karma is implacable! They are now on advice, and indeed the Asians will demand loyalty to the millions of dollars they are receiving. I've mentioned a few of them, but we know the list is quite long, with very well known individuals. University Rectors and Academia members are also on the list of payees.

Communist China is determined to replace the USA as the World's most influential Nation, and it seems that Trump is the only President that could stop them. That is why Democrats want to take him down.

We know that Joe Biden is one of the politicians benefitting from his deals with the Communists. Under his son, Hunter's front, as we already mentioned in the previous chapter, documented in several articles on the New York Post and Tucker Carlson Tonight TV show, among others. Twitter, Facebook, and other social media prohibited the reproduction of a New York Post article where a former business partner, Tony Bobulinsky, denouncing the Biden's family as the recipient of Millions of dollars from China, Ukraine, and other foreign countries.

Of course, if the suspect were Trump, the whole Media would be flooding the space with inquires and investigations -but because it is Biden, their silence is thunderous! No one is mentioning it. Every shady issue that shows, they sweep it under the rug. Uncertainty is keeping all of us and the World in suspense.

Meanwhile, Joe Biden assembles his eventual cabinet under severe demands from all sides of the Democrat Party. We know the Black Community is about 12 % of the United States population. Hispanics, the legal citizens only, are about 17 %. However, the Black Caucus and other Black political leaders' including the Majority whip, Jim Clayburn's demands are so ambitious that they indicate an attempt to escalate identity politics thru opportunism. "A muddy river is Fishermen's gain."

With greater proportional demographics, the Hispanic community is less demanding, despite being a more significant community in numbers.

As mentioned before, Biden will have some problems with the "most diverse" cabinet proposed. Many of the proposed cabinet members are known to be "warmongers." Others carry doubtful baggage from the Obama-Biden Administration, and their confirmation will depend on the Senate configuration.

156 -Following China's State Capitalism Model.

Democrats do not waste any opportunity to scourge the President and keep attacking him, blaming Trump for everything negative that comes to their sick mind.

Undoubtedly, they are using the Pandemic to try re-structuring the USA, pushing it to the left, far enough, to melt with Fascism, which will be equalizing it with Communist China.

Democrats are fascinated with Chinas "State Capitalism." They are anxious to copy the idea they want to apply in our country. When we look at tech corporations' employment strategy, we see a "herd" philosophy approach. They had the opportunity to watch closely, from the inside, how the Chinese manage their factories and their workers. They dream of a chance to imitate them, practically slaving the people, which they see as part of the factory's robotization.

Greed is the motivation; Power is the goal. Democrats are hungry for Power, absolute Power, to have the American People depending on the Government to survive, think as a mass without identity, and give up personality and individual values. That is the Democrat's goal.

For them, at the top, the ideal is a group of people, collectively thinking, obeying the middle managers, indoctrinated by a chosen elite in an absolute power position, who will dictate orders admitting no questions or opposition, and demanding total obeisance.

That is why, as many Democrat politicians, including Chuck Schumer, are repeating: "We cannot waste the Coronavirus opportunity, to change the country to fit our views." Moreover, those views are entirely authoritarian with a totalitarian approach from a modified left, and of course, a vision of eventual State Capitalism. It is not clear if, in the end, those Billionaires controlling now the US Corporation would agree to be under the Politician's rules, or they will rule them by bribes and widespread corruption. We will see.

Meanwhile, the options indicate that for us to imitate Communist China's production system, a herd of workers will have to surrender to the rulers. Syndicates will have to become "Yellow Unions," and working conditions subject to lesser safety and health standards. That is the way the Chinese Communist Government does it. Note that Labor Unions do not exist in China.

157–The Identity Politics Game.

The "Browning of America" is a fact, not open to discussion.

We commonly hear Democrat White people's rants against other Whites like they were not White, without a mirror in their hands.

Identity politics is a deplorable practice at this time, polluted by blind ignorance and immoral, unethical behavior.

It is unfortunate, part of our political system. It is polluted, full of hatred, and manipulated by people desperate for Power, reaching the lowest human levels to achieve political gains thru authoritarian actions. It is an actual weapon used by Postmodern Liberals in the Democrat Party; A corrupt practice.

The latest unfortunate drama with the "Coronavirus" is that some politicians from the Left try to gain cheap points instead of unifying people and keeping educated but positive information about the problems.

Democrats are using the actual Pandemic as a weapon to change our country and impose totalitarian practices.

However, they now have a nasty stone in the shoe:

"Trump's vaccine." A name I'm delighted to use to baptize the COVID-19 vaccine, totally developed and released under President Donald J. Trump's tenure.

The Democrat Party is no longer "Democratic." It became authoritarian, anti-Democratic, and instead of sustaining a free-will popular Democracy based on our Constitution, some politicians are pushing for a Congress that changes the laws or re-interpret them capriciously to adjust them to their views. They want not only to maintain Power but to escalate it to absolute Power. Authoritarianism will impose libertine practices against our three centuries' ever-evolving Conservatism. It is crucial to concur that our behavior has been hugely successful and a model to the World, imitated by most countries in freedom and Democracy lovers.

People should be aware that the present Government is doing its best to keep health as a priority. Both sides of the aisle must act together, and if the White House is assigning a smaller budget than the opposition desires to help the crisis, it is the House, with a Democrat majority, that can allocate more funds to it. Of course, it is intended to help people at these challenging times and not try to sneak millions in the stimulus plans to support their political agenda. That is precise, what Pelosi has been doing, consistently.

Such actions are delaying funds directed to help small businesses. Notably, after denying months a Republican proposal to an aid package, demanding 2.2 Trillion dollars, Pelosi accepts a 908 billion dollars offer from Mitch McConnell and Republicans, just because the election is over and it is convenient for Democrat's politics.

Nancy Pelosi is a despicable person.

159 -Totalitarianism: The Object In The Democrat Party.

Totalitarianism and keeping a colossal Government run by a small elite is unquestionably on their minds under a favorable Congress. That is the present option. The House of Representatives, filled with the most radical individuals of each region of our country, have been acting like a flock, raising hands to support the House's Speaker.

Nevertheless, the new House of Representative's configuration has 20 plus GOP members, women in its majority, bringing considerably down the past Democrat majority. Some of the Democrat Party's new members are not inclined to obey Pelosi and be friendly with Republicans.

However, Pelosi will try to manipulate the elite serving the "State Capitalism" in a modern China's style.

The CEOs already feel what they can do if protected by the Government, concurring with the Communists leaders, and they love it.

The experience of decades enjoying the privilege of being powerful "Oligarchs" partnering with Communists strongmen has been so rewarding that it would be difficult for them to go back to the US Democracy standards.

 Living under the US current Laws is no longer an option. They would be too limited, having to pay people the US standard salaries, and comply with the country's regulations and other labor laws; it would be unthinkable.

The new role of the old Capitalists will convert into Oligarchs under Communist Government. They have experienced the "State Capitalism" a Chinese invention, and they love it. Although they raised it lately, what Communist Chinese Government pays the laborers is still a fraction of what the USA Corporations have to pay workers under our current labor laws, plus the social and health benefits, inexistent in China.

China does not have such standards, and that is why the Chinese product is so inexpensive. The American Companies doing business in the Asian Giant have had the taste of such a convenient scenario. They surely do not want to go back to the USA for manufacturing. However, in my opinion, the USA should re-think the extent of the "Free Market," and as President Trump has often said, it should also be a "Fair Market." So, the taxation of product made in China by American Companies, and imported to the USA, should be taxed in a way which will discourage manufacturing abroad and encourage going back to US land, employing American workers.

Since the craze of manufacturing in China started, I think the US could let companies use Chinese labor to make everyday, inexpensive items. Still, reserve important, sensitive products, especially National Security components and military devices, to be made in the USA. It only makes old good sense not to trust our enemies to make those items that guarantee our safety. That includes, of course, drugs and medicine items.

Chinese Government is spying on us 24/7; they have an army of nationals spread across our Nation, in Universities and all kinds of enterprises, daily delivering information to the Communist Government.

Unfortunately, some of our politicians are receiving bribes from them, in a scandalous way, as never imagined before. The degree of corruption is so widespread that it is impossible to see the light at the end of the dark tunnel.

Money has become a poison, that unfortunately, we need in our system. Comparing it with the Chinese, well, they limit the individuals who manage fortunes to just a few politicians, military brass, and Oligarchs under a firm Government grip; Such a method minimizes the number of people handling big money and limits their Power.

In the USA, because of our old Market Capitalist way and some outdated laws, things are conducted so that the financial Power is personalized, allowing a few CEOs and Technology company owners, accumulating vast fortunes and, with them, exceptional Power. The bribes to State officials are so extensive that masked in campaign contributions, or merely using triangulation with different countries and other methods, are getting away with murder; it is the most natural cheat.

Morals are dead. Honesty is rare these days, and although I am not a negative person and still believe in Capitalism, I am not sure about humans preserving the good qualities in this World.

That is why as said before and repeated on many occasions; this time is an excellent opportunity to go back to the old Vedic standards for consultation, Vedic Philosophy, and what is called "Vanashram Dharma," the ancient model civilization.

If we do not apply a reliable brake to these deviations, we are bound to a derailing that will bring us back centuries.

As I always say lately, I am glad I will be 81 soon, rather than being 18. What a dreadful future our kids are inheriting!

161 -Obama Administration's Legacy Crumbling Down?

Finally, the DOJ withdrew General Michael Flynn's case after a set-up by some crooked FBI high profile agents was proved, including Obama's knowledge and approval of the procedures.

President Trump, tired of the dirty games played by Judge Emmet Sullivan, a Liberal Judge hating our military hero, decided to fully pardon General Mike Flynn, who is now a free man!

The criminal investigation by John H. Durham, the US attorney in Connecticut, seems to be reaching the end, and many indictments and prosecutions are expected.

The lengthy investigation of the origins of the FISA Court is about to end, and hopefully, some people will be going to jail.

As never seen before, high FBI officials seem to be involved in a real Witch-Hunt, now coming to light. Durham, supposedly, is uncovering the most incredible conspiracy of a political party's involvement trying to unseat a Constitutional President of the United States. Through many illegal issues, it would be hard to point in a few sentences. Surely it will be material for several books to be written. I will merely remark on the most prominent actors in this act of treason, including General Michael Flynn, George Papadopoulos, Carter Page, and others. Only because they were close to President Trump, the main target and most hated person by Democrats and the Mainstream Media, are the victims.

Trump's determination to "drain the Washington swamp" was the motive. It caused an obsession among Democrats because they saw all their under-the-table deals, bribes, and utter corruption jeopardized to come out to light.

As the reader went through previous pages, the corruption and determination to use the actual Pandemic to change our country's future are so real that it is scary.

Democrat politicians are desperate to cover their tracks and prevent the American People from knowing the status of corruption, bribes, and other conspiracies, especially with foreign totalitarian regimes, billionaires, and CEOs with factories operating in Communist China.

Some current events are irrelevant for me to include in this book. Because they are well known among the American People and the World, the readers probably already know them in detail. They are terrifying.

These new facts corroborate the Obama Administration's irregularities, conspiracies, treasons, a total disregard for our Constitution, and a despicable will to grab Power. The aim is to assure the conduction of American politics, in a totalitarian way, opposite to our way of life, our founding fathers' intention, and what they wrote in our Constitution and the Bill of Rights.

As an ordinary citizen, I am powerless to administer justice. However, I hope the loyalists in charge and able to do the right thing will punish the traitors who damaged the life of patriots like General Flynn, who put his life at risk, defending our country in the front lines for thirty-three years. Flynn lost his home to pay lawyers that supported him in court.

The case confirms the Obama Administration was ridden with illegal activities, manipulated by crooked FBI agents, informing President Obama in detail about any actions.

President Trump has been and is still a victim of the worse internal conspiracy against a President of the United States of America.

Everything is coming out slowly but surely.

As President Trump has said many times:

"What is happening to me should never happen again to any President of the United States."

Obsession for Power is a curse the Democrat Party is carrying on every member's shoulders. They are authoritarian in essence and totalitarian in the policies' application. Their closeness with the Communist Government of China has contaminated their souls, and the only language they talk and hear is money, as the means to reach total power and slave the people they suppose to govern. As I mentioned before, they are trying to use the present Pandemic as a tool to accomplish their evil means and take away any power the Constitution is granting to citizens, especially the ones that try to protect them from the State abuses.

163 -COVID-19 Is Bringing Out To Light Liable Errors.

Governor Cuomo begged other states' healthcare workers to come to NYC to help, and the response was tremendous. Hundreds of them came to New York to save lives.

Now, Cuomo shamelessly is paying the favor, trying to force those volunteers that save New Yorkers' lives to pay NY income taxes; Note that they also must pay income taxes in their home States.

At the same time, the Governor issued an executive order forcing nursing homes to re-admit sick seniors with the Coronavirus to facilities where healthy long-term patients were living, provoking thousands of lives lost. Cuomo has rivers of blood in his hands! He is responsible for the death of thousands of seniors condemned to share space in crowded Nursing Homes, unprepared and unable to separate sick people from the healthy.

The most outrageous thing is that Cuomo overlooked the facilities President Trump provided to New York, of the Ship-Hospital named Mercy, which was empty with 1,000 beds available, and 1.200 personnel.

Additionally, Trump Administration built an Emergency Field Hospital in Central Park, with 68 beds, also overlooked by the Governor.

It looks like a scene coming from a horror movie. However, it is real, and it happened in New York City.

Additionally, Cuomo recognizes that most people contracting the Coronavirus were to stay at home (66 %) through his executive orders. The less affected are the ones that preferred to be outdoors receiving fresh air.

Mayor De Blasio is attempting to curb the park's attendance, keeping a policy that has proven to be wrong and unhealthy. Fresh air is always the best to keep us healthy. It is an ancient, well-known activity and safe human behavior.

This new information corroborates what I have been writing in previous chapters, using different examples and sources. Democrats are no longer the old American Party, that honoring its old name: "Democratic Party," defended our Constitutional values, our charming lifestyle, and our Bill of Rights.

The change is horrendous. It dishonors the name and hundreds of American patriots that in the past called themselves "Democrats." Instead, the new politicians that took control of the traditional political party are wearing carnival-like masks, hiding their real intentions to grab absolute Power. The idea seems to apply a totalitarian way, enslave the American People depriving them of the most basic right that our Constitution grants us.

Forcing the American People to think collectively and act as a herd is not viable. Not even with an elite "pastor" working for the Government marking our way. Freedom or death! Those are the options.

Looking at the Chinese people's lives, although they may not know another way of life, those living conditions are far from the American way. Chinese Nationals who come to hour country immediately learn the differences and refuse to go back to their land.

Nevertheless, Billionaires and Millionaires holding the top economic posts in the US are working, siding with foreign forces, to destroy our liberties and impose us to accept their authoritarianism so they can fulfill their ego-trip.

Our Government should look into some laws and modify them to be a bit more nationalist, to curb the attempts by other political philosophies trying to destroy our way of life. Keep America first! As our President says: "Free market is OK, but if it is also a fair market."

A BRUTAL ATTACK ON DEMOCRACY by J. Pelegrin

J. Pelegrin

A BRUTAL ATTACK ON DEMOCRACY

(The All-Time Enemies on the March)

CHAPTER 5

(Philosophical Controversy-The Vedas vs. Islam)

"The United States of America, the country with the greatest Republican Democracy in the Planet, and enviable lifestyle are under siege. The vast majority of people who would love to be part rising a family, studying, working, and enjoying life, is at this time, endangered by three lethal enemies:"

1-Democrat Party (Presently hijacked by Postmodern Liberalism)
2-Socialism and Communism (led by China), and
3-Radical Islam (Led by Iran who at the same time has seized the rest of Islamists in the World, imposing their false interpretation of the Scriptures politically.)"
The Coronavirus Pandemic is only an occasional health crisis that our people will overcome and recover in a Champion's way; Of course, with terrible consequences.
Some will be permanent. The World, as we know it, will change radically.
We better acknowledge it and accept it.
As a reminder:

Islam is entirely against every single issue of Communism, Socialism, and Democracy, and the topics defended and promoted by the LGBTQ.

Any attempt to unite them will end with Islamists appropriating the booty, including the Government, by the numbers and 1400 years experience.

Additionally, they hate Atheists and any other faith different from Islam.

Postmodern Liberalism, including its Political Correctness, features the most dangerous philosophical evil; a sudden love for totalitarianism.

As we mention previously:

"Today's USA Business Elite, Democrats in the majority, has more in common with a totalitarian Communist Government than with the US Constitution and the American People."

168 -The Difficult US Relationship With Islam.
168 -Obama: Islam Has Never Been At War With The US.

Even if the reader thinks Islam's subject does not directly relate to Postmodern Liberalism, Democrats' invitation to Muslims to join the Postmodern Liberal Movement makes the issue a most definite link worth it to analyze in-depth.

A brief detail of why Democrats and Islam are not compatible is at the top of this page. However, a detailed explanation follows.

Koran and Hadith establish death penalties in many cases of rule violations.

So, it is like oil and water.

Democracy and Islam will never mix.

Democrat Party and Islam's only common goals are preventing President Trump's re-election and the destruction of the United States of America as it is presently.

Islam is a Theocracy and an autocratic form of Government that considers elections usurping Allah's laws.

Islamists believe the Scripture's words are the only valid mandates. They repudiate any other ruling as apocryphal and attempting to deny Allah's power and authority.

Many of us know Obama accessed the Presidency through a mixture of lies and the belief that many people wanted to give a Black person an opportunity at being Commander in Chief, especially the Liberal-Democrats.

Nevertheless, no one can blame Obama for it. He did not lie more than a regular politician does to obtain power.

First, people did not vet Obama properly or in-depth enough; neither the Media did.

Moreover, his baggage was not that brilliant to make it an exceptional presidential candidate, other than his race, socially desired at the time.

We must admit that Barak showed himself as a smart politician, with a convincing speech, and a clean appearance, proper of an IV-League scholar.

For years, the question of a Black race President possibility remained in the minds of many US Citizens. Suddenly, a popular TV series: "24", featured a Black President, patriotic, triumphant, fighting terrorism all the way and winning. The time and circumstances made the TV series feel like real life. The show's excellent quality and realism, as well as the actors, made it convincing. I was a big fan of the show, undoubtedly, a universal hit.

I also considered the chance, looking at a few possible candidates as Secretary of State Condoleezza Rice or Colin Powel, among others, since I was not comfortable with John McCain as the GOP candidate.

That "24s" fantasy, represented by the most successful TV series at the time, believe it or not, encouraged the thought in many American minds.

The possibility of a Black President came closer than ever and eventually real, mainly when the GOP was featuring a weak candidate as McCain, a former POW, without charisma and a conflicting personality.

Some TV series heavily influence the American TV audience, and "24" was possibly the most influential in a very particular moment of the World's events.

Radical Islamist Terrorist activity was at a peak, hitting the Western World the hardest in centuries since the Barbary Wars in the 18th Century.

The reader must wonder about our evaluation, but the TV screen, daily intruding people's homes, can make such a powerful influence and more.

Seeing a fictional Black President succeeding on the TV screen on a smash hit series like "24" was an incentive, and the chance to turn it real became plausible.

We must take into account that the majority of US voters are poorly politically educated.

Our great Albert Einstein used to joke about it. He had the understanding that '90 % of voters were not even qualified to think wisely.'

The frequent random street TV interviews, at the time, especially with young voters, showed a disturbing lack of knowledge even on essential issues.

Democrat's proposal to lower the voting age was the most idiotic idea, only in the minds of the bitter losers, desperate to recover power by any means, especially brainwashing the youth with Socialist and Communist ideology, contrary to our historical Democracy belief.

Nowadays, those youngsters cannot even decide what clothes to wear on a given day, so choosing our Government is out of any of their troubled minds.

Left-wing indoctrinators, now in command of education centers, manipulate the immature youngsters and the camp's operations.

170 -The Eternal Conflict with Islam. A War Declaration.

Although Obama has repeatedly affirmed that Islam has never been at war with the US, it is a false statement.

A few years after our Constitution was written, history narrates we had a severe problem with the Pasha of Tripoli, the most relevant Islamic leader at the time.

The Islamist chief ordered his armed forces (The Barbary Pirates) to stop and kidnap the US ships navigating the Mediterranean Sea, demanding that the US Government pay ransom for the kidnapped passengers and crew.

Besides, Yusuf Qaramanli, the Pasha of Tripoli, established a tax to the USA: 10% of the US Gross National Product, if they wanted to navigate the Mediterranean Sea; The charge was submissively assumed by the US Government, under President John Adams. They estimated that it was worth it to pay tribute to the Muslims to conduct business in the region, rather than engaging in a war with the Barbary States.

Some politicians, as Vice President Thomas Jefferson, disputed the idea. At the same time, he favored going to war with the Barbary Pirates, who were extorting the USA and the rest of the European nations who wanted to travel the Mediterranean Sea waters.

In 1798, the Pasha declared war on the US, demanding an increase in Americans' tax. Still, President John Adams, who was contrary to that measure, ignored the War declaration, saying: "If we go to war with the Muslims, we will be at War forever with them."

President Adams remarked:

"I do not know if the American people have the stomach for that."

However, the Islamic authority, at that time leading the Barbary States, was commanding an idea without a Country.

At present, the Islamic leadership keeps pushing for establishing a Worldwide Caliphate, with an armed branch called Radical Islamic Terrorists, a modern edition of the Barbary Pirates.

Note that Islam considers the whole World as its domain, just because Allah might have indicated it and revealed it to Mohammed in a dream or astral trip.

Meanwhile, they continue to attack and kill our peaceful citizens ruthlessly and brutally. We must remember that Iran somehow has assumed the Islamic leadership and named their land as "The Islamic Republic of Iran."

While Muslim terrorists kidnapped and killed innocent people worldwide as they continue to do today, Thomas Jefferson knew how to end radical Islam's bloodshed – with a classic American take-no-prisoners smack-down.

Later, after becoming President, Jefferson refused to play games when given the choice of appeasement or confrontation in the face of terror.

In his book "The Jefferson Lies," Historian David Barton wrote, "Jefferson led America's first war against radical Islam." Moreover, we can see many parallels between the novel American Republic struggle against the Barbary Pirates and the continuing conflict with Radical Islamic Terrorists.

Jefferson was very clear about protecting US property and people worldwide as he did within our land.

"The Jefferson Lies" was labeled so politically incorrect; the original publisher pulled it from the shelves, under uncertain situation! The book is now back on the Bookstores shelves.

172 -Islam's Goal: Establishment Of a Worldwide Caliphate.

During the American Revolution and the Early Republic, American merchants and sailors navigating the Mediterranean Sea were under constant threat from North African Nations, known as "The Barbary States," and their Muslim pirates.

More than one million White Europeans were captured and enslaved by the Muslims between the 16th and 18th centuries.

Baltimore, a village in Ireland, was famously ransacked, and its entire population enslaved by them, later sold in the Slave's Market auctions.

172 -Abd Al Rahman's Warning.

Jefferson and Adams, while in London around 1801/1802, spoke to the Tripoli Ambassador, Abd Al-Rahman, questioning him on why the Barbary Pirates thought they should declare war on a nation that had never done anything to harm them.

The Muslim ambassador's responded, "It is written in the Koran that all nations who will not acknowledge Islam's authority were sinners and that it was their duty to make war upon them, and to make slaves of all they could take as prisoners."

The Koran-quoting is one reason why the Muslims consider us their enemies and our people condemned to die unless they surrender to Islam.

After hearing the outrageous statement, Adams and Jefferson were encouraged to seek their copies of the Koran.

Jefferson, however, is believed to have owned a copy of the book since 1765. Notice that Jefferson owned 6.000 books.

Probably, the Koran writers (Mohammed friends) intended to say it philosophically. Note that Mohammed was illiterate.

Still, today's Islamists lack of education and their high grade of fanaticism have taken the scriptures literally, turning the politics in it as an authoritarian way to enslave the most uneducated fanatics of the "religion" developed by Mohammed.

In some cases, Muslims discourage Muslims, like women's, prohibit reading any other literature than the Islamic texts. Women are forbidden to read, even the Koran. They should merely listen to the quotes from their husbands.

Their brutally savage interpretation of the scriptures forces people to live in the past, under capricious rules, which have no place in our evolving World's Society of today.

Understandably, they are preserving the basics, but the highly fanatic practices of centuries ago, at present, only cause enmities with other religions. Moreover, when Islamists do not accept to share the space in our World with other faiths: an absurd, bully, and irrational practice appear.

It seems the Muslims mixed their faith with the World's reality, thinking that the verses written in the Koran could become the Law Of The Planet, dismissing any other philosophical documents. They adopted a totalitarian, selfish attitude.

The Vedas are a superior authority since fifty-five hundred years ago.

The Old Testament is some five thousand years old, and the Torah about forty-five hundred years old.

The Koran is only fourteen hundred years old and spoken from Mohammed's mouth, without corroboration of any kind, since it seems to be the product of a dream or Astral trip and subsequent alleged "appearances" of Allah in the Prophet's mind.

Moreover, the Koran shows strong similitude with the Vedic Scriptures.

Muslim scholars often say: "If you do not find it in the Koran, search the Vedas." Such evidence is not a negative one, except that there is no acknowledgment of the "borrowing."

Adams and Jefferson had a fundamental disagreement about Islamic Terrorism.

"John Adams, as President, refused to use the navy to fight the pirates.

He said: "If we get involved in a conflict with radical Islam, we will be fighting them forever."

"I do not think the American People have the stomach for it." We must remember that "Radical Islamists" were Pirates.

174 -The Jefferson's Resistance.

In contrast, Jefferson, as Secretary Of State under George Washington, and as Vice President under Adams, had long experience of dealing with the Barbary Pirates for 15 years, showing a different approach.

Jefferson wanted to put an end to terrorism. He had seen the future!: A potential Islamic Worldwide Caliphate was a terrifying possibility.

While Adams refused to go to war, Jefferson asked the United States to cease paying the Barbary States' tribute.

When Jefferson became President in 1801, the Pasha of Tripoli required a USA payment, which Jefferson refused to continue to pay. The result was the First Barbary War.

When the Muslims wrecked the USS Philadelphia and its crew captured, Adm. Stephen Decatur burned the ship, so the Muslims could not use it. That made him a National Hero.

Months later, the American forces were able to seize territory in the area and force a peace treaty, which freed the captured crew. The US Marines immortalized these victories by a verse of the "Marines' Hymn," which refers to the "shores of Tripoli."

175 -President Madison Finally Ended Muslim Extortion.

However, the Barbary Pirates or Islamic terrorists did not terminate the threat to the United States.

Within only a few years of the treaty, which ended the war, in 1815, the Barbary pirates were once again raiding American ships. This act drove the USA to the second Barbary Wars, until 1816.

Finally, President Madison would ultimately end the American payments to the Muslim pirates of North Africa.

If the United States had followed the European practice of just paying off the Islamic pirates, the problem could have continued indefinitely.

Unfortunately, and mainly because the Koran says it, Islamists continue to attack an "infidel America."

The old Barbary Pirates have become today's ISIS, AL-QAIDA, and other terrorist groups. They continue to attack our civilization aggressively, just because they read it in the Koran and obey the mandates in it.

Nowadays, we can see a similar pattern at work, in the USA and Europe latest Muslim invasions, performing massive assaults and raping European women. This practice, the EU Politicians are conveniently ignoring, looking to the side, and even hiding from the people, in an unsound Political Correctness practice. They prefer the cheap labor, if any, of the migrants, who are mainly uneducated and unskilled to their people's safety.

The Muslim penchant for the desecration of Christianity continues as scheduled. At the same time, they also proceed to attack Jewish and Hindu symbols.

Their old ways are stretching out, and wherever there is a biblical site, a Buddhist, Jewish, Christian symbol, or a Hindu Temple, Muslims mark it for desecration and demolition. After they level the land, they proceed to build an Islamic icon, which, of course, will generate a reply from the victims, and that attitude keeps the hostilities going on non-stop.
Once again, my writing is not coming from an Islamophobic position; I'm only highlighting history.

176 -History Education Is A Must.

Unfortunately, the Postmodern Liberal Movement is trying to hide history regarding our drastic inconsistencies with Islam, or better said, Islam's discrepancies with the US. Instead, they are conveniently siding with the Terrorist sponsoring groups against the US Conservatives.
Considering that while the United States is a formally established Nation with a Constitution, Islam is not a country. However, it pretends to hold ownership and authority of the whole of Planet Earth.
Postmodern Liberals are now pushing to allow people from obvious Terrorist Countries (all of them of the Islamic religion) into our country without vetting them.
However, the latest events have exceeded the Western side's patience, and we, in the West, need to confront the Radical Islamic Terror.
To have the people's support, we must spread knowledge of history and show how the old Muslim tactics are repeating.
It is incomprehensible why, in 1801, under the same US Constitution, our country repealed Muslims after they declared war against the US in 1798, and today the House and Senate are interpreting the First Amendment, including the Muslims as a Religion only.
Islam is an ideology, a mixture of Commerce, Military, Politics, and also Religion. Under our current Legal System, Islam is considered as a single religion, although in practice, it is a four-tier way of life:

1) **Trading Nation,**
2) **Military power,**
3) **Political Force, and finally,**
4) **Religion.**

In the final stage, they force people to accept Islam, as the 'Musselman' Ambassador in England said: because "it is written in the Koran."

The efforts by German authorities to conceal crimes committed by Muslims are nothing but submission. Something it appears to be in their DNA.

Angela Merkel undoubtedly is a disgrace to Western Culture.

The European leaders have an attitude of soothing, rather than confronting.

It seems the horrors of the Nazi's mistakes made them afraid to show pride and defend themselves from the bully Islam.

Political Correctness is also rampant in Europe, and unfortunately, our Postmodern Liberal Movement is taking those failing European Countries as the example they wish to follow.

Europeans decided to curtail their rights rather than secure them.

They are behaving just like they did 200 years ago. They have not learned a thing.

Meanwhile, after Jefferson's decision and Madison's confirmation, the United States became a World Power with massive growth.

Now, Europe is succumbing to a more significant invasion that is generating new natural citizens, by birth, with the Muslim's decision to impose their way of life, including their religion: Islam, which is determined to destroy any other faith philosophy.

Islamic Leaders continuously say:
"We will accomplish the task, either by our women's
pregnant wombs or by the sword, as the Koran states."

The German Court System is collapsing, having a backload of over 100,000 immigration cases, causing a complete breakdown of the system.

Although some European politicians are ready to fight the invasion, the majority are submissively placating it. They seem to enjoy the migrant's cheap labor more than protecting their people.

The bullies of Islamic Terrorists are inflicting fear among Europeans.

Politicians and the Security forces are hiding the public's attacks, while some independent TV Channels are leaking information to America and the World.

178 -Is The United States Ready to Combat Islam?

Luckily, the electoral victory obtained by Donald J. Trump, and his assumption as the 45th President of the United States, has brought us to the conviction that the most prominent Republic in the World is ready and able to fight the Radical Islamic Terrorists and win the war.

Unfortunately, that policy is in danger now, after the 2020 election.

There is a powerful enemy: The Democrat majority in the House determined to obstruct the President in any possible way. They wrongly consider Islam an ally. They ignore history.

The Trump Administration has accomplished the promise to eradicate the ISIS presence in Syria. It might not be entirely, because as we write, more ISIS fighters are being born, others are growing up, and they will not quit.

Still, there is some advancement.

The International Tour by President Trump delivered an unequivocal message that enough is enough.

The World needs to remember, and revise history, to see the similarities and patterns that continue to repeat on the Barbary Pirates today, acting with different names as ISIS, Al Qaida, Taliban, Hezbollah, Hamas, Boko Haram, and others.

The truth is, they are all driven by the same principle, and they all obey the Koran and the Hadith.

There is no difference between the followers of those books because the mandates and goals are the same. They are forbidden to read other books.

So, this is the reality, and we better acknowledge it and fight it right now.

There is a Muslim say: "The price for us is too high to pay. If you pay, we will back off and leave you guys alone." Unfortunately, Muslims are known for not keeping their word or promises. They will never cease to insist on advancing Islam at any cost, which, of course, includes violence. Lying is an established practice in the Koran, called 'taqiya.'

The Koran encourages its followers to lie (among other horrors) if it is for the advancement of Islam.

However, as in Presidents Adams and Jefferson's days, the question is "whether the United States has the moral and economic strength to confront Islamic radicalism."

As John Adams argued many years ago, "it is an open question whether the People of the United States of America has the stomach for an extended conflict."

We must remember Jefferson's attitude, something that it seems is in President Trump's mind too.

The recent dilemma, resolved by President Trump, by leaving the Iran Nuclear Deal, is an encouraging sample that the President is assuming a historical duty, firmly opposing Iran's leadership of the Radical Islamist World.

Iran is the modern leader of the absurd intentions to install a Worldwide Islamic Caliphate that will enslave the rest of the World and force them to become Islamists.

The enormous problem in our country is "The Postmodern Liberal Epidemic," and their "Political Correctness," something that only with education, the revision of the Mainstream Media attitude, and stopping the financial help from the Hollywood Elite and the Silicon Valley could end.

Still, both groups enjoy the third World workers with the H-1 and H-1B Visas and the convenience of migrant's lower salaries.

A full call to history and the 'memory refreshing' of the Islamist consisting of repeating patterns could help, maybe. People are lazy, with a short memory span, and that is a problem.

Meanwhile, the facts are here. The Muslim population keeps growing exponentially, while Western's procreation is descending.

Abortions, encouraged by Postmodern Liberals, and a lack of incentives by the Government to welcome newborns, are discouraging.

The Islamic invasions continue to overwhelm the European land, and the desecration and destruction of old non-Islamic symbols, including Christian churches, Hindu, and Jewish Temples, continue, frantically and unstoppable by the weak Western culture in Europe, exacerbated by the Middle-Eastern continuous invasions.

In the USA, the "Caravans from Central America" have become a National Emergency problem. Hundreds of thousands of illegal aliens, pouring through our borders, bringing crime, ignorance, diseases, rapes, and some good honest people. Immigration is good for our country, but it must be on a merit basis, not disorderly and illegal.

Fortunately, President Trump was able to stop those caravans with Mexico's Government cooperation.

180 -USA Must Revise Islam's Status In The Constitution.

The Postmodern Liberal Movement is our present real threat, the mole within us.

We must overcome a self-destructing thought because it proposes a distortion in our traditional values — the ones who allowed our Nation to be a successful World Leader for such a long time.

We need to renovate our patriotism, existence, pride, and the defense of our precious Legacy: The Constitution.

That is one of President Trump's goals: America First!

As he said, "every President in the World is elected to put his/her country first," as he spoke to a big audience at the UN.

Meanwhile, China is stepping on the gas and showing its hunger for the World's domination.

The actual COVID crisis is confirming the President's proposal. As we sadly see, previous Administrations have given away our National Security and Health safety by letting one of our primary enemy, Communist China, manufacture 96% of our medicines, health aid supplies, and even the ingredients to produce our prescriptions. China has a monopoly on antibiotic manufacturing.

We must realize our country has achieved success over the years and leadership in the World because of a firm Republicanism. (Not meant it in the Partisan way but the etymological understanding); by defending and enforcing the Constitution.

However, why, in 1801, the Muslims, who are Islamists, engaged in a war with the US? Two Presidents contested it, and now our Liberal Judges are defending them when they continue to decimate our people?

Postmodern Liberalism culture is playing a significant role.

I am no lawyer, but it makes common sense to me that we must revise our Constitutional Laws' interpretation and be more Patriots, rather than continuing to defend others to the detriment of our people.

Religious freedom, the essence of the First Amendment, is excellent, but the Koran and Hadith are not only opposed to our Constitution but aggressively attacking it. Their primary goal is to destroy our Republican values, our Democracy, and the Bill of Rights, which they hate.

Islamists believe that the only valid Law is written in the Koran, presumably spoken by Allah and received by Mohammed. However, there is no proof of that. Only the word of Mohammed, which is the Law for the Islamist, but not for us or for the Founding Fathers who established our country and gave it a Constitution to rule it.

Why, then, we continue to observe and grant Islam a privilege when the Koran's interpretation is definitively a threat to our lifestyle and what our Constitution says. They keep vowing it loud and clear! We need to rewind and replay history.

We have to bring up those old values to the sky as our flag and be proud of them because God blesses them. Not meant as religious thought, but as a scientific fact that consciousness is reminding us.

The United States is not trying to fight Islam; They are the ones trying to invade our country and force their convictions and religion over our beliefs established by our Founding Fathers.

Just by looking around, we can see God's creation, and we must be joyful and bow before it.

Thus, it is good to remember part of this book's foreword:

"Supreme Court Justice Robert Jackson, appointed by President Franklin D. Roosevelt, wrote in the preface of the book "Law in the Middle East" (1955): "Islamic Law offers the American lawyer a study in dramatic contrasts... (See foreword in page 11.)

182 -Insanity Continues.

The United States has always been a melting pot, and the ethnic cultures shared with fewer problems until the Postmodern Liberal Movement appeared to spoil our lives.

It is unbelievable our Land of Opportunity has become a bully society, intolerant and bigot in the hands of the new Liberals that have hijacked and entirely changed the Democrat Party. Silicone Valley Hi-Tech Billionaires are embracing the latest trend that adds to their power grab wishes.

Everything in the Democrat's tent is focused to "punish" the white majority, the Conservatives, and trying to impose a Socialist/Communist agenda, uniquely totalitarian, which is, as stated before, all based on a materialistic vision of life, based on sexual preferences and devoid of spirituality or family values.

The gender is mystified, transgender put before cis-gender, and everything turned upside down to satisfy a handful of "hypersensitive snowflakes" that pretend to make their way, to destroy the history of the most successful Democracy on the Planet.

Meanwhile, the World keeps turning, procreation is still between a female and a male, and the day follows the night, ever and ever.

The Creator's design is unchanged, although many nuts called Postmodern Liberals are attempting to disrupt it. Failure is assured, but we must be vigilant and active to remind them of the facts and truth.

Once again, I would like to reaffirm that I am not anti-Gay, anti-homosexual, or anti-Islam. I believe our Society should accept any possible lifestyle as a personal choice.

However, people who have different views and feelings must express their dissenting preferences without being deliberately offensive. Of course, there will always be disagreements that the rules of courtesy, civility, and culture must deal with in each case.

After all, we cannot see how living in a World Society could be possible.

We are here to share this Planet and this life under God. Believe in him or not. We do not have a choice, and we could call the 'Creator of all that exists' in any way or name we choose. He/She will accept the given name. It does not matter; it will still be our Creator.

I sustain the thesis that I have learned from the Vedas: God accepts any name people would like to assign to call him/her. After all, the Vedas say: God has no determined gender. He/She is omnipotent and possesses all qualities and both genders.

However, there is an ample warning for those who want to be equal to God, to Krishna. Be welcome to imitate God, but do not even think of being equal or superior!

184 -Postmodern Liberal Movement's birth.
184 -The Democrat Party Metamorphosis.

Although we can trace the postmodern era between the 1920s and 2000, the "postmodern style of painting" was defined, as a way to depart from French Impressionism and in Literature, the Existentialism lead by Jean-Paul Sartre, which had some brief featuring moments, was also a cairn marking the transition.

History tells that in the late 1970s, there was a significant change, taking place that shifted the period to contemporary or postmodern.

Several iconic signs happened in those years, where the revival of Rock & Roll in the US, introducing the UK Rock, was one of them.

On the other hand, the recorded music industry began to give way to the rappers, under Hip-Hop labeling. Also, in the academic circles, the works of various modern "philosophers" took center stage.

They were carrying different opinions and developing several new theories, influenced by many schools, especially in German and French thinkers' pens or pixels. They are familiarly identifiable as "philosophy speculators" (like the Top World Vedic-Scholar, Bhaktivedanta Swami Prabhupada used to classify them).

In September of 1969, The Beatles received Swami Prabhupada, founder of the Hare Krishna Movement as a guest in Tittenhurst Park, the eight-acre British estate owned by John Lennon, where "Srila Prabhupada" gave spiritual lectures three or four times a week.

Later in a tall building that was named "The Temple." The site is still untouched today, now owned by Ringo Starr; Prabhupada gave daily lectures about the Vedas, always proudly sponsored by the boys from Liverpool. John, Paul, George, and Ringo, who were having the time of their lives, learning the mysterious Vedic spiritual knowledge from such an extraordinary Guru, Srila Prabhupada.

However, a significant change in our World and the establishment of Postmodern Liberalism became prominent around the 1980s, with substantial shifts in popular music, art, fashion, drug culture, massive illegal immigration, and remarkable technological development.

Never before, the World had experienced such a radical change. Silicon Valley is the center of the evolution that also gave way to a commotion in the education centers and a weird politicization of the Campuses' life.

Not all Campuses responded to these changes. The State of California is leading the trend, once again, although now backward.

In 1968, Berkeley University, California was the leader of the "Free Speech" movement; however, in 2017, things dramatically changed to a regressive level.

Some Universities' Faculty members maintain that "to protect the student's identities," they must ban Traditional speakers from avoiding "hurting the tender students" with "aggressive" Conservative speeches. This action is undeniably an infringement of our Constitution First Amendment and a highly controversial change on the Faculty members that fought in the 1960s for the same First Amendment standing.

During the 2016 post-electoral period, groups of Liberal extremists organized many violent and bloody rallies, destroying private and public property, never seen before in our country's history.

The violence, the pre-planned destruction, mainly in dissatisfaction with the 2016 election's result, pushed some groups of leftists, illegal aliens, and Democrat Partisan members to the streets near the University Campuses (Especially in the State of California) in a savage and destructive rampage. Today, we can say the Postmodern Liberalism fanatics are suppressing Free Speech.

Thus, the Postmodern Liberal Movement was born in America. Such a change was more than welcome by the Hig-Tech billionaires, who already loved the new trend of Communist China and their innovative "State Capitalism." They were conveniently sharing with the High-Tech industry owners, doing massive business in China's factories with unbelievable profit.

186 -Conservatism Ideal Keeps The Balance.

Let us pause here to establish that the Conservatism role is not to go back in time to the sole search for the entire old values, and yes, to keep a rational attachment to our spiritual and material roots.

If we lose the primary benefits and correlation to the development of life on our Planet and the Universe, we will be lost in space without a point of observation. We are entering a permanent degradation of our identity that may be suited to a few but won be a positive change for all.

Materialistic life needs to stand on the ground rather than flying in space.

It is too dangerous. Especially being that Postmodern Liberalism is trying to force an experimental way of life, disregarding Science and experience, to replace it with just following unstable human feelings. It is a dangerous way of transiting uncharted terrain.

Understanding that the only permanent changes are 'changes' themselves, it still is not enough to justify the loss of many values inherited from ancient cultures. The experience proved to be beneficial to our human race, so we must preserve it.

Let us remember that Quantum Science has changed our lives, and recalling Albert Einstein thought,

"Everything is relative to the point of observation."

Values like Family, Friendship, Loyalty, Fairness, Goodness, Humanity, and so many others have proven beneficial to humankind, highly appreciated, and revered by generations. We cannot define these values mathematically or scientifically, but they make so much sense; we must regard them as axioms and part of our existence.

I want to reassure the reader that I am not talking about "religion" at all. However, it is the legacy left by our Creator.

We must regard the old instructions because it is Science, the Science of creation. Call the "Creator" whatever you want, but accept there is one. Things do not happen by chance.

187 -The Personal Hatred Against Donald J. Trump.
Asked many of them, the Liberal protesters, they say to be determined to bring down President Trump, and they will not settle for less. That is their only goal, though when asked why the majority cannot explain the reason. It is a personal hatred against the Commander in Chief whom they blame for Hillary Clinton's failure. (?) How dare you, President Trump?
Liberals were desperate to see the President impeached and brought down.
They were dreaming and waking up with that possibility. After the failure of the recent Impeachment, Democrats keep looking for more ways to continue it.
The possibility of a Trump second term is the Democrat's worse nightmare.
Although they rapidly adopted the health crisis to impose a Socialist agenda, the Pandemic has paused the effort. "This is a tremendous opportunity to restructure things to fit our vision," House Majority Whip Jim Clayburn expressed to Democrat Lawmakers. "This opportunity cannot be wasted," he added.
After four years from the first accusation of Trump's campaign being in collusion with the Russians, there is no evidence at sight. Although the Postmodern Liberals continue to accuse our President of wrongdoings publicly, there is not a shred of proof or an indication of said accusations.
Let us make clear that collusion is not a crime.
At the transition, Obama told Trump that the two worse dangers he faced were North Korea and Michael Flynn. The 44th President knew that Gen. Flynn was aware of many dirty 'secrets' from his Administration. After Trump took the Oval Office, many inconveniences will come to light by the Three Star General experience in the previous Government.
Therefore, Gen. Flynn became the target of the rogue FBI agents covering for Obama.

Durham's Russian collusion origins have investigated a horrendous treason plot and may expand when we read the final report. Who knows?

Researching for data, we can name some actors in the broad Postmodern Liberal movement that, since the middle of the 20th Century and probably before, began departing from modernism, searching for new horizons, altered and influenced by technological developments.

So, no names, because it is not the idea of discussing those different speculative theories that have left little influence in our daily lives.

It is preferable to overlook the various names assigned to those temporary changes. As usual, while considered relevant at the time, history also shows us that their overall influence in real life was insufficient to be considered fundamental.

However, the stomping of the Postmodern Liberalism in our lives, politically and socially speaking, is the real change affecting us today and the product: hatred, recklessness, and division.

188 -The Snowflake's Complaints.

The social evolution that gave us Postmodern Liberalism provided some results and produced some regional leaders who are like "snowflakes" falling in the middle of a snowstorm that melts at the touch of the ground.

They leave no traces, other than the memories when falling.

So much has been going on through the years while life offered a few little changes. Some, we must admit, attempting to make some sense.   While entertaining, the speculation could be a waste of time and may keep people from using their energy in a much valuable way.

Although some individuals need to occupy their lives learning from others or experiment with other people's thoughts, following them is a personal option.

It is not about criticizing other people's works of their minds, trying to understand life and human behavior.

We all have our preferences and aspirations, and of course, the right to develop them.

Drugs, especially the hard ones, are a significant component of the present social debacle. The overwhelming opioid crisis, generated in part by irresponsible doctors that began writing painkillers prescriptions recklessly without considering the evident addiction consequences, is insane.

Moreover, the excessive sexual liberation promoted by the Postmodern Liberalism, as Lenin wrote and recommended in his Decalogue of 1913 as an essential part to take control of Society by Communism, has also added some fuel to the fire.

However, while the USSR, with their experience, showed us a rudimentary application of Marx and Engel's theories, with their failures, the Chinese Communism experiment has surpassed the most dangerous features of the political philosophy to the human beings.

Chinese ancestry is Confucianism, not a religion, but a set of social rules of behavior. First, family, second State, and individuals are down below. However, the Communist Chinese Government's treatment of human life is despicable.

During the Coronavirus lockdown, they force held people in their apartments or rooms, letting them die without any physician's help, in hideous criminal behavior.

Mao Zedong, a ruthless ruler, left a vile legacy and a fierce determination to lead the entire World by force.

Unconscionable, Democrats, now under the Postmodern Liberalism spell, are adopting many features from Communism, especially the way they manipulate the masses through totalitarian practices.

The horrible Chinese behavior regarding the Wuhan Virus has not discouraged Democrats to adopt the disgraceful political philosophy. Still, confirming their thirst for totalitarianism, at the special request of some Billionaires owners of technology companies, who desperately want to get as many foreign workers as possible, to take advantage of their cheap labor requirements. Greed is the new mantra after Globalism failed.

An exasperating hunger for absolute power leads the Democrat Party, now in the hands of the Postmodern Liberal movement.

These are some of the issues that the Postmodern Liberals today are trying to enforce, suppress, restrict or re-direct under their terms. They have an apparent determination to "guide" or influence people on what to think and how to live. Collective thinking is preferred.

They adopted the idea from Socialist, and Communist regimes, now seen in the Chinese experiment of "State Capitalism."

Billionaires and their 'salaried Democrat politicians' are the answer.

They are strong supporters of "Big Government," that will imagine and do for the masses, which of course, will obey without questioning.

That is their ideal.

Ashamed of their own intentions, the individuals are fighting for the long -for absolute power, hiding their greed by becoming puppeteers inside a big Government, in the Communist style.

Absolute power is still the ultimate goal of a corrupt society.

We live in a regression of our culture, where the Postmodern Liberal Movement is trying to suppress rights that a few years ago, the traditional "Liberals" were fighting to bring up and defend.

However, as I always say:

"I would give my life defending the right to allow others to differ with me."

But do not take me wrong. I will also defend with my life the right to express my dissent with injustice.

190 -The Vedic Philosophy Teachings.
190 -The Genders.

Bhaktivedanta Swami Prabhupada, a true scholar of the Vedas, prolific author of dozens of books sold by the millions, and translations from the old Vedic Scriptures, has taught us, his followers and alumnus unforgettable lessons.

Undoubtedly, the massive influence those lectures transmitted among his disciples and students carry an exquisite wealth.

We should not forget that he was who philosophically formed the four members of "The Beatles." The guys from Liverpool were never the same after Prabhupada entered their lives and left a deep Vedic mark in their souls.

Even nowadays, science bows down before the Vedic Literature, Vedic Philosophy, and Vedic Sciences in the broad approach.

One can go back and forth in time to realize that life's basics are unchanged, unchangeable, and the speculation can alter the terms temporarily. Still, at the end of any cycle, we go back to our roots, and the fundamental values remain the same, although some progress stays.

That is why Conservative thinking must be preserved and remembered as the stem that will guide humanity's evolution.

Life, among the species, spreads and multiplies through male sperm and female egg, except for some animal species and their uniqueness in their reproduction styles.

About humans, we still depend on females and males as the joining forces to procreate newborns, and regardless of the multiple attempts to change it, we keep coming back to the original.

A man having sex with a woman may open the opportunity for a sperm to enter the egg and start the process of procreation that, after nine months on average, will bear another human being unless some exterior incidents or organ malfunction stop it.

As we all know, there are alternative forms to bring to life the conjunction of the sperm and the egg, but the origin remains the same. A female is a receptacle, and a male is an impregnator.

Even in the extreme cases, now under development, scientists could manipulate human genetic material and give way to the appearance of a "different human form," be sure that if consciousness is present within such entity, God's spiritual energy will be near.

Genetic manipulation, although morally questionable, will be material. However, spirituality and conscience will be present, even if it is not seen mainly because of the scientist's inability to detect the Spirit Soul.

Still, there may be some scientists capable of knowing some facts of life.

So, here we are, that after millions of years of the same, a group that calls themselves new Liberals, Postmodern Liberals to the writer, in conjunction with different political sectors but with a common enemy, called Conservatism, have lately joined forces to pick a fight.

They deny the usual way we denominate things, as simple as women and men, male and female, the unique actors that confirm the Gender definition.

Gender is a word that the new Liberals hate, and they are frantically trying to eliminate from the Language, any Language. I ignore the real reason. Maybe attending the needs of some who, unsatisfied with their genetic form, would like to change it, and they find it impossible, so, tired of being signaled as weird, they are looking to solve their frustration with an implausible. Living a fantasy is the only option they find. Still, not enough, they persist in an imaginary world.

This Liberal movement, we call now Postmodern Liberalism, has taken over the Democrat Party, with the consent of their leaders at the time, who, because of their weakness showed in the 2016 election, allowed and promoted a metamorphosis that ended with the essential values of their traditional Old Democrat Party.

The main reason Hillary lost the election was the absence of a platform, the inexistence of real issues, the lack of communication with people, desperately looking for a clue, a missing guide in Clinton's speech. "Stronger together?" It did not work.

Let us face it: The Democrat Party is today without a-head. Being a Political Leader requires many features; the most important one is credibility. Still, as in the case of the entertainment or sports stars, or even a politician, it is a condition not only invisible but projecting a personality, a sense of trust, and an image impossible to describe with words accurately.

Bernie Sanders is the leader of the Left, Socialists, and Communists. But definitely, Democrats do not consider him their leader. They share a hatred for Donald J. Trump, but that is it. If they were to think of the issues, a future Government, and the consequences, their support is not there, They may agree on some Socialist matters, but not in many others; they consider too radical to the Left and toxic to many voters.

Joe Biden is a product of massive Media pounding daily, brainwashing uneducated people and politically ignorant, which was overwhelmed with a gigantic propaganda anti-Trump, based on a lie, after lie, after lie. Donald Trump, with his sarcasm, analogies, metaphoric and figurative expressions, allowed the Media to take some thoughts negatively, to reproduce them daily to the already manipulated minds of the politically and culturally unprepared regular people. The Media's powerful megaphone proved to be, still, a mind indoctrinator.

Whatever it is, the Democrat Party does not have that kind of person at this time. "Uncle Joe" is pending from a thin thread that, at any moment, can be cut and bury Biden. That is the primary problem but not the only one.

Since the 2016 election, after Hillary Clinton's defeat, the Democratic politicians have spent 100% of their time exclusively deprecating Donald J. Trump, and they continue it as of today.

Democrats never talk about the Party's platform ideas. They might not have any. Trump has already taken and flagged the most critical issues. Only throwing dirt against the President, each day a new one is what is left for Democrats to handle.

Throughout the Pandemic, Democrats and their partner, Mainstream Media, are frantically lying, slander, fabricating fake news, taking the President's words out of context, attempting to manipulate the Constitution and Laws to force the election's numbers.   Those are the only activities occupying their time.

Speaker Pelosi keeps the House members in their homes, avoiding doing what we, the People, are paying them handsomely to do: Legislate.

Long forgotten is the point to benefit the Middle-Class, the economy, job creation, taxation, and other relevant matters. They are all flags already successfully in use by President Trump.

We are not even talking about Islamic Terrorism, which Obama took out of the list, or any other relevant issue on Foreign Policy or National Security.

Democrats are for open borders and no National Security.

Recently, Majority Speaker Nancy Pelosi has declared that the Democrat Party must stop deprecating President Trump because the voters do not see the approach as favorable; thank you.   However, she is the one insulting and throwing dirt at the President daily.

194 -The Mainstream Media Fake News.

The Mainstream Media is increasing the infamous "Fake news," based mainly on what they call "Undisclosed sources" or "Anonymous confidential sources." They claim that to preserve the flowing of tips and information that would become news, they must maintain those sources anonymous, adding a great deal of "fake news" to try damaging the Republican Government.

George Soros and some Islamists groups are financially aiding the Postmodern Liberals to travel, getting weapons, propaganda material, and lately, providing technical support to make websites and spreading hatred through Social Media.

A significant part of corporate America, especially Silicon Valley, led by some Postmodern Liberal executives, has joined the Trump Administration's fierce opposition. They adore totalitarianism, the primary aim of Democrats, at this time. Still, it is in their DNA.

195 -Democrats and the KKK. The year 1865.
They will never tell or recognize that in the past, Democrats were for Slavery and defended it even with fury and violence. They engaged in the Civil War against the people that wanted to stop slave trading and ownership.

We must recall, Democrats also founded the KKK Movement and opposed every civil rights act in US history. General Nathan Bedford Forrest, a Democrat, in 1765, co-founded the KKK and was its first grand wizard.

No, they will never admit that. However, it does not change the facts. It is part of history. Anyone can read it in any history book.

The Mainstream Media keeps a dedicated hatred toward the President, suppressing information about his victories and occupying their time with hateful rants and fake stories. This unfortunate behavior has never been seen before in our country.

However, it is working against the Media outlets whose popularity is continuously decreasing. The latest polls show them way under the President's numbers.

195 -What Democrat Party and Postmodern Liberals Want.
The 2016 election was hard for Democrats and Liberals. The American People changed how they think and taught them a hard lesson: Our Land's safety is critical, and open borders are a threat.

However, it might sound cultured attractive, and very progressive; it is a danger to our established way of life.

Newcomers, especially the illegals, want to force what they believe are their rights to jump into an already developed, prosperous society without being invited or earning access to it.

Oddly, many of them, primarily Middle Eastern, are carrying the totalitarian practices they escaped at home, which they want to impose on us.

It is hard to understand, although they are taking instructions from their Scriptures.

Except for skilled laborers and professionals, they bring a much lower culture and poor education, or none at all.

Most illegal immigrants, especially those coming from the Middle East, refuse to learn English and insist on preserving their old habits, notably opposing our Constitution and our way of life. Most of them even have the determination to impose their culture, as the Sharia Law, which is entirely against our Democracy and our Constitution.

How they treat the women is mean and opposite to our observance of Human Rights and our way of life.

It is incomprehensible how women in the Democrat Party could defend those practices that clash with years of efforts to conquer women's rights in a full battle against the male-dominated feudal system seen within Islam.

Postmodern Liberal leaders have found a way to manipulate the values and change the issues to their advantage by making the ones they favor the most prominent and trying to hide or dismiss those they oppose.

We know psychology manipulation can do that and more.

An ancient proverb says:

"The enemies of my enemies are my friends."

However, in the Islamist's case, they will never be satisfied with just the "friends" victory. They will continue to seek their own until they get it. They have been doing it for thousands of years.

It is hard to know if the Postmodern Liberal Leadership is "naive" looking at the big tree but not seeing the forest, or they genuinely believe they could "use" Islam's support without consequences.

The fact is, they are getting trapped in the Islamic "devouring machine," and their hundreds of years of experience.

Meanwhile, the astute Islamic Leaders are jumping on the Postmodern Liberal wagon, expecting, at least, to be among the supposed winners.

Muslims hate the LGBTQ, but acting smartly, they know, in the end, they will win the contest.

Meanwhile, they are making strides into our Society. Their goal is destroying our country from inside our Constitution, and they are on the way to achieve it.

Democrats managed to elect two congresswomen: Ilhan Omar, and Rashida Tlahib, that already, in a few months in their offices, are causing troubles trying to advance their Islamist ideology.

As soon as they reached the Congressional podium, they attacked Israel and our President, defending Islam and its totalitarian ideology.

Meanwhile, congress-people are under the intimidation that criticizing Muslims would be considered "racist, or Islamophobic, or xenophobic;" That is a myth we must eliminate.

Reality shows us that Islamists are our enemies at heart, by their own declarations thru history and written in their scriptures. Do not trust me. Read the Koran, Hadith, and Sharia Law and find out the truth.

We did not declare war on Islam. They did it to the USA in 1798, under President John Adams, who decided not to fight them and pay their imposed taxes to be able to do business in North Africa. History comes in handy when one reads it.

J. Pelegrin

A BRUTAL ATTACK ON DEMOCRACY

(The All-Time Enemies on the March)

CHAPTER 6

(The Vedic Knowledge)

199 -Why The Vedas, Now?

Allow me, please, to repeat a paragraph from the Prologue:

"Since the beginning of the nineteen century, the founders of the Quantum Mechanics: Nobel Prize winner, Laureate Niels Bohr (1885-1962) and Erwin Schrödinger (1887-1961), and later Werner Heisenberg (1901-1976), stated that "Quantum theory will not look ridiculous to people who have read 'Vedanta.'" (the conclusion of Vedic thought.)

Schroedinger went a little further, writing in his biographical work: "Vedanta teaches that consciousness is singular, all happenings play out in one universal consciousness, and there is no multiplicity of selves."

The brightest mind of our times: Albert Einstein, acknowledged his regular reading of the Vedas, recognizing the absoluteness of Krishna, the Supreme Being.

Robert Oppenheimer (1904 – 1967) stated: "The Vedas are the greatest privilege of this century."

Strangely, Vedic philosophy has remained apart from the main discussion; I ignore the reason."

'Or maybe such knowledge changes one's life in such a way that drives you to replace mundane pleasures with spiritual ones. Of course, if one can understand the Vedic philosophy, something not everyone can digest and even enjoy, without proper guidance by experts.'

The above is a reminder of how some geniuses of our era thought and felt about the Vedic Scriptures.

If we choose to act smart, it is wise to follow their lead.

At this time of commotion, a present danger is with us, and we have just begun a new era in our Planet Earth, in dire conditions.

The facts are unmistakably telling us we must change many aspects of our daily lives, our plans for the future, our kids' education, and re-education of ourselves, or the times will be replacing them anyway in the most challenging way.

Also, international politics, new geographic frontiers among countries because of political actions, and why spiritual knowledge's achievement will inevitably help our lives take the right pathway ahead.

To me, being intimately involved with Vedic Philosophy for fifty years, not shaking hands anymore, will not be a problem.

I remember, after reading the "Bhagavad Gita as it is" by Bhaktivedanta Swami Prabhupada, one of my Godbrothers sarcastically told me: "Ok, Prabhu, (a common expression in Indian culture meaning 'master,' as a courtesy." 'Your material life is now ruined, but welcome to the spiritual life! A much better choice.' The man was joking, although the most brutal truth is many times said as a joke.

Soon, I confirmed my friend was right. Such knowledge changed my priorities. Material things became less critical, and spiritual goals became essential, and many mundane pleasures turned to be unwanted or irrelevant.

For years I have practiced the Eastern style salutation with some people, pressing the palms together with the fingertips facing upwards (i.e., in a prayer position) and bowing down the head and chest. Also, saying Namaste, or merely the act of lowering one's head or the upper part of the torso, is a widely accepted sign of respect toward the other person and a courteous salutation.

Of course, I continued to shake hands with people who otherwise would have been rude, not doing it; But not anymore. Courtesy rules have changed.

For most of the American people, it probably will be difficult at the beginning, but a reminder of the possible consequences will teach them rapidly to adopt the new style.

However, that is the superficial part of the latest recommended social form. There are more aspects of Vedic knowledge coming to the surface, much more crucial and vital to this Earth's survival.

Based on cures through traditional cooking spices, roots, and other vegetables, Ayurvedic medicine is proved to be very useful. The Internet is full of recipes and suggestions.

One of the issues I learned right at the beginning of studying Vedic Literature was the need for humans to stop killing animals, especially cows. Each one gives us, on average, 13 kilos of milk daily throughout their lives, in the mode of goodness, without violence. That could partly feed several families daily while killing a cow for food, you will have to support her for many years with food and medicines, and in the end, the meat would only feed about 50 to 70 people once. Even as a business is much better to keep the cow alive than killing her, but of course, the problem is people's tongue, too attached to eating the flesh. It also comes with a tag price— many illnesses related to eating red meat cost money to cure, as most of us know. Some times are even lethal.

It is not my intention to preach about not eating meat. It is an individual decision related to Karma, and I prefer to keep my opinion to myself. The above was more as a half-joke than a criticism. Once again, I am no one to judge anyone.

However, I can give my opinion and the experience of 60 years being a vegetarian while looking 25 years younger in perfect health.

Dairy is a battled nourishing item by some; others are lactose intolerant, but undoubtedly the preferred way that the Earth population in its majority has survived for thousands of years, especially at an early age. Myself included.

We can argue the modern practices of Dairy farms, but at the end of the day, they are much more humane than slaughterhouses.

At least that would be the cow's opinion if we could understand them. I like cows. They are beautiful animals and very helpful to society. Even their stool is an excellent fertilizer, antiseptic (also the urine is), and for some people, a good source of fuel to cook.

We got to think not everyone can live like us, in a city like New York or another big city. Millions live in dire conditions without luxury.

It is utterly painful to change this aspect of Western people's diet, for centuries accustomed to the "convenience" and the unarguably good taste of a stake or other kind of meat product, especially the convenience to get it anywhere, at present times, at a reasonable cost.

Also, the different regions of our Planet, where vegetables are not available for various reasons, and eating meat is the only means of survival, is an issue to consider and respect.

I remember asking Bhaktivedanta Swami Prabhupada, my dear Spiritual Master, about those cases. His answer was simple:

"There are all kinds of souls incarnated in material bodies. Not all of them are fortunate enough to become vegetarians. That means that for some people, achieving a spiritual body in the next life will not be possible. Some will have to re-incarnate several times, or at least once more to meet the requirements to get rid of the material body and become spirit-souls essentially."

The explanation sounded reasonable to me and directly related to Karma, the Law of action and reaction, which means that the person's activities create reactions directly linked to the future life, and re-incarnations. The place of birth, parental qualities, and other features of existence are also modifiers.

In other words, performing certain acts during a lifetime forms the individual's next life personality and the commonly defined: Destiny.

Of course, it is not that easy—the complexities of life we don't need to explain in detail. Most people know them.

Some Vedic volumes clarify that at the moment of death, a person's last-minute desire will determine what kind of body and activity will be in their future. The Vedas say: "you carry your last wish in your mind into the next material life or incarnation."

A Spirit-Soul can re-incarnate in various, different kinds of bodies, from an insect to an advanced Spirit-Soul and the absence of a material body.

They could be passing through all kinds of animal lives, accordingly with one's Karma or even the unfulfilled desires in their last material body incarnation.

Vedic philosophy assures that Krishna wants his devotees to fulfill their wishes. If they would be frustrated by unfulfilled desires in the present life, and the person's will is firm, the Supreme Personality of God will have the individual taking the next birth in the kind of body that would allow them to live the type of life they desire.

That, of course, means that all sorts of material desires, like wealth, health, position, family, and other mundane features, will require a physical body. At the same time, they will be subject to their talents and abilities to succeed.

Now, thinking about the World's status right now and guessing the future, who wants to go through another material existence?

Not me, for sure.

Once again, I would like to reassure the reader that it is not my intention to preach to anyone. However, If I know anything, I consider it my duty to expose such awareness, as a good neighbor should do, so my fellows could grasp it.

However, in my case, born in Uruguay, widely known to produce the best red-meat quality in the World, where the population is a high consumer of cow's meat, it was not easy to become a vegetarian. Still, I did it sixty years ago, and I did not broke the rule since, not even once. In the beginning, I gave up red meat, then poultry, and seafood, and at last eggs.

One of the almost immediate benefits was: My chronic sinusitis, which I suffered for 20 years, disappeared after a few months of refusing to eat meat.

Later, I learned that cows' meat carries the viruses that transmit the disease, linked to the common cold. Consider that cattle are washed various times before the slaughter, so they get sick, and poor conditions are prevalent.

Recently, after more than forty years, I now consume eggs again, especially recommended for helping Diabetes II. Also, most of the eggs are unfertilized at this time.

I know many readers would think these are extreme measures and do not apply to all.

It may be the case, but personal opinions are just that: opinions, including mine.

Facts are hard proof. The benefits of stopping eating red meat are widely accepted, healthwise, humanely, and respecting life in general.

Nevertheless, when we compare the effects and come to conclusions, those become elements that will influence and inspire changes in people's lives.

After becoming a dairy-vegetarian, I found myself being less aggressive in general.

Faith, yet, becomes the filter and the options of life.

While I am not even trying to dictate a course on spiritual life, I hope, for some people, it would be a teasing moment to dabble in the deep field of the inner-soul. Start reading the Vedas, please!

205 -The Need To Consult Conservative Standards.

Murphy's Law is in effect right now, at the most controversial moment in our country and the World's history.

Unexpectedly, in the middle of a National Election campaign, the most important since the establishment of our Nation, this plague and its consequences are shaking our very foundation, our life standard, and general culture. Nothing will ever be the same.

Our political parties, divided into two different partisan philosophies wholly opposed to each other, are confusing the generally 'civilly uneducated citizens' driving the emotions to the extreme, sometimes unfortunately violently.

Once again, we all need to rewind and recall history for consultation.

Vedic Scriptures are among the best source of ancient reference if one can transport it to the present with adequate adjustments. Common sense indicates that although the primary understanding of the Vedas will be impossible to apply it in its original version to modern times, the fundamental philosophical depth is the cornerstone for any review of our current standards.

They are primary requisites to common sense and a good understanding of the principles of life.

Vedic culture is full of guidance that, even though it is not visible at first sight to all people, carries wise knowledge, no one can deny because it makes sense.

As mentioned before, it will be necessary to understand the concepts and adjust them to contemporary times.

It is a task that we must perform intelligently to be successful. Not an easy one.

In my personal experience, before starting to read the "Bhagavad Gita As It Is" by Bhaktivedanta Swami Prabhupada, I was reluctant to operate any change in my life.

After I reached the end, I had some different thoughts about it. I knew many issues I read; others, I assumed them, and by reading, I confirmed them, some others, I had suspicions about it, and a few were new to me, although all of them made a whole lot of sense.

However, none of the Scriptures' issues were far out there, weird, or even strange. Reading the Vedic Literature has been the most rewarding experience ever, especially to evacuate any doubts I had before.

The Bhagavad Gita is primarily a novel, narrating a war between two branches of the same family, a pious sector and an impious.

They engage in a contest, for power, in the battle of Kurukshetra, where millions of people died. The armies were lead by two Chiefs with the distinctive appearance of Lord Krishna, who educates Arjuna, in charge of the Pious branch, to confront the enemies with Philosophical knowledge, which will lead him to victory. A classic situation we can relate to (saving distances) and no personal allusions, please.

It is an entertaining and highly educating reading.

206 -The Vedas, A Source Of Ancient Wisdom.

When a person reads and gets into the philosophy embodied in the Vedas, one realizes that the men who wrote these books, fifty-five hundred years ago (however, the spoken words came from several thousands of years before), there were special people, very advanced beings. Some incredibly knowledgeable enlightened men spoke the Vedas initially in local dialects.

Then, once the Sanskrit Language became available, a group of Sadhus (wise men) wrote the Vedas in the form of rhyming words, like songs so, it made it complicated to change the meaning of a phrase without altering the whole purpose.

Sanskrit is the first full language known in our World, with an alphabet, a verb structure, and other significant features. In the beginning, It was transmitted, transcribed by word of mouth for centuries.

That assures nobody tampered with the Scriptures. They are keeping the original substance unaltered.

With that said, the Vedic Scriptures are the most trust worth ancient documents, written by exceptional men, with an incredibly vast knowledge that amazes modern scientists and religious scholars.

Also, they are the cornerstone of other old records as the Bible, Torah, and Koran, as well as the Greek texts.

A friend of mine, possessing high Vedic Knowledge, recounted that years ago, he went for an appointment to speak with a big Lab CEO. At the company's front desk, he saw a large painting representing Danvantari, the Demi-God in charge of Science and Medicine in the Hindu religion.

He asked why the art was there, to the woman at the front desk, but she ignored the meaning. Once in the meeting, my friend, a Hare Krishna devotee, asked the CEO why they had that painting in such a prominent place. The man said: "Well, revising the Vedas, we found out valuable information about our scientific investigation, that amazingly matches our modern studies, so that helped us to come up with some new drugs, following the data found in the Vedic Scriptures."

Several contemporary scientists have found similar data, reading in between lines, putting ideas together, and utilizing ancient concepts, including Ayurvedic medicine, to developing new products that save lives and add new knowledge to our Civilization.

I humbly sustain that by reading the scriptures, it is possible to find great information hidden in between lines, usable these days to improve our lives.

Take, for instance, the tremendous knowledge these people wrote fifty-five hundred years ago, and who knows, coming from how many centuries before. The information came about Cosmology, the Big Bang Theory, the origins of the Multiverse, as well as the diversity of planets our Scientific studies just confirmed a few years ago. An almost exact concept, although with different terminology, it is found in the "Srimad Bhagavatam," Fifth Canto, also part of the Vedas. It is undoubtedly no pure coincidence.

Whoever read that book can confirm my experience. It is fascinating to validate the knowledge displayed in those volumes, especially when present scientists match distance measurements, speeds of the planets, how old they are, and other technical information with their current studies.

Scientists now consider that in most cases, the data seems so accurate that little by little, is confirming a high knowledge, and principally, the recognition of many philosophical issues, until now regarded as "merely philosophical," escalating to "Scientific facts."

A significant milestone is now being accomplished for the Sacred Scriptures' value acknowledgment.

208 -The Most Trusted Source Of Knowledge.

Unfortunately, these days people are not reading the vast source of knowledge not only in the Vedic Literature but also in modern History books.

The USA's education system is minimal and exclusively geared to prepare students to get a job, so it only feeds them with basic math and language, and even that, our students are way low in the World's rating. But ask them about drugs, and they can write volumes about it. It is regrettable.

Our country is in 39th place in math and 13th place in reading according to the 2018 PISA ranking.

It is, frankly, a shameful position for a country like ours. Maybe the Liberal inclination of teachers and professors, as well as Dean's, has something to do with the failure.

World History, American History, Geography, and other essential subjects that kids in Latin America usually study in primary schools are missing in the US education system nowadays.

Such a situation impedes people to vote wisely. Today, the Postmodern Liberalism, now embedded in the Democrat Party, insists on indoctrinating people instead of educating them. The new leadership in Postmodern Liberalism prefers massive obedience instead of personal thought. Massive thinking is preferred.

There is a drastic change of directions in the Postmodern Liberalism philosophy, where docility is the principal goal, leaving the big resolutions to a small elite in the 'Big Government.' They do not propose anymore. Now, "suggestions" are becoming decision making for the masses to follow without questioning.

Conservative advocates are fighting those changes, defending the individuality and self-pride of individualism over mass thinking.

However, due to poor education in the early stages and kids needing an immediate job, it is challenging to elevate the standards unless individually desired.

Once again: Education, education, education is a must at this time.

Although Vedic Literature is very advanced, there is a part focused on religion that is also complex and not very popular because of cultural traditions.

In a country (the USA) where Christianity, with its uncomplicated philosophical concept, is the most popular, and Judaism is sectarian and kept in the family, as a tradition, the Vedas remain a subject to the elite, interested in cultivating higher knowledge.

Still, the complicated metaphorical language in the Vedic Scriptures keeps away a good portion of the population.

There are cultural issues that prevent the ancient scriptures from becoming more popular and challenging to overcome. Only people interested in a higher experience will ultimately reach the incredible knowledge exposed in those marvelous books.

Islamic scholars always say:
"If you do not find it in the Koran, search the Vedas."

Fortunately, there are many commentaries from highly trained scholars that help the understanding of the Vedas. Bhaktivedanta Swami Prabhupada is, without a doubt, the most trusted of all. However, and by my experience, people not interested in the Indian religions would have to be guided by expert help to understand the valuable data in it, or be patient and examine the books without rushing. The truth will prevail, and complete satisfaction is assured.

As an example of the high standards read in the Vedic Scriptures, in contrast with the Chinese Confucianism tradition and Western civilization practices, Vedic culture considers animals as valuable and respectable as humans.

No animal eating is allowed or even abused. A whole different lifestyle reigns in the ancient Vedic culture.

Since times immemorial, Western Civilization, out of 'convenience,' although disregarding spiritual and somehow materialistic humane concepts, began acquiring food for survival by killing animals.

Out of ignorance and laziness, people preferred to bypass sowing seeds, nourish them, wait to harvest them, and learn how to prepare foods without meat.

Instead, they found out they could have the animals feeding on plants, processing the nutrients, and growing to the point of becoming suitable to be killed for human consumption.

But those actions create Karma in humans that will affect their lives in the future, including re-incarnations into who knows what type of life.

You may not believe in the Law of Karma; however, it does not change the facts. You are welcome to try learning about it.

It is frankly incredible, the excellent, tasty preparations we can make without utilizing any meat, although there is plenty of meat substitutes plant-based at this time.

Nowadays, with the increasing fashionableness of Vegan cuisine, which lacks some essential proteins found in Dairy, an expanding amount of new vegetarian or vegan lovers are helping to operate a drastic change to a much wholesome diet. Of course healthy for animals too, since they don't get killed. The West coast people are big fans of not eating meat.

The recent outbreak of the COVID-19, out of China's experimental Lab and wet markets, shows us the utterly inhuman mistreatment of animal life. However, the Karma reaction is in plain sight. A Pandemic; Believe it or not.

210

Such practice unequivocally creates a highly negative Karma for the people involved, as well as utter ignorance.

The Chinese' "rubber stamp" Parliament seems that is trying to correct the ancient practice of killing animal wildlife either for medicinal uses or for food. Still, it is unlikely such an old habit the population would drop it without fighting, even in a Communist State.

We will see.

211 -The Vedic Philosophy Teachings.
211 -The Genders.

Bhaktivedanta Swami Prabhupada, a true scholar of the Vedas, prolific author of dozens of books sold by the millions, and translations from the old Vedic Scriptures, has taught us, his followers, and alumnus unforgettable lessons.

Undoubtedly, the massive influence those lectures transmitted among his disciples and students carry an exquisite wealth.

We should not forget that he was who philosophically formed the four members of "The Beatles." The guys from Liverpool were never the same after Prabhupada entered their lives and left a deep Vedic mark in their souls.

Even nowadays, Science bows down before the Vedic Physics, Vedic Philosophy, and Vedic sciences in the broad approach.

One can go back and forth in time to realize that the basics of life are unchanged, unchangeable, and the speculation can alter the terms temporarily. Still, at the end of any cycle, we go back to our roots, and the basics values remain the same, although some progress stays.

That is why Conservative thinking must be preserved and remembered as the stem that will guide humanity's evolution.

Life, among the species, spreads and multiplies through male sperms and female eggs, except for some animal species and their uniqueness in their reproduction styles.

About humans, we still depend on females and males as the joining forces to procreate other people, and regardless of the multiple attempts to change it by Postmodern Liberalism, we keep coming back to the original, as the only possible way to reproduce.

A man having sex with a woman may open the opportunity for the sperm to enter the egg and start the process of procreation that, after nine months on average, will bear another human being unless some exterior incidents or organ malfunction stop it.

As we all know, there are alternative forms to bring to life the conjunction of the sperm and the egg, but the origin remains the same. A female is a receptacle, and a male is an impregnator.

However, here we are, that after millions of years of the same, a group that calls themselves Liberals, Postmodern Liberals to the writer, in conjunction with different political sectors but with a common enemy, called Conservatism, have lately joined forces to pick a fight.

They deny the usual way we denominate things, as simple as a woman and a man, male and female, the unique actors that confirm the Gender definition.

Gender is a word that the new Liberals hate, and they are frantically trying to eliminate it from the language, any Language. I ignore the real reason.

This Liberal movement, that we call now Postmodern Liberalism, took over the Democrat Party, with the consent of their leaders at the time, who, because of their weakness, showed in the last election, allowed and promoted a metamorphosis that ended with the essential values of their traditional Party.

The main reason Hillary lost the election was the lack of a platform, the inexistence of real issues, the lack of communication with the voters, desperately looking for a clue. People could not find a guide in Clinton's speech. "Stronger together?" It did not work.

Let us face it: The Democrat Party is today without a leader. Instead, Democrat's leadership is collective, and of course, controversial and multi-faceted, mostly chaotic. The real leaders are mostly not seen. They hide behind some High-Tech applications.

Being a Political Leader requires many features; the most important one is credibility. Still, as in the case of entertainment or sports stars, it is a condition not only invisible but projecting a personality, a sense of trust, and an image impossible to accurately describe with words.

However, Hispanics have the right word to define it: Caudillo. Unfortunately, there is no adequate English translation.

Whatever it is, the Democrat Party does not have that kind of figure at this time. That is the primary problem but not the only one.

Since the 2016 election, after Hillary Clinton's defeat, Democrat politicians have spent 100% of their time exclusively deprecating Donald J. Trump, and they continue it as of today, mainly through lies.

Helped by Mainstream Media, together they have raised a rare kind of hatred, never known before, against a Constitutional President of the United States of America, an unfortunate innovation.

Democrats never talk about the Party's platform ideas.

They might not have any. Trump has already taken and flagged the most critical issues, according to our traditions.

Only throwing dirt against the President, each day a new one is what is left for Democrats to handle.

Long forgotten are the subjects to benefit the Middle-Class, the economy, job creation, taxation, and other relevant matters. They are all flags already successfully in use by President Trump.

We are not even talking about Islamic Terrorism, which Obama took out of the schedule, or any other relevant issue on Foreign Policy or National Security. The Democrats are for open borders and completely disregard National Security.

Recently, Minority Speaker Nancy Pelosi declared that the Democrat Party must stop deprecating President Trump because the voters do not see the approach as favorable; thank you.

However, she is the one insulting and throwing dirt at the President daily.

Her only goal is to continue the witch-hunt, the impeachment, and now the distrust of President Trump and his scientific, economic, military, and social team of dedicated citizens trying
to help to combat the actual Pandemic, that in essence, it is an unknown disease caused by a virus, unknown to all of us, including scientists.

The so-called 'journalists' at the press conferences are nothing but MSM paid 'claque,' only trying to embarrass the President, mostly taking sentences or words out of a concept.

214 -Jesus Christ Learning the Vedas?

There are serious indications that Jesus Christ's disappearance from the public for almost three years, before the crucifixion, was spent on the East (the Indian subcontinent), studying the old Vedas and learning the immense knowledge recorded in those scriptures.

Because of the vast material distances, time frame, differences in cultures, idioms, and means of communication, it is evident, in the beginning, the Vedas were not a substantial part of the early Western Civilization.

The Roman Empire had limited data about what happened in the Indian sub-Continent region. The distances were too significant for the communications available at the time to help.

The Greeks contributed with some information, theories, and meaningful advancements in Medicine, Social Sciences (Democracy.) They committed to building Western Philosophy.

The use of rational argument was probably the nexus helping to connect the Vedic and the Greek philosophy and, therefore, to begin an influence on Western Culture.

The Hellenistic city of Ay Khanum, situated on the border of Russia and Afghanistan, is not far from China; the city was mostly Greek, but its population shared philosophies and religions.

Alexander the Great was later a uniting factor when he pioneered several regions between Greece and India, leaving entire cities connecting his empire.

However, there were some privileged minds and souls that, since the beginning, helped to connect the dots between East and West, providing information that built the foundation for modern philosophy's link to ancient knowledge.

Slowly, the Spiritual part of it made in rows into the Western culture, and people began to change their minds from the first wild, and mythical approach to the reality and profound meaning of the information received.

Jesus Christ was not to be unaware of these facts.

215 -The Great Western Civilization.

As the Century advanced and the core of Vedic knowledge began to be credible to the eyes of the elite and the scientific community, the Vedas commenced a definite trend that these days have satisfied in excess all kinds of challenges.

The scientific community has compared and certified many of the information written in the Vedic Literature, utilizing them as an intrinsic part of current studies and experiments.

However, Postmodern Liberals decided to ignore any information concerned with the Spiritual World, God's Science, and only rely on the material life and the feelings, although many of their intellectuals may give credit to the Old Scriptures.

However, Postmodern Liberal politics insist on demonizing Western Civilization, accusing it of being a White Supremacists tool.

The actual controversy is their ignorance about the composition of the mentioned Western Culture.

While there were a strong influence of White race individuals in the past, history does not always specify people's depicting different skin coloring.

Many ethnicities intertwined since time immemorial.

Whites are inevitably bound to mix the skin colors, darkening the tone, every time they mix. They contribute to developing a less than pure white race or ethnic group, only apparent at sight.

Despite this fact, the White race, by different means but mainly political, economic, and educational, maintained a grip on the tenancy of the land and control of the human-made Law.

Besides, the somehow "purity" of the White race was kept among the royalty and Nobility, while the lower caste tended to mix with other ethnicities faster.

However, even the White Royalty is, at present, mixing with other races. Prince Harry has married Meghan Merkle, and their royal descendants will not be 100% white.

Also, we are aware that the royalty had in the many past incidents procreating "out of the marriage," babies that, in many cases, lost track of them and just ended mixing with the commons.

However, for Postmodern Liberalism, it is more convenient to apply the adjectives: racist, xenophobic, homophobic, supremacist, bigot, and other pejoratives to the White race in general, even if they are misused, generating mostly ignorant comments.

At the same time, they are the real bigots, utterly intolerant of those who hold different opinions.

Of course, this approach was to benefit their survival as a group (identity politics) and principally to keep the privileged status acquired by various means, some of them not near humanistic or even legal.

No civilization on our Planet is free of guilt. They are all tainted by ignorance, greed, insensibility, and all kinds of human trash. Nobody is perfect.

Our Western Civilization has earned credits like no other in the World, except the Vedic Civilization, definitely a higher level.

We ended slavery; we helped art development, sponsored Science, promoted technology, supported human rights, improved health care, founded the industrial revolution, introduced a fairer judicial system. We facilitate other prominent World advancements like Social Science, and also, unfortunately, helped some forms of human degradation.

Western Civilization is not perfect, but an aim to perfection drives it. It is evolving, even considering the claims from the ones who oppose it.

Life on our Planet is not simple, nor the people on it are. Although we are created equally in practice, not all can enjoy living in the same way.

There are differences, of course, according to the Law of Karma, and the natural gifts of life as intelligence, skills, virtues, and talents.

In consequence, the word equality cannot apply to all to the same extent.

Although we are all created equal, we need to earn anything material we want or desire, although Karma influences it. It is the Law of fairness, the Consciousness within.

Postmodern Liberals believe people have the right to grab anything they want without any effort to obtain it. It is to their convenience, which after our country's founders and their descendants built an entire productive society, and applied their collective knowledge. Then, added intellect and hard labor to maximize our land use, these new liberals think otherwise. Furthermore, that is the intention of the Postmodern Liberals. Despite being systematically attacked by Islamists, they promote their fake religious philosophy because they share hatred against Western Conservatives. They dismiss that Islamist's goal is to confiscate our traditions and destroy our Constitution.

Our country is in a troublesome situation. The only ways to revert the dangerous path is referring to history and educate people to learn from past experiences.

One of the sadly ignored parts of history is in the XVII and XVIII centuries, especially regarding the Mediterranean Sea's happenings and notably "The Barbary States," As we mentioned in other chapters.

218 -Democrats Need to Find an Identity.

The Postmodern Liberal Movement must be stopped and disbanded.

An essential part of the strategy is that the Democrat Party renews its leadership and ceases to be an obstacle to the present Government.

So far, Conservatives are doing their job, with the annoying obstructionism from the Democratic House of Representatives and the ominous obstacles from the MSM that keep inventing fake news and opposing any President's initiative, regardless of whether they are right for the country. That is got to stop in the name of justice and patriotism.

Right now, although Chinese Communists have failed the World hiding the origins of the Coronavirus, Democrats and their servants, the MSM, are siding with China instead of condemning them for their careless and criminal handling of the COVID-19, that killed hundreds of thousands around the World.

We know, several CEOs, Liberal politicians, and entrepreneurs are profiting from the Chinese totalitarian practices that enslave their people to have cheap labor. That has to stop.

The Hollywood elite also needs to do a soul searching and review their values. Postmodern Liberalism might not be that good for business.

Before the Pandemic, polls indicated Hollywood films were experiencing a decrease of up to 70% in revenues at the box office. Some theatre conglomerates have gone bankrupt already.

Maybe the audience does not enjoy their political and social views. Besides, the wrong messages sent by many members of the Hollywood elite lately are damaging their credibility, exposing excesses, sexual misconducts (Me too), and now, despicable attempts to push their children to success through bribes and other illegal acts.

Some supporters of the "Me Too" movement ignore a particular group of women who create situations to take advantage of men's weaknesses and advance in their careers, especially in the entertaining business, Movies, Theater, TV, and even Sports.

It does not mean that they are all alike. Still, in many cases, some actresses and singers have taken advantage of male producers, agents, managers, and other executives, enjoying their business advancements, and years later accusing them of sexual misconduct and even rape.

Today, most Democrat Party's significant issues of the past are gone.

The DNC has lost the connection with many voters. The main reason is, after having eight years of the worse Government possible by Muslim Obama, where they lost thousands of government officials, including the majority in the Senate, the House, and several Governorships, the voters left on their side are the uneducated, fanatics and Trump haters.

Today Democrats are desperately looking for votes among the lowest educated immigrants, mostly illegal. That is why they are trying so hard to give them free stuff and other favors attached to greeting cards in the name of the Democrat Party. That has a name: Demagogy.

Of course, they do not mention that before the 1960s, the Democrat Party favored slavery; against the Civil Rights Law. They fought a bloody Civil War against President Abraham Lincoln and his followers' Republicans. A Democrat assassinated Lincoln. (See page 79)

Moreover, the most significant Democrat Party's mistake was leaning to the Left in search of a political philosophy that has been a failure all over the World.

Hillary Clinton has said lately that the 40% leftist within the DNC was the cause (another one) of her defeat.

The Leftist ideology has been spreading death, corruption, human degradation, including slavery, labor exploitation, absolute poverty, and other known facts, which past Leftist Governments have left around the Planet as a legacy of their corruption and failure.

Democrats need to get inspired and consult the American people about hearing their needs and change the "all the way leftist political philosophy" and then hiring a damn good publicist.

Democrats must come with a smashing phrase capable of topping the "Make America Great Again," which catapulted a newcomer to politics, Donald J. Trump, and made him the 45th President of the United States, or the new slogan for the 2020 campaign "Keep America Great!"

Meanwhile, although Democrats are united behind the "resist" movement to derail Trump's Government, there is no visible "fabulous" political leader at sight or in the making capable of leading the DNC to victory. Biden? I don't think so.

For over eight years, Democrats were exalting and worshiping one only leader: Barak Obama, which in the end failed to keep the Party's leadership.

Presently, some unfaithful FBI high profile agents and CIA former officials accuse Obama of setting up a conspiracy to make General Flynn fall into a trap. Finally, the DOJ withdrew the accusation, and Flynn is now a free man after President Trump fully pardoned him.

The former Obama Administration is in serious trouble, and the ex-44th President's Legacy compromised.

Let us remember that Senator Sanders is not a Democrat. Bernie is a Socialist in a Communist body and mind.

We cannot forget that his newer idea of granting a job to every American is a ship full of holes. Mr. Sanders has not provided a hint of how he is planning to finance such an idea, which by the way, in the one hundred and forty years of Communism existence, was never put in practice nor seriously tried by any country in the World. It is just an impossible dream without acute feasibility.

Maybe Sanders is dismissing the fact that the Trump Administration's unemployment rate was the lowest ever, until the COVID-19 crisis. Let us hope it will come back.

We must also remember that never in history, a Communist regime has been successful in making workers happier. The

Chinese experiment is part capitalist, with a selected leadership connected to the Government's Oligarchy, and a workforce under slavery, driven by the political elite.

We must remember that Democrat's Socialist and Communist ideas are keeping regular people receiving government assistance. In contrast, the addiction to such "gifts" keep them surviving, at the same time that indefinitely postpones their hopes for success. The Left does not want many successful people. They are the most challenging to manage. Instead, they prefer a collective mass, submissive in the making, and without any success expectations.

Also, now Bernie Sanders wants to allow all prisoners in jail to vote from inside their confinement. Bernie is as crook as the prisoners. People in prisons pay their debt to society for their illegal acts, and their citizen's rights are suspended until they do time.

221 -A Fierce Battle: Traditions vs. Postmodernism.

The country is in a terrible spot. Socially and politically divided like never has been before, its population is sick and tired of political division. The clear breakdown shows on their side, the Postmodern Liberals, integrated by Democrats, Independents, Socialists, Anarchists, Communists, Mainstream Media, LGBTQ, Hollywood elite, helped by the Islamist wearing a ship's skin, under a wolf's identity. On the opposite side, Conservatives and moderates are defending the traditional trenches, with an increasing dose of "old-style Liberalism," meaning studying the new proposals, accepting the coherent ones, and refusing the rest.

Democrats keep arguing in favor of open borders to invite Illegal Immigration but do not allow them to live near them. There are no poor people's shelters in Beverly Hills, West Hollywood, or Malibu, of course.

On the other side, the Conservatives, working people, Middle Class, Christians, Hindus, Asians, Hispanic, and European and Russian heritage-related and, of course, the unavoidable 1%.

Very different philosophies of life well define the two sides. Ancestry plays an important role, especially in keeping the traditions and old culture, opposing radical changes that will be demeaning not only for Western Culture but also for Spanish, Blacks, Asians, Russians, and Hindu traditions.
It is a battle between the old customs and the radical new attempts to dismiss the safety standards of life, to try some crazy experiments, playing with feelings, and new unexplored games that could end damaging society to irreversible results.
Our Creator established by which kind of ideas in our Universes, we must live to keep an orderly growth. Unfortunately, many Postmodern Liberals deny Creation.
God has delivered a conscious Legacy, perfectly coordinated and defined.
We must continue developing it safely, maintaining a common sense based on past experiences, and future guidance following tradition. Balance is the key.
However, Postmodern Liberals are ignoring the examples of recent degradation caused by some severe mistakes. AIDS is spreading through unsafe sex practices and sharing needles.
At the same time, some insist on continuing to ignore the red lights and promoting a libertine lifestyle, which has failed in all past experiences, causing, at times, considerable damage to our society.
Maybe they aim to a re-edition of Sodom and Gomorrah.

J. Pelegrin

A BRUTAL ATTACK ON DEMOCRACY

(The All-Time Enemies on the March)

CHAPTER 7

(Our Future - China's danger)

223 -The most significant hoax -Russian collusion.

We all know and lived the details for four years.

We were told that Russia intervened in our 2016 election, with the sole purpose to elect Donald J. Trump as the 45th President of the United States. They even affirmed Donald J. Trump was a "Russian Agent."

Democrats under Postmodern Liberals leadership pounded daily, lying and manipulating information through the Media, massively.

We, Americans, were forced to believe that was the truth.

The new Government, with a President that wasn't a politician, per se, a successful businessman, with a Cabinet, integrated mostly with inexperienced politicians, was unprepared to fight the attacks of the Left.

Russians have been our political adversaries for a long time, and the type of accusation seemed real; Although, Russia does not have the economic power to overwhelm the US economy.

After three and a half years of the Mueller investigation, we learned that although there was collusion with the Russians, it didn't involve Donald Trump. Hillary Clinton and other Democrats were the ones compromised.

We believe the hoax was to uncover the real aggression to undermine the US World's influence; A diversion to cover-up the real intentions.

They were working on behalf of the Communist Government of China, our real enemy.

We already wrote about the connections established by Hunter Biden (Joe Biden's son) going around the World selling the then Vice President, collecting millions of dollars from foreign countries, including China.

Unfortunately, the Media swept the issue under the rug.

Now, we are learning through the TV show Tucker Carlson Tonight that some interesting evidence is detailing the facts.

From Beijing, China, a leaked video featuring a University Professor Di dan dong Chen, recorded on November 28, in a Beijing TV show about Wall Street and the international trade. Beijing removed the video immediately from Social Media.

Translation of Professor Chen, already corroborated by several Chinese Language experts, is self-explanatory:

Here they are: "The Trump Administration is in a war with us, so why can't we fix the Trump Administration? Why, between 1992 and 2016, did China and the US use to settle all kinds of issues? No matter what kind of crises we encountered, be it the (Container-ship) Yinhe incident, the bombing of the embassy, or the plane's crashing -things were resolved in no time, like (a couple) do with their quarrels starting at the bedhead but ending at the bed end. We fixed everything in two months. What is the reason? I'm going to throw out something maybe a little explosive here. It's just because we have people at the top. At the top of America's core inner circle of power and influence, we have our old friends." Said situation has been going on for decades.

So, who are those "old friends?"

Well, the professor didn't say precisely, although he suggested that some Chinese agent was working as Vice President of a financial institution. He said: "I can't say more without causing political trouble." He described her as a person that is now a Chinese citizen. China doesn't allow dual citizenship. Professor Chen seems pleased that the US Government is foolish enough to allow this type of situation. Ding don Chen expressed his satisfaction that the mentioned agent is part of the "invasion" that helped the Government of China's propaganda in Washington in 2015. The Obama Administration was easy to manipulate. The Chinese had many friends, he suggests, until Donald J. Trump was elected. Then, everything changed. The Video translation continues:

"For 30 - 40 years, we have been utilizing the core power of the United States. As I said before, since the 1970s, Wall Street has had a powerful influence on the domestic and foreign affairs of the United States. So, we had a channel to rely on. But the problem is that after 2008, Wall Street's status has declined, and more importantly, after 2016, Wall Street can't fix Trump. Why? It's very awkward. Trump had a previous soft default issue with Wall Street, so there was a conflict between them, but I won't go into details. I may not have enough time. During the US-China trade war, they (Wall Street) tried to help, and I know that my friends on the US side told me that they tried to help, but they couldn't do much.

Since the 1970s, Wall Street has had an enormous influence on the Government and the way it operates.

The Chinese Government has a tremendous influence on Wall Street. That arrangement worked very well for a long time. Until Donald Trump was unexpectedly elected, they tried to fix it, but they couldn't.

Then, China changed the attack's nature and flooded our streets with Opioids, Fentanyl, and other drugs, decimating our population. But that was not enough, so they tried a more potent weapon: The COVID-19.

If I had doubts that China sent the Coronavirus's intentionality on purpose or by errors committed unintentionally, the subsequent events would evacuate my suspicions. Unfortunately, we can't prove it—no evidence in our hands.

I want to especially thank Tucker Carlson, a most patriotic TV Anchor and a shining star in our society, for his effort to inform us of the truth that, unfortunately, the Mainstream Media keep hiding from us, the American People. Thank you, Tucker: God bless you and your family.

226 –The Most Urgent Measures.

From the previous section, we can see that while we've been deceived for years by our leaders, at the same time bribed by the Financial community, also bribed by China.

Of course, Donald J. Trump was the worse thing it could happen for those taking advantage of the situation and enriching them; at the same time, they were helping the Asian giant to grow. That is why they hate Donald so much in such in-depth. They can't buy him; he is a patriot. He is smart enough to be a billionaire on his own, without bribes from China or Russia.

The United States must immediately work to weaken China in all ways possible; it is of genuine National Security interest! They are our lead enemies.

We know now that some of our past political leaders failed to look up to the American People. They sold us out for the generous, quick profits that the Communist Government of China offered, taking advantage of their national workers enslaved to operate for pennies, paid in rice and some veggies, and unspeakable, dangerous meat. The enslavers are the Elite of politicians in charge of the Government and the Oligarchs worldwide doing business with China.

Besides the despicable actions described above, the Chinese saw that money was the most powerful tool to acquire absolute power, adjusted their political philosophy, and reverted Mao's hatred for Capitalism, turning the economic style into a State-owned Capitalism. They magistrally applied to their society, the new version of State Capitalism drawing a line that separated the two country's economy; One for the regular workers, enslaved and abused, and on the other side, the elite, close to the CPC, governing China.

Due to the laws enacted during Mao's Great Leap Forward (1958–1962,) about 40 to 45 million people died of starvation.

At the time, famine was widespread, appalling, forcing Chinese people to eat anything they could find to survive. Some of those eating practices are traditional, which increased the need to endure; they added many wild species to their diet.

 Humans need to get aliments from foods to survive and be healthy. The requirements of energy and nutrients vary depending on race, age, sex, and physical activity level. Different living places take nutrients from different kinds of food, making nutrition a cultural, regional, and biological process other than a simple physiological, biochemical method.

Food intake influences people's vital functions throughout life. When and what people eat affects economics, politics, culture, religion, and many other factors.

Historically, China always had difficulties finding nutritious food.

Wild animal consumption, as well as rodents, insects, including cockroaches, ants, locusts, other bugs, and also snakes, bats, and any other unimaginable wild species, have been common in their diet.

Some of them are part of an ancestral tradition, religious reasons, and everyday necessity to get the protein amount to survive.

The Asian Giant's terrain is rough and challenging, so people's survival became a kind of artistry skill since times immemorial.

After Mao Zedong passed, powerful Chinese men, backed by the military, realized that Capitalism was the only way to advance economically and have a better chance to feed the people, to keep them quiet without even thinking of revolt against the Government.

So, the new CPC (Communist Party of China) invented 'State Capitalism." While they maintained China's center territory under strict Communist rules, keeping workers and peasants under slaving conditions, sleeping in ultra-crowded rooms, without the minimum sanitary requirements, they had other plans. They allowed a few cities in the Coast to enjoy some Capitalist privileges, always in partnership with the Communist Government Officials, with the primary purpose of exporting Chinese production.

Later reinforced by the recovery of Hong Kong from the UK, under some conditions, that China was not too happy to accept, but they manage to somehow follow with some tumbles.

The Chinese Communists Leaders successfully sold their new idea to the real Capitalists of the World, with the help of some Oligarchs from the West, hungry for money.

The latter found in such offering a new way to exploit workers without the apparent guilt now transferred to Chinese Communism—it is a very convenient thought.

Globalization then forced to spread out, at a time when most of the World was not prepared yet for the experience.

In a way, the Coronavirus Pandemic suggests an end to premature Globalization, forced by greedy CEOs and hungry Entrepreneurs, avid of generous profits offered by the Communist Government of China.

America led the manufacturing migration to the Asian Giant, followed by Japan, and later the rest of the World, which helped them enrich the Communist Government. They dangerously grew in only a few years after the famine and poverty scourged them for centuries, much worse under Mao's ruling years.

Simultaneously, thousands of American factories closed, leaving millions of American Workers unemployed, and the US Treasure exhausted and indebted, mainly to the Communist Government of China, now our largest creditor.

A great paradox, stupid and criminal on the hands of some of America's Capitalists, and many crooked politicians had begun.

The motives were strictly selfish and unpatriotic. Greed is the only reason they did it, and the Chinese outsmart them largely.

Business people, and some of our politicians, who got blinded by the false gold shining, sold us out to the Asians.

We should add stupidity to the main reason which drove them to such a disastrous idea: Pure greed, indeed.

The new American entrepreneur's generation has lost the sense of patriotism so severely that we, as a Nation, have lost credibility around the World, and every country on the Planet is abusing us in any possible way, China at the head. Of course, the inadequate education provided to the American People made the difference. Today, as we said before in this book, even students in universities are so ignorant that it is hard to believe.

Abundant heavy drugs helped to numb the inexperienced youngsters and Millenials, with the Chinese help. At the same time, they were helping themselves by continuing to sell them illegal drugs.

A significant part of the United States of America's people has lost its patriotism, sold for money to the Asian World labor force under the last few Administrations, mostly Democrats. It is sad but true.

For Postmodern Liberals, an educated community is hard to handle. So. they prefer the uneducated.

The United Nations, while the US land is, besides its headquarters host, also the most significant economic support, lately, consistently is ruling in favor of everyone else and against us. China is bribing its way through modern times utilizing the old Capitalist technique: they buy every single politician, government official, university Deans, and even Judges, to economically grow and advance their power, including the military.

China's fast growth is scary. The US must take advantage of the Pandemic situation to start to revert the trend. However, we have a powerful obstacle right in our country: The Democrat Party, which lately sides with the Chinese, including several of their politicians doing massive business with them.

Hunter Biden, son of the "Elect President," as the MSM likes to call him, is an example. He has collected at least 1.5 Billion dollars from a Bank in Communist China, originated by an unknown transaction, and also, through a dubious triangulation, received a similar amount from an energy company in Ukraine, with external commercial links. Also, Senator Dianne Feinstein and her husband, Richard Blum, have grown extremely rich. One could be suspicious of the $25 billion deal the Federal Deposit Insurance Corporation struck with the senator's husband's real estate company during the housing crash of 2009. Additionally, several high-rank Democrats, including Speaker Nancy Pelosi, are enriching themselves doing business with Beijing, and there are no indications that they are willing to stop the trend.

The new Democrat Party, as I have been telling in other chapters, are dazzled with Chinese money, and they dream of having in the United States, a similar totalitarian Government.

In previous US Administrations, politicians' errors or why not, their deliberated actions helped to erode our leadership and increased Beijing's power around the Globe.

Lately, the UN has supported our old enemies, especially Terrorists, and Communists, including China, and against the USA and its allies.

Our enemies, now labeled as "developing countries," and their contributions minimized. Simultaneously, the USA provides generously, accommodating the UN offices' housing, along with free parking and other privileges that our New York citizens do not have.

America's political leaders, investors, entrepreneurs, and financial operators have made severe wrong moves and horrible deals, detrimental to our people.

The market crash of 2008 generated by the unforeseen excesses by Banks, Insurance Companies, and Real Estate operators did not teach us a good lesson, and right after a difficult and expensive recovery, the economic community drove us into the ".com" crisis. Technology advances in computer science introduced the possibility of using processors to generate new businesses.

However, the new ventures were not easy to develop. Some investors had the technical knowledge, but they did not know how to use it yet. Very few entrepreneurs had a clear idea to profit from the new trend or turn the latest technological evolution into substantial businesses, so a massive bankruptcy occurred.

As usual, our economy recovered, and with the 2016 election that gave us President Donald J. Trump, an experienced businessman, rapidly, we achieved goals like never before were imagined.

The lowest unemployed numbers, the highest employment figures on Hispanics, Blacks, Asians, women, high GDPs, and other healthy economic signs became a reality. Our President fulfilled his promises.

Everything was fine until another import from China delivered us the worst ever: The Coronavirus Pandemic, right out of Wuhan, China in a combination of an unsafe experimental Lab, and a traditional 'Wet Market,' selling all kinds of exotic animal wildlife killed on the premises for food; a gross error or deliberate action;? We will never know the truth. I am inclined to the latter. We already disclosed the facts.

However, the result caused a debacle that cost tens of thousands of American lives, indescribable pain and suffering, besides the economic damage inflicted on the best finances our country ever has had.

231 -Our Dependence From China.
The one item at the top of the list is that we need to bring back our manufacturing. It is vital to our survival.

Unfortunately, the uncertainty of the next US Government indicates that if Democrats are in charge, doubtfully, they will stop China from advancing their world power. Let's keep in mind that Joe Biden's Family is highly suspicious of collaboration with China and also receiving bribes from the Chinese Government.

It is not wise, safe, commercially viable, and lacking common sense that our people's health depends on almost 100 % from China's Communist Government, our primary enemy, politically, militarily, socially, technologically, scientifically, and financially speaking.

The American People need to wake up and see the aberration of the actual status of our National Security.

If our country, God forbid, would enter a war, our military force, Radars, Nuclear Submarines, War Vessels, Warplanes, and other military equipment depend on parts manufactured in China. Said action means that we are entirely at Beijing's will. They could stop us from defending ourselves in a second. They could even disrupt our electrical grid and annihilate our country.

We just had a sample of this. After the Coronavirus spread, the Communist Government of China suspended any shipments of safety equipment like masks, gowns, goggles, protective gear, and any other component to keep our doctors and nurses healthy, creating panic among our people.

Besides suspending exports to our country, including American manufacturers' prohibition to ship their product home, they hoarded massive production of those items worldwide.

After they secured the items, they gouged the prices and sold them to the World, including the US, profiting some times up to 500 %, or used them to coerce some countries to avoid criticism on China's behavior.

Recently, the California Governor signed a deal with a Chinese electric car manufacturer to purchase one billion dollars of masks similar to the N95, which initially cost cents from the inventors, paying two dollars each. Outrageous!

Because their inventory was enormous, they utilized the rest of the equipment to influence other countries, making them look politically, heroes.

At the same time, they were hiding facts on how the Coronavirus started in their own Wuhan City. The unsafe Lab, experimenting with bats, and other wildlife specimens, may be the source of different types of viruses and strands or experimental gene manipulation.

The Wet Market is only a few hundred yards away from Wuhan Lab. It is not strange that the virus transmission had occurred, from one place to the other. Consider that bats originally inhabit a region thousands of miles apart from Wuhan but are sold in the market for food and used in experiments at the Lab, as we have seen in several pictures from the site. The closeness prompts any accidents to happen.

Also, the Communist Government, as soon as they learned of the first people infected, ordered the destruction of any samples, articles, papers, or data about the virus. They sanctioned the doctors that blew the whistle on the danger of transmission. Also, they publicly denied the contagion between humans, dismissed manipulation of the strands, and minimized the consequences.

At the same time, China forbade traveling from Wuhan to the rest of their country while encouraging trips to Europe and America.

If those orders and actions are not criminally punishable, then I don't have a clue what it would be.

Of course, we will never know the actual truth. The Communist Government just released an order to stop all investigations about how the Coronavirus started, issuing threats to Australia and other countries to halt shipping Chinese products to them if they insist on continuing the search for the truth.

However, we are intelligent people and able to come to our conclusions.

The main one is that our Government should revise our manufacturing practices.

While I have no problem buying plastic toys, kitchen appliances, furniture, clothing, and other consumer's articles from China, we must take back our manufacturing of sensitive items. Especially the ones involving medicines, medical equipment, military parts, security, especially National Security components, and any other accessories or objects that, at one point, could mean dangerous consequences to our Nation.

We got to stop being "penny wise and dollar foolish."

When we realized that China monopolizes the World's antibiotic manufacturing, makes 96% of our medical prescriptions and other types of medical supplies, 'the horror' enters my mind.

But when we learn that by a strange Law, the Labs in charge of distributing our daily prescriptions don't have to include the drug components' origin, we realize that our Lawmakers are not doing a good job.

Moreover, they are receiving bribes and privileges from the Communist Government of China; In my opinion, treasonous behavior.

When on June 16, 2016, Donald J. Trump announced his determination to "drain the Swamp," operating in Washington, while I cheered the proposal, I thought to myself:

"Hmm, it is going to be a tough battle for one man!"

Facts are corroborating my suspicion—too many kids feeding on one the same teat. And they will fight to the death to keep it that way.

232 -A Different Communism - Worse Than The USSR.

President Ronald Reagan helped to destroy the 'Axel o Evil,' as he named it after fighting the 'Cold War' against the USSR, finally, and in agreement with Mikhail Gorbachev,

By the Russian leader's brave actions, the Soviet Union collapsed after a series of events. Gorbachev's decision to loosen the soviet yoke on Eastern Europe's countries encouraged an independent, democratic momentum. These actions led to the Berlin Wall's demolition in November 1989 and subsequently overthrowing the Communist rule throughout Eastern Europe.

However, Mao Zedong (December 26, 1893 – September 9, 1976) was a Chinese Communist leader, Chairman of the Communist Party of China (CPC), from its establishment in 1949 until he died in 1976.

He led the Communist Party of China to victory in a civil war against the Nationalist regime.

He founded the People's Republic of China and transformed the Asian Giant radically.

In 1958, Mao decided to change its agricultural economy into a Communist society by forming people's communes, a significant change for the Nation.

Mao named the move: "The Great Leap Forward." It was an economic and social campaign by the Communist Party of China from 1958 to 1962, which Mao Zedong launched to reconstruct the country's vast, impoverished agrarian style.

However, things did not turn all well. The Chairman's plans collapsed, leaving at the end of the period, estimates say 40 to 45 million people dead, between the famine and political punishment by the execution of opposition.

Mao admitted that problems had occurred. He blamed most of these difficulties on bad weather and natural disasters, acknowledging that there had been policy errors too, for which he took responsibility for them.

After Mao's death, the country was left without a political head. They continued to revere the Chairman's figure and considering him a symbol of China's rebirth.

A power struggle after Mao's death began, and the arrest of the Gang of Four, in 1976, started a series of political changes.

Without the figure of Mao to protect them, the Government imprisoned the Gang of Four.

They, the CPC, reinstated Deng Xiaoping, and in 1977 was appointed General Secretary of the Communist Party.

In 1978, the CPC appointed Deng as Chairman of the Committee in charge of economic reform. It accepted Deng's policy of the 'four modernizations' and resolved to restore the "Party's democracy," Communist style.

Rather than trying to attack Mao, Xiaoping proposed a compromise; The Party considered Mao as a great leader who, although he had made some 'gross mistakes'… 'his contribution far outweighs his errors' – The Central Committee declared that Mao had been '70 % right 30% wrong.'

In 1981, the Gang of Four was put on trial for the deaths of hundreds of thousands of people during the Cultural Revolution.

Deng Xiaoping introduced a set of policy reforms called the 'four modernizations' (agriculture, industry, technology, military)

-In agriculture, peasants were allowed to rent a plot of land and farm it, almost as a private farm, provided they gave a quota of the product to the commune.

-In industry, each State-Owned Enterprise had to produce a certain amount for the State, after which any extra profit could be used to award higher wages, bonuses, etc.

-A Reform of the Economic System Resolution, in 1984

did not allow private businesses, but it permitted more freedom to State-Owned Enterprises (SOE) managers to run their businesses as they wanted, along capitalist lines.

-They created four Special Economic Zones:

Shanton and Xiamen (north), Shenzen, and Zhuhai (south); were granted autonomy and tax deals and were told to concentrate on exports. -Exports quintupled between 1978-1988.

-Imitating Gorbachev in Russia, Deng introduced 'Reforms and Openness' (the Beijing Spring') and set a policy of reform called the 'four modernizations' (agriculture, industry, technology, military)

However, Modernization was not accompanied by political change. – Deng Xiaoping opposed Democracy and recommended upholding 'the Socialist style,' "democratic dictatorship," as the CPC leadership and Mao Zedong thought.

At one point, the CPC was accused of corruption when scandals like the Heilonjiang fraud. They discovered SOE managers of a power company stealing the profits.

The so-called Democracy Wall was a place where reformers posted their ideas. – From time to time, the Government would arrest them and clear the posters.

In June 1989, the Tiananmen Square Massacre took place.

The former CPCD Secretary-General (1982-1987) famous reformer Hu Yaobang's funeral and Gorbachev's visit to Beijing prompted a student hunger strike and occupation of the Square. After the tearful pleadings of General Secretary Zhao Ziyang were ignored, the People's Liberation Army moved in and massacred thousands of students, leaving the World outraged.

Even after Mao died, Chinese media were not allowed to attack his record; Chinese schools do not teach the past failures. The 1981 declaration of the CPC Central Committee – '70 % right 30% wrong' – is the current official Chinese assessment of Mao's legacy.

From the above, they highlight one issue as the most detrimental outcome from the changes: The regular people of China, the commons, the workers, farmworkers, and students lost all possible rights, human rights, and health privileges. Only the CPC servants could have some rights, according to their intelligence or servitude to politicians.

Although the World has controversial opinions about Mao Zedong and his philosophy, there is no doubt that he transformed China radically.

Helped by the US Capitalists, the Asian Giant evolved in a half-century, more than several centuries before.

His legacy, together with some reformers that, after Mao's death, operated dramatic changes in the once rigid hierarchy inside the

CPC, finally made possible Mao's dream of "The Great Leap Forward."

Today, China is, momentarily, the second-largest economy and Military Power, of course, before the Coronavirus Pandemic.

237 -The US Greatest Challenge.

If a sense of patriotism in the USA does not find resurgence over the unbridled greed driving it now, the US future is severely compromised.

The new direction in the Democrat Party (the recipient of the coalition votes, and politically responsible) dramatically hijacked by Postmodern Liberalism, has successfully seized the once a Democratic Party and is operating a severe change of directions in its policies and political philosophy.

The Pandemic's appearance has emphasized a deranged "Power Grab," which has changed how almost one half of the country thinks and wishes for the future. Democrats, with the help of the powerful Mainstream Media, through fake news and lies, have influenced a part of the population that could not find the truth and surrender to the Postmodern Liberalism manipulation, leaning to the Left.

Greed, a search for absolute political authoritarianism, Big Government, dictatorial, totalitarian, and unprecedented ultra-liberalism that will replace traditional society standards are at the top of the list.

I call the new movement that has hijacked the Democrat Party: Postmodern Liberalism, which I explained in detail in previous chapters.

Echoing Democrat politicians, the Mainstream Media is responsible for our society's deep division and a radical increase of hatred, insults, and slander. Other negative feelings, especially against President Trump, who is being demonized and blamed for anything the Press decides to invent, prompting the confused Lawmakers in the Democrat Party, to follow like a herd.

The main instrument is FAKE NEWS, a creation of the so-called Liberal "journalists" acting as Democrat political hacks instead of real Journalists featuring the news as they are.

The damage such folly is causing to our country is so appalling that it is hard to understand why. After all, our Nation is at stake.

The Communist Government of China has influenced Democrats, which manipulated by Postmodern Liberalism, is trying to dramatically change the basic democratic philosophy for one based on feelings and fantasy, denying science and reality.

A dangerous trend that also embraces Totalitarianism, authoritarianism while indoctrination of youngsters is replacing education.

They want to change the way our Government functions, according to the Constitution. They prefer adopting China's Communist system, where people are deprived of individuality, compelled to collective thinking instead of a personal approach. It is a blatant power grab, to seek absolute political authority, to destroy our two and a half centuries-old Nation, the most successful Republican Democracy experience on the Planet.

The aim is to subjugate the American People and deprive them of the Bill of Rights, individual thinking, and freedom of choice. They also are against the First Amendment Free Speech, the Second Amendment to carry weapons and in favor of curtailing other Constitutional Rights.

They are enamored with the economic development of China. However, they haven't thought that while the Chinese are a "collective society," based on Confucianism, where Family is first, second comes the State, and personal is way down the list.

Overall, they forget that China holds its status now, because of the incomparable help gotten from the United States, to build the colossal economy they are showing nowadays, while our country entered a dangerous dependence on Beijing.

The United States of America is naturally opposed to that totalitarian way. For over three centuries, our leaders have been fighting for individual freedom, justice for all, as our Bill of Rights reads.

Although Democrats are trying to mask this new philosophical thought as "Democracy," an astute observer sees 'authoritarianism' written all over. Indeed, Totalitarianism is down the road.

Unfortunately, most American People lack the proper education, historical knowledge, political experience and show profound ignorance about political manipulation.

Americans should educate themselves on how China got to the place they are now and where they are coming from as a country. Also, what is the people's nature, ancestry, education, and lifestyle?

America is, without a doubt, the country most people, including Chinese nationals, would like to live, raise a family, study, and work. Looking at our streets, we can see hundreds of thousands of Chinese people enjoying the freedom their country denied them.

Chinese students are fascinated with our Liberties, Bill of Rights, and our Constitution, which gives them what China won't grant them: FREEDOM.

Democrats, in exchange, want to revert the rules and dismiss our lifestyle to adopt the Communist Government of China's style. They are dazzled by the profits gotten by exploiting their population of workers.

It is a deranged idea.

Hundreds of thousands of Chinese Nationals are taking advantage of our Universities. The Communist Government pays for their tuition and living expenses. At the same time, the students enroll in courses teaching Sciences, Technology, and Computers Science, exploiting our openness and stealing our secrets that they consistently deliver to the Communist Party of China.

Additionally, the CPC keeps bribing Universities, granting them billions of dollars, to maintain good standing with the Faculty and University directors. Simultaneously, politicians, mostly but not exclusively Democrats, are bribed generously, while in exchange, they perform tasks to facilitate the Asian's penetration in our society.

While the spying, pilfering, appropriation of secrets, and technology is going on openly, the sense of patriotism has disappeared from our political scene and replaced by greed, power grab, and imitating the totalitarian practices of our worse enemy: China.

My sincere intention writing this book is to open up minds by narrating parts of history, comparing philosophies, marking differences, and trying to go back to Conservatism, not to hung out on it, but recalling it for consultation these troubled times.

I ignore if people have a sense of the disaster that is entering through our doors; nevertheless, it is wise to be alert, and that is the primary purpose of these writings.

240 -Democrats Obsession With Absolute Power.

The Leftist magazine The Atlantic recently published something in these terms:

"...Government should make sure that the options align with what the political power wants."

It sounds to me like a blunt Communist statement.

Thus a political regime keeps power because people accept and obey its dictates, laws, and policies. However, any power structure relies upon the people's obedience to the ruler's orders. If subjects do not obey, leaders have no power.

Therefore, Democrats are trying to grab absolute power by forcing people to avoid individual thoughts and engage in collective thinking.

Moreover, if possible, avoid thinking at all and just obey the decision made by elite Government workers, which in the future will think and resolve issues to relieve the subjects from having to think and make choices. That is the Postmodern Liberalism's plans to govern our USA.

To achieve their goal, Democrats are engaging in a massive illegal immigration effort that allows mostly uneducated people to enter the USA under a "catch and release" policy. They would spread out and melt with US Citizens. At the same time, they will have in their minds that Democrats allowed them to be in the country to enjoy privileges that supposedly are for Citizens. Those include healthcare by Medicare/Medicaid, Food Stamps, Housing, Free Education, Child Care, and other perks. Democrats expect migrants to give back by voting once they are legal and can vote, or like in 2020, encouraging illegals to vote Democrat illegally or fraudulently.

It is a despicable plan to break all the rules possible for one only reason: To get absolute political power.

Remember Chuck Schumer's cry! "Now we get Georgia, and then we change the country!"

It is incomprehensible that after over two hundred and forty-some years of enjoying the most successful experiment in the Constitutional Republic practicing Democracy, under a Bill of Rights, the Democrat Party would want a Totalitarian rule. There are journalists, who supposedly would've been well educated, knowing World's history but with a little patriotism, would root to change our status to Socialist Authoritarian regime, one step away from Communism, an enslaving way or life.

Indeed they have not lived in a Socialist or Communist country like I was for some time.

Living under a Socialist or Communist ruling is oppressing, exhausting, suffocating, and frustrating because talents, God-given grace, skills, intelligence, personal achievements, wishes, and overall, dreams are not possible unless you accept to become a slave of the political system, cease your individual thoughts, and succumb to massive thinking; Just like a herd or a flock does.

For Democrats today: Fear is their weapon. Lying is their tool.

They practice massive thinking even in Congress. Nobody is allowed to dissent or to express a different opinion. Democrats act in unison, even when out of tune, which makes them sound awful.

241 -Market Capitalism Clashes With State Capitalism.

The essence of Market Capitalism is freedom. The Market regulates the offer and demand. State Capitalism is rigid and ruled by politicians, not always smart enough or with the knowledge that business-people have.

Of course, there are the Oligarchs, which Communist leaders trust and share personal profit with them, coming handy to help.

Oligarchs are tacit Capitalists, acting inside a Communist Government, enjoying privileges that others cannot. They are part of the thrill.

In China's case, many oligarchs are American citizens who decided that money is their Constitution; greed is the only object, and profit the superior satisfaction in life. There are plenty of them.

Some well known, others masked under Complex Company structure, and some politicians included too.

They are philosophically numbed, anesthetized, drugged by wealth, and the ultimate stage: power.

Because as I said before, money is only the means to achieve power, the ultimate elixir that provides control, authority, influence, dominance, mastery, sovereignty, jurisdiction, sway, weight, leverage, hold, grasp, say, clout, pull, and other perks. They are not a bad collection of heavyweight elements of material life.

That is why money is so critical to many individuals hungry for power. Money, in all cases, grants access to the accessories that make power.

However, to be absolute, power needs to be enforced.

And then is when the totalitarian philosophy comes in handy, and Communism is the optimum political system to provide it. But they are not alone. Islam is also mastering the absolute political power within. We will discuss it separately.

However, at the end of the line, it is never enough. There is always room for more, and on the way to the achievement, many people lose their minds and sometimes lives, searching for the insatiable greed that has destroyed so many lives, families, countries, and hopes.

I am not against wealth, I want people to know, but without a component of Spiritual Life, everything turns so hollow, so inconsequential, that in the end, it turns happiness into depressive life.

Most suicides occur among wealthy people.

240 -America's Future Is At Stake.

There is no doubt the coalition wanting to destroy America as it is today; strong, well organized, and working like a clock.

Postmodern Liberalism, under the LGBTQ's strong influence, Socialism, Communism, Totalitarianism, Islam's authoritarianism, are the tools. Democrat's inability to maintain its traditional platform has become a powerful brotherhood.

They count on the inexperienced youngsters, avid to explore new options. What the elders told them, they think is not wise to try. They do not trust them and exert a traditional rebellion that we all had at one point in our youth. (I remember my math professor saying: (If you are not Communist at eighteen, you don't have a heart. If you are still Communist after 25, you have no shame or a brain.)

The confusion of ideas is also developing a strange philosophy that is rapidly building a conformist society out of the millions of youngsters who already accepted that their chances to succeed are so slim that it is not worth trying the traditional way. They prefer crazy changes.

Most juveniles ignore their possible hidden talents, overwhelmed by competition, lacking proper support from their families, or merely natural weakness. They think that being part of a vast government that will make all decisions to shut up and obey will pay them enough cash to survive and get older without having to think. But I have news for them. Government pay, especially in Communist-style, is so low that it will discourage anyone. Isn't that great?

Well, not for me, but I know there are many candidates for that kind of life. Life?

Wait a minute! I almost forgot that for the system to work, the Government would train them to avoid having responsibilities, including children, for what they will have to learn how to prevent them or abort the pregnancies. Even killing them babies after the abortion fails, and they are born—just like the Governor of Virginia, Ralph Northam, approving a Law to Kill babies after a failed abortion. I call it infanticide!

244 -The Conspiracy Is In Full Speed.

The COVID-19 Pandemic came as a blessing to Democrats.

Liberal TV personality Bill Mahers has publicly said:

< I'm "Hoping" For "A Crashing Economy" So We Can Get Rid Of Trump, "Bring On The Recession"> Really?

And that is the mood in the Democrat Party, now commanded by an insane group I call Postmodern Liberalism.

They don't give a damn about the American People.

Lately, other Lawmakers have expressed their satisfaction with the economic crisis caused by the Coronavirus.

Majority whip, Jim Clayburn said: "Coronavirus Bill Is 'Tremendous Opportunity to Restructure Things to Fit Our Vision.'"

The offensive words of these "Democrats" tell volumes about the lack of modesty, and disdain for the American Public, when the Democrat Legislators refuse to go back to Congress to work, claiming that their doctors counsel them to stay home because of the Virus. A big lie.

Everything works for Democrats under the Postmodern Liberalism spell. The hatred for President Trump is more significant than their love for our country.

Power, control, and authoritarianism are the primary goals.

The coalition members are determined to change our country, how the Government functions, its structure, and imposing an undoubtedly Socialist political philosophy mixed with Fascist practices ultimately to exert control over the population. Absolute power is the goal, quoting Congressman Jim Clayburn, "to Restructure Things to Fit Our Vision."

This vision is totalitarian, with the primary objective of having an elite inside the Government, which would impart orders to people, to obey the decisions previously taken by the DNC Leadership.

Regular people would serve the directions without any possibility to question them. Those are part of the 'visions' that Democrats are planning to enforce, taken directly from the Chinese Communist Government, which have Democrats fascinated.

A close examination of the latest Democrats' plans for an eventual Government will confirm their intentions.

As I mentioned in a previous chapter, the instructions imparted by Karl Marx and Fredrich Engels in the Communist Manifesto: "Destroy any country government to rubles, and on top of them, build a Communist Paradise."

The insane project called "Green New Deal," basically the Democrat's platform's core, is very explicit. It calls for the ban of any fossil fuels. Under the Trump Administration, the US has made our country the number one producer in the World, consolidating the economic power embedded in it.

A measure like that will weaken our country, decimating our production capabilities, and driving millions of business to bankruptcy. Additionally, that move will assure the absolute World's dominance of China and Russia. They will never stop drilling for oil.

The idea to ban cows because they release methane gas is as crazy as the proponent, Alexandra Ocasio Cortez, inexplicably now, acting as the leading voice of the Democrat Party.

Also, the elimination of private health insurance, which we discussed in another chapter in detail, is another sign of insanity.

There is no doubt in my mind that the USA's destruction is in every Democrat politician's mind. Their voters are also the victims.

Their plans are frightening and aligned with State Capitalism in practice by the Communist Government of China.

Over the last decades, Democrat Billionaires, Entrepreneurs, and CEOs of manufacturing companies operating in China have collected large profits, taking advantage of cheap labor by Chinese Workers, which are under strict laws imposing slavery conditions enforced by the Communists.

Democrats, learning from the experience, now want to install a similar practice in the US, which is in absolute violation of our Constitution and the Bill of Rights.

The infatuation with these excesses of power is the new philosophy Democrats want to impose in our country.

Their behavior in the House of Representatives is a token reflecting their intentions, and the recently failed Impeachment hoax attempted against our President is a sample of their evil plans.

It is hard to believe how a political party that in the past defended women's rights now adheres to Islam's philosophy, totally contrary to those fundaments.

It is also regrettable they dishonor the Party's name: "Democrat," adopting totalitarian ideals.

President Trump's hatred has poisoned the entire Party and turned their minds so insanely wasted like it is hard to understand.

Democrats' obsession with power is part of a deranged syndrome that Donald J. Trump's victory in the 2016 election created.

The frustration for the loss of power has grown into desperation, which added to the passion for achieving a similar people's control Chinese Communism style has brought a desperate race to seek power.

Fear is the tool to scare people and, through lies and intimidation, get results; The "anti-American Media helps with fake-news" to enhance the Power-grab obsession. Control is the new mantra!

The object is a society unable to think for themselves, except for a few which the Government will employ as "herd handlers" who will make choices to order the ordinary people to obey without questioning.

Through deceiving headliners, the MSM delivers half-true notes, taking advantage of people's bad habit to only read the headlines without getting into the rest of the news.

Today's so-called journalists are increasingly taking advantage of the fact and delivering a distorted message in the title. Simultaneously, they clarify the rest of the information, so they are not lying but exaggerating the headline to make an impression that leads the "headliners readers" to get a misrepresented message.

The Mainstream Media is a stalwart Democrat's ally.

They often take advantage of people's lack of curiosity who lately only read the headliners in a dangerous disinformation habit that will lead them to make severe mistakes in the election, choosing the wrong political leaders.

The LGBTQ, well represented in the Media and also among the politicians, is stirring the pot to gain acceptance to their questionable fantasies and now pushing a scientific hoax like Trans-genderism, an obvious illusory life decision. I believe people have the right to live an illusion without involving children and not trying to force acceptance by the rest of society that doesn't believe in fantasies.

However, what beats me hardest is the notion that while the US needs more people to help our economy, they kill millions of newborn babies through millions of senseless abortions. At the same time, our country has an actual foreign invasion, including children, babies, and youngsters. Democrats hate our American-born babies. They prefer imported ones.

It would make a lot of sense that instead of promoting abortions like Democrats do, which are, in fact, murderers of human life, Congress should legislate and provide financial help to pregnant women to help them to deliver and raise their babies. The country needs them.

Even in the case that the mother desired not to keep the newborn, I am sure there are plenty of women in this country that unable to get pregnant or, for other reasons, cannot have their own babies, that would love to welcome in their homes a newborn, especially saved from being murdered by abortion.

I hope politicians on both sides of the aisle can pick up the idea.

Vladimir Putin recently passed a law that provides financial help from the Government to new mothers giving birth. A policy we could imitate!

247 -Evolution, Not Revolution.

While Postmodern Liberalism, driving Democrats and the rest of the coalition: Socialists, Communists, and Islam are pushing for a Revolution, Conservatives are making sense by proposing a continuous Evolution, consulting history, the sacred Scriptures like the Vedas, The Bible, and Torah, not to stay on the old thinking, but to bring the wise advice to present and revise our society and lifestyle to adjust some issues to the modern civilization, to enjoy a better life.

The differences between the two sides are so profound and fundamental that hopefully, the American People will choose the right option.

However, the masses are easily confusing issues. The political operators on the left side of the aisle are getting massive help from the Media, controlled by billionaires desperately seeking cheap labor, like they see every day in China, lusting to increase even more the colossal profits they are getting at this time.

They dismiss that the American People are part of a society conformed by individuals, and that is what our Founding Fathers had in mind when they wrote our Constitution and the Bill of Rights.

The differences with the Chinese society, which is, as said before, a "collective society," won't take the 'poison-pill,' and if it does, a few months into the new experiment proposed by Democrats will revolt and reject the changes with passion and probably violence.

I hope such an option will not pass after the November election, because besides destroying a significant part of our values, almost impossible to recover, it will open wounds in our veins that will take generations to heal.

So, let's come to the senses and do the right thing. We are enjoying a strong economy like never before; Our society is currently politically induced by some manipulators to hate each other. However, our roots, our people are peaceful, love our country and its lifestyle, and the wounds, so far are not difficult to heal.

Most people believe in God, although false prophets abuse others. Some have difficulties in discerning between God's spiritual power and material life.

I hope the American People will listen to the inner voice and make the right choice.

Being on God's side is always a guarantee because believing is positive while denying, you need proof, that many times is not available.

Communist China's plans are clear. World domination, Economic, Cultural, Geographic, Military, Scientific, Technological, and anything else they could control. There is no limit to their ambitions. Money, always repealed in the past, repudiate it as the evil of society, lately has become their greatest ally. Chinese learn fast, and Market Capitalism finally conquered their brains. Although against the core of the Communist philosophy, they changed one bit on the structure and converted it into "State Capitalism." That slight move, in a short time, turned hunger into enormous wealth. Like in the USSR before, workers only changed their exploitation from Aristocracy to State, and similarly, they got a worse deal; The State is a much worse boss.

Nevertheless, workers are China's backbone, a strong one. Unlike in the Czars' Russia, Chinese workers were dying by famine and political repression. Any improvements, even adding some vegetables to their poor diet, would improve their lives, so a wealthy State is a plus; people are content with it and proud of the country's progress. Everybody is proud of their birth country. They ignore any other different lifestyle. Remember that China is one country, two systems, and workers live in the Communist system.

China's CPC's Government learned fast from past mistakes. Their rigid, obsolete philosophical ways, instead of keep fighting them, admitted some techniques from Market Capitalism and unified the businesses owners into one prominent entrepreneur: the State. A simple, fast, and clean move transformed a poor Communist, Mao Tse Dong style, to the Planet's most vibrant economy, with one and a half billion potential consumers.

Billionaires, Millionaires, Entrepreneurs, Business-people, and even foreign countries, got marveled and enamored with the result, especially the fantastic operations' low cost.

Unlike the USSR, where the product was low quality, awkward design, and overall disliked by customers, Chinese people, with an ancient culture, passion for details, and natural eagerness to learn, produced inexpensive goods, the market welcome, and the Merchants enjoy profits like never before.

Of course, in the Western culture's view, the victims are Chines workers, with a slight change. They are enjoying a better life, compared with the famine and death of Mao's times. In the future, they will surely learn that Western culture has better things to offer, but that is in the long-range.

In my mind, I always have learned from eastern wise business-people that the Japanese were at the top of the Pyramide, followed by Taiwanese, and Mainland Chinese at the bottom. However, Japan and Taiwan have an inconvenient reduced land of their own. That limits their operations.

Chinas' expansion is in full motion, although they face some opposition besides the USA from Japan, Taiwan, and lately Australia, where their pressure is increasingly threatening to cut some of the countries' vital imports from the Asians. Meanwhile, the European Union is like a lamb. They prefer comfort to the competition, and the UK is weak after leaving the EU. Latin America is a target, although its people are not too crazy about the Chinese. They enjoy the inexpensive imports, but they resist a take-over.

India is a competitor. Its labor force is High-Tech oriented too, but manufacturing is way behind. Africa, so far, is too wild to manage it, and not very desirable for China to spend much time on it.

It is a complex World. We will see.

Unfortunately, Democrats spoiled Donald J. Trump's initial attempt to solidify a partnership with Russia to build an alliance against China. They used the Trump-Putin closeness as a political weapon against our President, probably unaware of the primary intention, but because it was what they had at hand, easy to manipulate into a dark conspiracy theory: The Russian Collusion.

I am sure Trump could have used Russia's partnership as a deterrent against China. Democrats know how to divide. That's what they did with Trump, maybe a little naive coming from the Business World into Politics.

251 -Important Words From The Author.

In the next chapter, there is an Epilogue with some additional information and more historical facts. It's a bit long but worth it to read.

The reader is welcome to explore the writing, although it may be a bit charged or religiously challenging for some.

However, it is consistent with the rest of the work you just read.

Thank you for reading it. You can always leave your comment through my email: <mayavadi@aol.com> or, preferable, on the Amazon page where the book is selling. Your comment will encourage potential readers.

J. Pelegrin

A BRUTAL ATTACK ON DEMOCRACY

(The All-Time Enemies on the March)

EPILOGUE

(Islam: An ever-present danger)

253 –Three Contenders In The Battlefield.

Two foreign powers and one interim group are partnering to dominate the World at present—America's Democrat Party, the Communist Government of China, and Islam.

Two of them, commanding over one and a half Billion people each, all they slaved under authoritarian and totalitarian philosophies. The third one is an interim partnership: The Democrat Party, now obeying Postmodern Liberalism, which at the same time is constituted by local Liberals, Socialists, Communists, Fascists, Islamists, Atheists, LGBTQ, and other ignorant, mostly undocumented fools hoping for handouts.

China; its Government is Atheist and totalitarian, although among their subjects are various religions involved. The State dismisses as against their laws while having over one million Muslims in concentration camps; they call "re-education facilities."

Islam considers the whole World as their land or country, which is entirely the opposite regarding Religion; Although we do not know how many could be hiding Atheist thoughts or even other religions. The rest seem to be Muslims.

The first two want to destroy the United States and rule the World in very different ways or at least strip us of authentic leadership, economically, politically, socially, religiously, and others.

The third one: America's Democrat Party, shares with the other two totalitarian ideals and authoritarianism. They also became Atheists, in its majority.

We know that in Technology and Sciences, China, which has stolen many secrets from the USA, has developed and, in many cases, improved the fundamental knowledge, technical designs, and other information, always with the collaboration of some rogue US Scientists and Investors.

A close "partnership," 'design-manufacturing' between both countries, is clouding the scene and makes it difficult to know the actual status.

The United States was the initiator of the scientific/technological development, although some we share with the Asians.

China has been stealing secrets and spying for decades at plain sights without any former US Government leaders trying to stop them. Bribed them? Hmm.

China's product, exploiting their subjects to work for pennies, incentivized US entrepreneurs and investors' greed, blinding their views of our country's future.

One thing is clear: both group's leadership have the same goal, although utilizing different methods.

China wants to rule politically, using its Military to enforce it and technology to develop leadership.

On the other hand, Islam, which has persistently attempted a take-over for 1400 years plus, wants to rule the World religiously. They exert a stiff authoritarian theology that slaves people, abuse women, abject and kills homosexuals, and attempts to go back in time. They insist going back to when ignorance was reigning, and Islam was banning education, other than reading their scriptures, limited to some men only.

Democrats now hijacked by Postmodern Liberalism, which I explained its formation and goals in previous chapters, came out as the unifier, putting together a coalition with a joint plan: to destroy Donald J. Trump and the United States of America as it is now. Moreover, of course, China and Islam are willing to help, hoping, in the end, they will also get rewards.

It is intrinsically an internal battle for power; in essence, a powder keg, ready to explode at any time, and who knows who could be the winner.

The effect is also unknown. China and Democrats (USA) possess nuclear weapons, and Islam is on its way to achieve them. A dangerous game they are playing.

All of them are determined to gamble their lives to win.

However, if Democrats are the winners, one of the partners, Islam, will challenge the trophy, claiming the right to take the portion allowed for Religion. Also, considering that Democrats are primarily non-believers, I cannot foresee and end of the rivalry. Islam has 1400 years of experience, against two hundred and some years on Democrats. The outcome is written all over.

China has a place assured. They are already bribing US politicians, Education Centers, Entrepreneurs, Investors; they have plenty of money they continuously stifle their workers to continue the pattern.

At the same time, they will insist on the World's domination.

Here are some facts and historical data.

255 -Postmodern Liberals/Islam, US Constitution's Enemies.

Perhaps, nobody informed our Founding Fathers about Islam as an ideology rather than a mere religion, neither on their destructive intentions against the US.

They never imagined how the Muslims would behave in the future, now a dreadful reality.

The Constitution Framers' purpose was to establish a non-religious government, wide open for all faiths.

It seems their primary desire was to leave engraved in the Charter the freedom to worship God in any form, separate from the Government, and mainly to prevent the States from choosing one Religion to be the absolute ruler of the land.

It sounded good, fair, and promising. We believe that Thomas Jefferson, who penned the clause about religious freedom, did not intend to include Christian faith so severely in the State's separation.

He was a frequent supporter of building new Christian churches and other charities; the Government also usually helped.

Historical records documented those of Jefferson's money contributions to Christian organizations. Neither foresaw the Islamist escalation in the form of military force to conquer our land and destroying our Constitution and lifestyle.

History tells us, many things began changing around the country by the end of the 17th century, opening some doubts about the generous offering in the Constitution's First Amendment.

Two hundred and forty-some years passed by, and we can see the ambiguity in the concept of what Religion is and what ideology is. Ideology or Theology, for instance, political power, military force, and those pooled under a religion's umbrella, would-be enemies to the fundamental Law of the United States? No, they never expected something like that, although, at the time, there were various indications through the Islamist's behavior that raised doubts about their real intentions.

Presidents Adams and Jefferson got a taste of the problem.

The Islamist's bullies gave way to the Barbary Wars.

However, it is still happening nowadays, and with the advances by these enemies, we can see them clearly at present. They even managed to plant a couple of spies as House Representatives, recently.

Revising the Constitution, we encounter a duality in the wording, causing severe problems regarding Islam's behavior concerns.

Mohammed founded Islam around 610 AC when he was forty years old.

He was a warlord, a bandit, mass murderer, and employer of torture, polygamist, slave trader, and slave master. He commanded himself about thirty military campaigns killing thousands, appropriating other men's wives, wealth, and homes. It is all recorded in history.

Mohammed died in 632 AD, but before he passed, he left a legacy of some precisely determined future conquests that his disciples should continue to pursue in what we call: the Islamic invasions and the World conquering to establish a Worldwide Caliphate.

The goal is: forcing the conversion of the whole World population to Islam.

From the Eighth Century to Eighteen Century, Muslims devastated the World with their continuous destruction and genocide at the end of the Ottoman Empire.

History indicates that those invasions only had periods of less activity but never stopped. Even right now, with the War explosion that sent to Europe over ten million Middle Easterners from Syria and Lebanon, in what appears to be a pre-planned Islamic mega-invasion of Europe and America, is a confirmation of their long-term plans.

While the Europeans accepted the vast majority of refugees, the USA resisted such a massive invasion, socially and politically, allowing only a few thousand at the end of the Obama Administration entering the US land.

Still, the Democrats or the people who voted for Obama did not realize the damage caused by the pro-Islamist President.

The harm posed by Islam over 1,400 years since its creation is inestimable, 'Dantesque.' It seems history has not been able to convince people the firm determination of Islamic ideology/theology must end. Or soon, we all be slaves to the incumbent Muslim Government or Caliphate. That is the prophecy the Islamists are determined to accomplish. They do not deny it. They indeed brag about it.

Muslim Leaders are saying: "In the end, we will prevail and dominate the World: By the pregnant wombs of our female, by peaceful invasions or by the sword."

Their women give birth at the highest rate possible.

The militants are using females as a relief for their sexual appetites with the inevitable consequences: pregnancies and newborns, in my opinion, pre-meditated and encouraged by the leadership.

258 -Islamic Laws Are Clashing With Our Constitution
258 -The Postmodern Liberal Ideology is against Islam.

Our Constitution says:

"Congress shall make no law respecting an establishment of religion, or prohibiting the free exercise thereof, or abridging the freedom of speech, or the press, or the right of the people, peaceably to assemble and to petition the Government for a redress of grievances."

It is evident that the Founding Fathers did not have complete knowledge of the Koran and Hadith, or they misunderstood the wording in them.

Although Thomas Jefferson and John Adams owned copies of the book, no one knows how well they knew the content. (Jefferson owned a library with 6.000 books)

They supposedly acquired the Koran's copy after the Ambassador of Tripoli in England told them the famous phrase that explains the reason the Islamists hate and persecute all nationals of Nations that refuse to accept the "Koran Holy Book" as the Universal Ruler.

Once again, "Jefferson and Adams, while in London, around 1801/02, spoke to the Tripoli Ambassador, Abd Al-Rahman, questioning him on why the Barbary Pirates thought they should declare war on a nation that had never done anything to harm them.

The Muslim ambassador responded:

"It is written in the Koran, that all nations who will not acknowledge the Islam's authority were sinners and that it was their duty to make war upon them, and to make slaves of all they could take as prisoners."

The Koran-quoting is one reason Islamists consider us their enemies, and our people are condemned to die unless they surrender to Islam. It is something impossible to change since no one can alter the Koran. In my opinion, Islamists should adjust their interpretation to the modern World and our social evolution if they want to live in peace and share this World with others.

After hearing the outrageous statement, Adams and Jefferson were encouraged to seek their copies of the Koran" (although some historians affirm that Jefferson got a last copy of the book in 1765.)

The critical fact is that the concept maintained by Jefferson, Washington, and Adams was hypothetical, wishful thinking.

Jefferson and others defended and insisted on including Mohammedan rights in the Constitution for the principle of "imagined Muslims," and the idea of promoting them to be theoretical citizens would reaffirm the truthful universality of American rights.

Unfortunately, there are few chances that would happen.

Muslims come to the USA with the firm conviction to lay low until the time comes when they could do something to hurt our country and our lifestyle, with the sole purpose of conquering it and advancing Islam.

Some may enjoy the perks offered to them in our free society, and some could even get used to them and enjoy our culture for a while, but at one point, the Islamic ideals will prevail. They are tattooed in their brains.

That is what the Postmodern Liberals are ignoring or carelessly dismissing, or maybe just trying to take advantage of them. They are bound for a surprise at the end.

259 -Dangerous Islamic Infiltration To Destroy The USA.

Our country is experiencing a silent Islamic invasion, fortunately, lesser than Europe, but significant. In the form of students, merchants, refugees, visa-overstay, and other means, an increasing number of Muslims are growing in the US. They are all actual or potential terrorists, just waiting for the opportunity to be useful, like the 9/11 perpetrators did.

Moreover, even now, by invading our Congress, as the recent election of two House Representatives: Ilhan Omar and Rashida Tlaib, who after only two months in their offices in the House, they are already showing that their primary purpose is the advancement of Islam, and not to help the American people. Their only goal is fulfilling the words and the instructions in the Koran and Hadith.

Those parameters are engraved in every Muslim's DNA, and they will remain like a tattoo to their souls, their entire lives.

Admittedly, when the Framers wrote the US Constitution, they lacked a clear vision of Islam's future; Mainly the absence of in-depth scrutiny of the Islamic way of life and its goals. They disregarded their plans.

The Framers evaluated the behavior of most possible immigrants correctly. However, maybe they never thought of the Islamist as such a fanatic group with an incredible birth rate growth as they are or the strength of their fanaticism in applying the Koran's ideology, and worse, the Hadith's directions.

Of course, nobody could have imagined at that time what kind of life was expected in our World today. Indeed they did not foresee the Coronavirus Pandemic.

History shows us time and time again that the mandates engraved in the Koran, and the practical enforcement of those orders to despise and hate people who do not surrender to their faith and harm them as revenge, are real and unchangeable. Any attempt to reverse the thought would be considered a rebellion against the Koran, and therefore punished by death. The rules are clear. The present Islamic leadership by radical Mullahs is the most fanatic interpretation of the Islamic Scriptures.

The non-Islamic World always had problems evaluating the vital link between Muslims and the Koran. However, notably, they dismissed the fact that blind obedience to the book and its mandates is the only way.

The detailing is in the Hadith.

No other Scripture affects their followers as the Koran does for Muslims. The obedience to the "Holy Book" is of life and death. The Koran indicates violent punishments and procedures to the violators. For Muslims, nothing is more important than the Koran and its rules.

Maybe one-day Islamic leaders would understand that the confusion of philosophical and material issues is a matter to be addressed and modified if they want to share the World's space peacefully. Nevertheless, it seems the Islamists are not willing to share the World with other religions. They are absolutists.

However, God is too big to be owned by Islam only.

The Hindus saw the Vedic Scriptures' ambiguities and knew how to separate them and live a peaceful and harmonious life in this World.

The Vedas also say:

"God's names are as many as his devotees want to call upon him. God is unlimited, and also his names are, as far as they pronounce them and use them with respect, love, and devotion."

Also, I believe the undeveloped scientific knowledge and utter people's ignorance of the times are one reason for the Mohammedan's evaluation's grave mistakes.

There was a candid Framers' expectancy that people strictly following the Koran's ideology will turn to an eventual "American Citizen's" behavior and displaced the Koran to obey the American Constitution.

Again. The Islam Ideology and its expansion work in four parts:

1) The Traders penetrate a foreign land looking for business,

2) Then, the Military invade.

3) Politicians appropriate the conquest, dictating laws, and collecting taxes.

4) The three sectors oppress and force the locals to accept the Islamic Religion and the Koran as their only ruling or face slavery and death.

There is no other option with Islam. The "Holy Book" message says it, and it is hard to imagine how and why Adams, Jefferson, and the rest of the Founding Fathers disregarded such a basic fact.

Was it a lack of vision or only the "desire" that the Mohammedans (Muslims) would change their philosophy and adopt the new US Country's ideal of democratic life.

Maybe some would do it, although the Islamic Religion is not like other faiths that admit discrepancies and different philosophical streams.

The Koran is very strict and precise, not allowing any differences or questioning the rules. Also, the children born in Muslim families are trained since a very young age that they are Islamists, and they will be such forever.

"Mohammed stated:

"Whoever changes his Islamic religion, kill him." (Hadith Sahih al-Bukhari, Vol. 9, Book 84, No. 57).

When Mohammed founded Islam, he searched for followers among the most accessible people around, the poorest and uneducated.

They were easy prey to believe his fantastic stories that made a smashing influence on their mostly empty minds in need of something superior to believe, and Mohammed was there to tell the story.

He founded Islam on top of philosophically empty minds and mainly illiterate people, which was not even identifiable as philosophy.

It seems Jefferson, Adams, and the rest of the Constitutionalists might have overlooked that abandoning Islam's Religion was punished by death, as the Hadith says.

So, hoping Islamists will obey our Constitution, it was only "wishful thinking."

Over and over again, Muslims living in America or other parts of the World are not only passionate about Islam, but their only purpose in life is the advancement of Islam. It is their obsession and the sole purpose in their minds since they cannot get knowledge from any other source.

It is also unthinkable to imagine why they would disregard the Koran's quoting given by the Tripoli's Ambassador to Jefferson and Adams. Even substantial evidence was surfacing from the Barbary Pirates' actions.

They would sink ships, sequester crews, kidnap passengers, sell them as slaves, burn entire towns, and rob what they encountered on their path. History tells the story with undoubted details. We can also see nowadays, they are still destroying all non-Islamic traces of history.

263 –Old Barbary Pirates Are The New Islamic Terrorists.

We should think of the Barbary Pirates as today's ISIS, Al-Qaida, and other terrorist groups. The similarity seems so close to the facts that we can only see one difference now.

Muslims have learned that it looks better to the World to think of the Terrorists, like a dislodged sector, which acts independently, while the core of Islam attempts to look peaceful and friendly; an ugly lie, in any case.

The error shows at the mere sight. Both groups read, abide, and obey the same books: Koran and Hadith. Their mandates coincide; the punishments and rewards are also the same for all Muslims.

If the leadership could appear to be different when in private, they meet or communicate, both parts unite in one point: Koran. There is only one Islam, ruled by one book: The Koran, and with its Law: the Hadith, a record of the traditions and quotes from the Prophet Muhammad.

Also, the Sharia Law added later, after Muhammad's death, is what they use in daily life to push for the replacement of the local laws or Constitution to the lands they invade.

They are doing it in the UK, Europe, and wherever they manage to establish their communities. This nucleus ignores and disobeys the local authorities. By violent behavior, they force their own "justice" in private Sharia Law courts of the communities they manage, disregarding, and violating local and Federal Laws.

Therefore, we must understand from the above that Islam is not 'only' a "religion," but theology, ideology, and it uses a trading activity, a military power, and a political force to establish them. Those are the weapons utilized to push the last stage: surrendering to the Religion.

When the Constitution was written, there was a different understanding of strategies and systems to practice a religion.

Islam's misinterpretation by such giant figures as the Founding Fathers remains a mystery. We cannot judge people's behavior two and a half centuries ago by today's standards. It is not fair or wise.

Their wishful thinking seems to be the answer.

The Framers expected in good faith, Muslims were going to be happy to be freed from the oppression of their totalitarian way of life and quickly adopting our Democracy. The rest of the religions did it, but Islam will not accept otherwise.

President Bush, the 43rd, had a disappointing experience when he sent Ms. Karen Hughes, an Undersecretary of State for Public Diplomacy with the ambassador's rank on a job focused on changing foreigners' perceptions about America, especially women.

After a few months of traveling, primarily around Middle/East countries, and receiving all kinds of rejections and negative feedback from women, Ms. Hughes returned to the US.

In response to her comment to a group of female students that Muslims oppressed women, the answer was: "No, we are delighted." After the tour, Karen Hughes resigned from her post and went back to private life. Of course, we ignore if those students were influenced or feared punishment from Islam's clergy if they had answered otherwise. It is a possibility.

The Bush Administration, Ms. Huges included, overlooked the root of the problem that is brainwashing and the imprinting in their brains, that is, Islam or death! They are born under that rule.

Moreover, death is desired for the male to go to heaven to enjoy dozens of virgins waiting for them, as they expect. Of course, women's role is disregarded and only used for sexual pleasure, procreation, and servitude.

Some historians picture Jefferson as a dedicated reader of the Koran. However, no one knows how deep Jefferson got into the "Holy Book's" spirit.

Only he could have known. He owned 6.000 books!

Moreover, Jefferson was a dedicated Christian who helped many religious projects with money and other means.

It is easy praising the Fathers of the Constitution because they did a marvelous job structuring a new Country like ours.

For two hundred and forty-some years, the USA has been the Leader of the Free World, admired by many, hated by some.

However, its society has managed an excellent way of life on justice, human rights, equality of opportunities, and economic development.

Naturally, when we see Islam, a totalitarian idea that contradicts all aspects of Democracy, and the Constitutional Republic, it is doubtfully a match for our idiosyncrasy.

Islam is the only so-called "religion" that denies sharing spaces with other faiths. Their ideas are confiscatory, and World domination is their only goal, never sharing, always imposing, and the worst, being violent when disobeyed. That is the core of their beliefs. They might apply "taqiya" at some point (lying to advance Islam,) but the core is the essence.

Every other Religion is tolerant of others. Although they compete for followers, there is tolerance and acceptance of other people's beliefs sharing only one God's original thought, perhaps with different names and worship styles.

The quality, power, and capacity of God are undeniable. Although there are many worshiping styles, the creation's concept is shared at one point, although the discrepancies are mainly at the beginning.

However, the problem is that if Muslims cannot get their way, the order is killing the "infidels." Murder is their way, and there is abundant proof available throughout history.

Postmodern Liberals and the Democrat Party should note this behavior and be aware of their alliance's consequences.

265 -Some Additional Highly Controversial Facts.

The Koran states in Sura 4:89: "Those who reject Islam must be killed. If they turn back (from Islam), take hold of them and kill them wherever you find them."

Our Constitution's First Amendment states: Congress cannot take away "the right of the people to peaceably assemble," yet Islamic Law says: "non-Muslims cannot repair places of worship or build new ones. They must allow Muslims to participate in their private meetings; they cannot bring their dead near the graveyards of Muslims or mourn their dead loudly."

The above sounds bigot, discriminatory, and exclusivist, clashing with the idea of Democracy and equality. Islam's disdain for Democracy is well known.

The First Amendment also states: 'Congress cannot take away the right of the people "to petition the Government for a redress of grievances." Nevertheless, Islamic Law says non-Muslims cannot shelter any aversion towards the Islamic State or help those who disagree with the Islamic Government.

Accordingly, this is a precise clash with the Democratic principle of equality. One more proof that Islam is not only a religion but also a totalitarian political force.

The Second Amendment states: "the right of the people to keep and bear arms shall not be infringed," yet Islamic Law says non-Muslims cannot possess swords or weapons of any kind.

Also, in the Towns conquered by Islam, the locals not converted to their faith are forced to pay taxes to the Islamic Government, while Muslims are spared from paying taxes.

The Eighth Amendment of our Constitution declares: there shall be no "cruel and unusual punishments inflicted," yet the Koran states: "Cut off the hands of thieves, whether they are male or female, as punishment for what they have done – a deterrent from Allah." (Sura 5:38)

A woman who has been raped is also punished "with a hundred stripes." (Sura 24:2)

Women can be beaten: "If you experience rebellion from the women, you shall first talk to them, then (you may use negative incentives like) deserting them in bed, then you may (as a last alternative) beat them" (Sura 4:34).

The United Nations have denounced honor killings of wives and daughters who have embarrassed their families in Muslim populations of Egypt, Jordan, Lebanon, Morocco, Pakistan, Syria, Turkey, Saudi Arabia, Iraq, Yemen, and increasingly Western nations.

The 13th Amendment states there shall be no "slavery or involuntary servitude," yet the Koran accommodates slavery, as

Mohammed owned slaves. Also, Mohammedans were known to be slave owners and traders.

The Constitution's 14th Amendment guarantees citizens "equal protection of the laws," yet the Koran does not consider Jews, Christians, and other non-Muslims as equal to Muslims before the Law. Referring to Jews as "the People of the Book," Mohammed said: "They are those whom Allah has cursed; who have been under his wrath; some of whom were turned into apes and swine" (Sura 5:60, 7:166, 2:65).

The 15th Amendment guarantees "the right of the citizens ... to vote shall not be denied ... on account of race, color, or previous condition of servitude." However, a strict interpretation of Islamic Law does not allow voting, as Democracy is considered people are setting themselves in place of Allah by making the laws.

The 16th Amendment has some similarities with Islamic Law, as "Congress shall have the power to lay and collect taxes on incomes from whatever source derived." Mohammed said, "Fight those who believe not in Allah, until they pay the 'jizya' [tax] with willing submission, and feel subdued." (Sura 9:29)

The 18th Amendment has some similarities with Islamic Law also, as "the manufacture, sale, or transportation of intoxicating liquors for beverage purposes is at this moment prohibited."

The 19th Amendment allows women to vote, yet in strict Islamic countries, women cannot vote.

The 21st Amendment permits liquor sale, yet Islamic Law states non-Muslims are not to sell or drink wine and liquor openly.

One would assume that to swear upon a book implies believing what is in that book. As Mohammed was not just a religious leader but also a political-military commander, Sharia Islam is a religious practice and a political-military system.

Since no one has the authority to demand Muslims worldwide cease imitating Mohammed's political-military example, when Sharia-practicing Muslims bow in prayer, they are also pledging political-military allegiance to Mecca.

Therefore, inviting the Islamists to the United States is inviting a Trojan horse loaded with warriors ready to take down our Constitution and replace it with the Koran, Hadith, and Sharia Law.

268 -Koran Is Incompatible With Our Constitution.

Swearing to defend the US Constitution upon a Koran book that promotes entirely different values presents a controversy.

Supreme Court Justice Robert Jackson, appointed by President Franklin D. Roosevelt, wrote in the foreword of the book "Law in the Middle East" (1955): "Islamic Law offers the American lawyer a study in dramatic contrasts. Even casual acquaintance and superficial knowledge reveal that its striking features relative to our Law are not likenesses but inconsistencies, not similarities but contrarieties. In its source, scope, and sanctions, the Law of the Middle East is the direct opposite of Western Law."

The Koran's recent use to swearing Rep. Ellis and others is not valid because the Koran's spirit is opposed to the Constitution.

Therefore, it is invalid, as well as ignorant.

As we can see, the inconsistencies of the Islamic philosophy, the Laws, and the goals are contrary to our Constitution. The object and ultimate accomplishment of Islam are, in fact, contrary to our Democracy emanated from the Constitution.

Not only that, but if the Koran, the Hadith, and the Sharia Law, at some point, could be enforced to become the ruling Law in our country, we will be violating the Constitution's writing and spirit.

We will also be negating all the efforts throughout three hundred years, and rivers of blood spilled to establish our Democracy and the Bill of Rights.

So, to be clear, Islam is not a viable option for our country. The push to advance it and the violence shown in their public demonstrations, as well as the adherence to the heinous terrorist acts, are a sample of its dreadful intentions.

The firm determination to impose their Sharia Law attempts to abolish our Constitution and replace it with their totalitarian theocratic laws and ideology.

Our political community and the Supreme Court must revise these intentions and evaluate the possible outcome if they manage to be successful.

It seems ridiculous to help the development of such an enemy in our home. So, knowing that the Islamic followers are working into forcing such a vicious theocracy, entirely against our natural laws, our lifestyle, and our Constitution, is frankly absurd.

It is like inviting the fox to oversee the hen's House.

The US must stop Islam's growth in our country by all means. We should not allow their closed communities, certain Mosques where they preach subversion, practices against our way of life, and cruel treatment of women, which clashes with our culture, such as the female organ's ablation.

Also, it is necessary to watch closer the marriages between grown male and underage girls.

In the Koran, the marriage of nine-year-old girls, and in some cases, six-year-old, to older men in their forties and fifties is recommended, something that our society rejects as abnormal and despicable.

Mohammed himself, in his 50's married a six-year-old Aisha.

269 - Postmodern Liberalism/Islam: An Unholy Tie.

The Islam adherence to the Postmodern Liberals is scandalous, being they are opposite philosophies. In the case the Postmodern Liberal Movement could get its way, the firm determination of the Islamist will wipe out any vestiges of the initial Liberal's intentions, just because they are incompatible and opposite.

The previous is another proof of Islam's Military-Political nature and a menace to the United States' existence.

We must prevent Islam's intentions of appropriating our Nation through their religious, military, and political tricks.

The well-known Richard Dawkins is no friend to Conservatives. His raucous Atheism, for decades, has clashed with many. His negative comments about Christianity and Judaism are famous. His statement: Even moderate religious people "make the world safe for extremists" have earned some enemies on the Postmodern Liberal's side.

He has criticized the murdering of apostates for no crime other than their disbelief in the Koran and denounced the appalling misogyny and homophobia of Islam.

Berkeley University recently barred Dawkins and canceled his scheduled speech.

The Left is frankly disenchanted with him because his hatred of Conservatives is no match for his "offenses" to Islam. The Liberals are enamored and count on it for their "resist" movement.

Postmodern Liberals are suffering from a mental disease. However, principally, the Muslims' alliance is precisely the same as inviting a Trojan horse full of Radical Islamic Terrorists to their party.

Once inside the targeted land, the horse will open up, and the radical fighters will eat up the lefty snowflakes even before they touch the ground.

Postmodern Liberal's greed is a rooky politician's dream.

They do not have the slightest idea about Islam's intentions, which means they are also poorly educated in history.

They ignore what Muslims have been carrying and exercising for fourteen hundred years.

270 -Identity Politics, A Failed Strategy.

Since the 1970s Movement for the Human Rights and the African-American Civil Rights era, at that time, some minority groups used Identity Politics as an aid to forming coalitions with the majority.

The feelings of oppression lead to the consciousness-raising sense. In a way, it helped them to advance on the recognition of their demands for equality.

Specific groups took advantage of it in the wrong way, and slowly the movement dwindled.

However, in the Postmodern Liberal Movement today, their leaders try to keep it present to exploit the Illegal aliens and undocumented migrants who need any help. They see the initiative as golden.

The American Citizens already know the old movement's melodramatic tones. They ignore their demands, mainly because they are part of the strategy to help people that violated the US immigration laws by entering the country without the proper documents.

Already, Minority Leader Senator Schumer has expressed his opinion by saying: "I would not mind for the Democratic Party to get away from Identity Politics."

Author James Schlesinger warned us that for the Liberal Movement to be successful; unity was fundamental.

Indeed, in the Democrat Party, there is a kind of forced integration generated by the 2016 election results. However, in the broader Postmodern Liberal Movement, the feelings are entirely different since there is no personal Leadership at this time or even the benefits of being a legal recipient of votes. Votes belong to the Democrat Party.

Because many of its members are illegal and cannot vote, unity is fractioned by each group's personal needs and desires, being Hispanic, Middle-Eastern, European, or other origins.

Identity Politics.

This scenario complicates the strategy, which for the moment, as a "resist" group, if it fulfills the purpose of rallying against the mildly dismembered Conservative Movement, Donald J. Trump administration (including the "Never-Trumpers"), and Swamp members.

It is a total mess, which the President is trying to overcome and keeping his Government running.

Although knowing him, Mr. Trump never imagined this scene, and it would not have mattered or changed his intentions.

Donald Trump is a fighter, and the problem for the Postmodern Liberals, Democratic Party, the Left, and Islam is: Donald is used to winning. He is a winner and has proof of it all his life. He frequently looks as he is losing, but in the end, he usually wins.

The 45th Presidency is for Mr. Trump, his last fight, the biggest one, the mother of all battles, and there is no doubt in our mind and most minds in the World that he is a most favorite in this odd war the Postmodern Liberals started.

However, the present declared Pandemic of the COVID-19 has wholly changed the board, prompting the President to declare himself: "A war-time President," allowing him to use some unique powers.

Although we cannot see our main enemy, we can feel it in the air! Our country and the World are shutdowns until a new order! Fortunately, the re-opening has begun. It will take some time, but we will succeed and come up better and stronger!

272 -The Inevitable Talk Involving Islam.

Writing about the problems with Islamic Religion, in my thoughts, I was wondering if the subject belonged to this book.

Many readers may be unsure of the relevance. However, after reviewing our research's results and the actual controversies with our Constitution exposed in it, I believe it makes sense to add it to the idea of "A BRUTAL ATTACK ON DEMOCRACY" and the sub-title: "The All-Time enemies on the March." Islam is part of it. On my Facebook page, I have the opportunity to intervene on many blogs, many run by Democrats. Far from insulting or spreading fake news, I propose unity for our country. It is not easy, but that it is my goal.

The Liberal Movement used to be a decent effort to advance new ideas, bringing up fresh concepts, and discussing their usefulness to improve our passage through this complex World.

However, a balance is necessary to keep the route to success, something Postmodern Liberalism does not offer.

Since the day after the 2016 election, the new Liberals established hatred as the primary weapon to fight Donald J. Trump and his Government.

Not only hate has influenced all aspects of the battle. They took racism as their favorite tool to mud the field. They are forcing the racial confrontation on every inch of the way. It has become an obsession.

For many years, American citizens who had worked to achieve a fair amount of peace in the old discordance involving the racial issue are now finding accusations of racial behavior every minute. Postmodern Liberals and their subdued Democrat politicians want to keep a political disagreement alive against Conservatives. For Democrats, everything in the Republicans is racially motivated. They scrutinize every sentence to find a racial discrepancy, and when they do not see them, they invent them. Fake news is a favorite.

Democrats find every Word on the President's mouth offensive, ignorant, racially intended, bigot, or a lie. It is becoming tedious, and many people are watching and beginning to react negatively to it. The Mainstream Media TV hosts' opinions are the worst. Especially MSNBC, CNN, CBS, and ABC, as well as The New York Times and Washington Post.

Meanwhile, President Trump is achieving accomplishment after accomplishment of his campaign promises.

Unfortunately, the Corona Virus brought sad news to our country and the World, pausing our lives.

Before the Pandemic, the economy boomed; unemployment was at the lowest level for the last 50 years. Although Trump is Internationally recognized for his success bringing the two Koreas together and have issued a score of executive orders that are helping our economy, Democrats keep lying and slandering our President.

Unfortunately, the people who used to old ways to conduct business misunderstand his approach to fairness in other countries' trade. However, the actual Pandemic has stopped our country's growth, and who knows what the future could bring.

Every other country in the World is abusing the USA.

Trump has been talking about it for years, and now, he is committed to ending the negative balance on our trade agreements. He is saying: Free Trade is OK, but it must also be Fair Trade.

However, some countries dislike Trump's new approach to trading and menacing to start a trade war.

It is wise to remember that the USA is the most robust economy in the World. Doing business with us is the bread and butter to many countries, so they must understand that unless it is a Fair Trade, we will modify the business deals, and tariffs may apply.

Trump's approach is like a salesman's thinking.

He threatens, and then he opens up to conciliation. He goes back and forth until he finds a way to his idea.

Not everyone understands his ways, which showed in his dealings with North Korea, where he had been tough, soft, and in between, but he is getting what he wants in the end.

Trump is patient and reminds us of a predator patiently waiting for its prey, something many politicians, especially his foes, do not seem to understand or like.

So far, the President has achieved more triumphs than deceptions, and the country is transiting through a period of bonanza like we have not seen in many years. It may not be luck only.

Donald J. Trump is applying a business-like technique to run our country, something that I have loved and carried in my mind for years.

The understanding of how the current leaders of the World are doing business has changed. Nowadays, countries are being managed like private businesses, with the people's welfare in mind, in some cases, of course excluding the hideous Dictators that oppress their nationals for personal reasons.

Balance is essential to achievement in any endeavor, and our country has handled to preserve the direction that has led us to be the most prosperous Nation on Earth. That is not a small performance.

As I grew up, first, my parents, then my teachers, taught me that anything in the material World works because of its balance.

So, it is my goal to remain in the center, as long as I can help it.

Imagine the Universes without a perfect balance.

The planets and stars would be crashing against each other, and the Multiverse would collapse to rapid destruction.

Material energy annihilation is part of our existence, but the creator has established a precise chronology.

The Vedas have a name for the Multiverse destruction driver: Lord Shiva; he is in charge of the Material Energy destruction and returning to the Unmanifested form.

It is not easy to imagine the Spiritual World because its grandiosity is so potent that it brings an indescribable feeling to poke at it.

I do not know how the Postmodern Liberals manage to live in a fictitious world, driven only by sexual desires and false emotions, which we know are only fantasies.

There are illusions that, like snowflakes, disappear at the touch of the ground.

However, Islam is not our only danger at this time.

Communism, in the past represented by the USSR, now led by China, is much more dangerous because they added some Capitalism features (State Capitalism). They have also learned to bribe foreign politicians masterfully. Bribing is their new weapon, and the Democrat Party, shifting to the radical Left, are the latest components of the menace plotted by the three mentioned groups:

- Democrat Party (Postmodern Liberalism)
- Communist China
- Islam.

I hope President Jefferson's spirit would guide us to preserve our identity and keep the written Constitution to prevail over the authoritarian, totalitarian, and fanatic theological forces opposing us with evil intentions.

In the end, God will prevail, and we, his devotees, must help with our effort, persistence, and strength.

God makes 50 %; the rest is up to us.

ABOUT THE AUTHOR

J. Pelegrin creative history goes back to the beginning of the group "LOS 4 BRILLANTES", formed in Uruguay in the 60's: Yvonne <Lead Singer> Roberto <bass>, Ricardo <guitar> and me, Jorge <keyboards>. Then, a little later we added Hector (drums), who accompanied the Group and later was an integral part of it until the end, by 1970's.

They began playing and singing in Uruguay, their homeland, traveling to Argentina, Brazil, Chile, Venezuela, Perú and landing in Mexico, in 1964, where they remained until 1970 when decided to go separate ways.

CBS Columbia Records Mexico hired Jorge as a Producer-Artistic Director. After two years, working for the label, having produced several successful projects, encouraged by his Boss, he decided to move to New York, where he founded a successful new home. Jorge's relationship with New York City was "love at first sight." Since 1974 to the present has been his home, except for eight years, between 1989 and 1998, were he had to take some time off to attend to family matters, back in Uruguay.

New York City has been a great deal in Jorge's life. It brought him the opportunity to develop himself into a better musician, a writer, and a better person, giving him the recognition and success in the English Language market, that to these days had helped him to complete many of his dreams, including writing Newspaper articles, books, and making movies. He is very grateful to New York City and its people.

In New York, he had the fortune to have produced five hit records for the American Market and some others in the hit parade top 40's: "WALKING DOWNTOWN," featuring "Black Ivory," "IF YOU WANT ME," by "Ecstasy, Passion & Pain." "FEEL GOOD, PARTY TIME", by J.R.Funk & the love machine." "ROCK YOUR WORLD", by "Weeks & Co" and '"I DON'T WANNA LOSE IT", featuring "Wayne Cooper", former late "CAMEO" lead singer.

In 1998, returning to his beloved City of New York, destiny took him thru various ways until he came back to his heart and soul: the music. In 2005, with best friend Sue Samuels, a dancer, choreographer and multi-talented NYC icon, they approached something new. They began to write a; Broadway-bound Musical Play, (THE DREAM FACTORY).

By 2008, they finished the writing and composing the music and lyrics. Some Broadway producers read the script and listen to the music of the play and immediately showed interest in producing the show. They offered to assign an expert budget director and Executive Producer, thinking on a production budget of 5 million dollars and the request to do it fast since they needed to replace their fading Broadway play: "Spring Awakening," after seven years on stage.

Unfortunately, 14 days later, the Real Estate "Market Crash" surfaced. Jorge and Sue received a notice saying that due to the World's economic situation, the project had been postponed indefinitely (All the investors were people affected by the Wall Street collapse). The market crash shattered their

Affected by this disappointing fact, Jorge began a life reorganization, which besides the Musical Play setback, that leads Jorge to his personal life collapse, ended in a bankruptcy and three consecutive brain strokes.

Changes in the entertainment market took him to other new ways, were taking advantage of the Electronic Music escalation, he began to produce Music Videos, Film production and, combining his music creativity, the writing and the new visual aspect of it.

He released his first Music-Video production on Youtube by April of 2012.   Being that the Music business is in frank decadence, the music production has fallen to an unrecognizable mediocrity. A few productions in today's market have a decent quality and the rappers, managed by obscure characters who own most record labels or managed to merge with unscrupulous big Media Corporations CEO's, have monopolized the pop music market, it became irrelevant to keep producing music for the American Market as a way of living.

Instead, the book industry has begun to pick-up, and Jorge now dedicates his time to the book writing. He has written a Musical Film Script, with 23 original songs, titled: DREAM FACTORY, selected by the 2015 Beverly Hills Film Festival, as the best Musical. Then, he wrote a political/Religious book: "SAVING AMERICA THE BEAUTIFUL, a Fiction Novel: "DEATH IS ONLY AN ILLUSION", "Postmodern LIBERALISM," and "America Is Great Again!, published on Amazon Books

A BRUTAL ATTACK ON DEMOCRACY by J. Pelegrin

Other Books by J. Pelegrin:

AMERICA GENIAL! POR SIEMPRE Versión en Español de AMERICA IS GREAT AGAIN!

"URUGUAY PUERTO LIBRE" in Spanish Language, an essay on local Uruguayan economy.

"DREAM FACTORY", a Musical Film Script, Selected as the best Musical at the *2015 BEVERLY HILLS FILM FESTIVAL*. Include 23 original songs.

"SAVING AMERICA THE BEAUTIFUL", a "current affairs" narrative about Jorge's arrival to New York City, the process of integrating to the community, his progressive interest in politics, and the Donald Trump stomping the grounds in the political arena. J. Pelegrin predicted the election's result on July 4th, 2016.

"Postmodern LIBERALISM" (An Obsessive Epidemic)

Postmodern LIBERALISM" (An Obsessive Epidemic)

"America is Great Again!

"DEATH IS ONLY AN ILLUSION", A Fiction Novel.

Synopsis 1

When Martin Frost, a Philosophy professor at an NYC University closes his class and lecture year, in a speech to his students, he quotes "DEATH IS ONLY AN ILLUSION," from the Vedic philosophy. Some curious students want to know more about the subject and invite the Professor to expand on the theme privately. A visitor from an alternative Planet appears on the scene, looking for help to stop an imminent invasion by Earthlings' Terrorists to take over his Planet.

The Alien invites Martin and friends to visit his Parallel World; the group enjoys what they see and commits to helping. Some student's parents, former CIA operatives, join the Professor and friends to form a "Garrison" to aid the man from the Parallel Planet to defend his remote homeland. Exciting action, high in Philosophy, Sciences, Religion, Morals and unexpected developments in an electrifying thrilling plot.

ALSO AVAILABLE: - TAMBIÉN DISPONIBLE:

"LA MUERTE ES SÓLO UNA ILUSIÓN"
"DEATH IS ONLY AN ILLUSION's", en Español

"UN BRUTAL ATAQUE A LA DEMOCRACIA"
"A BRUTAL ATTACK ON DEMOCRACY" en Español